# Medieval Society:
## 400–1450

The Structure of European History
*studies and interpretations*

NORMAN F. CANTOR and MICHAEL S. WERTHMAN, Editors

*Volume I*
ANCIENT CIVILIZATION:
4000 B.C.–400 A.D.

*Volume II*
MEDIEVAL SOCIETY:
400–1450

*Volume III*
RENAISSANCE, REFORMATION, AND ABSOLUTISM:
1450–1650

*Volume IV*
THE FULFILLMENT AND COLLAPSE OF THE OLD REGIME:
1650–1815

*Volume V*
THE MAKING OF THE MODERN WORLD:
1815–1914

*Volume VI*
THE TWENTIETH CENTURY:
1914 to the Present

# Medieval Society: 400-1450

*Second Edition*

edited by NORMAN F. CANTOR

*State University of New York at Binghamton*

and MICHAEL S. WERTHMAN

*Thomas Y. Crowell Company*    *New York*

ESTABLISHED 1834

**ACKNOWLEDGMENTS:** The editors wish to express their gratitude to the following publishers and individuals for permission to quote selections from the works designated:

Marc Bloch, *Feudal Society*, translated by L. A. Manyon. Copyright © 1961 by The University of Chicago. Reprinted by permission of The University of Chicago Press.

A. C. Crombie, *Science in the Middle Ages and Early Modern Times*, Vols. I & II, 2nd ed. Copyright © 1959 by A. C. Crombie. Reprinted by permission of Heinemann Educational Books Ltd. and Harvard University Press.

Deno J. Geanakoplos, *Byzantine East and Latin West*. Copyright © 1966 by Deno J. Geanakoplos. Reprinted by permission of Harper & Row, Publishers, Inc.

Friedrich Heer, *The Intellectual History of Europe*, translated by Jonathan Steinberg. English translation copyright © 1966 by Jonathan Steinberg. Reprinted by permission of The World Publishing Company.

Friedrich Heer, *The Medieval World*, translated by Janet Sondheimer. Reprinted by permission of Weidenfeld (Publishers) Ltd. and Praeger Publishers, Inc.

Johan Huizinga, *The Waning of the Middle Ages*. Reprinted by permission of Edward Arnold (Publishers) Ltd.

Robert S. Lopez, *The Birth of Europe*. Copyright © 1962 by Max Leclerc et Cie, Proprietors of Librairie Armand Colin; © 1966 translation J. M. Dent & Sons Ltd. Published by M. Evans and Company, Inc., New York. Reprinted by permission of J. M. Dent & Sons Ltd. and M. Evans and Company, Inc.

Henri Pirenne, *Economic and Social History of Medieval Europe*, translated by I. E. Clegg. Reprinted by permission of Harcourt Brace Jovanovich, Inc. and Routledge & Kegan Paul Ltd.

R. W. Southern, *The Making of the Middle Ages*. Reprinted by permission of Yale University Press.

# Preface

&#x2767; *The Structure of European History* is a six-volume anthology series whose purpose is to present to the undergraduate and lay reader leading interpretations of fundamental political, economic, social, and intellectual change in European history from the advent of civilization to the present day. The six volumes are devoted to the following eras of European history:

I. Ancient Civilization: 4000 B.C.–400 A.D.
II. Medieval Society: 400–1450
III. Renaissance, Reformation, and Absolutism: 1450–1650
IV. The Fulfillment and Collapse of the Old Regime: 1650–1815
V. The Making of the Modern World: 1815–1914
VI. The Twentieth Century: 1914 to the Present

Every volume consists of eight relatively long selections, each of which is preceded by an editors' introduction that outlines the problem, identifies the author, defines his methods and assumptions, and establishes his interpretation within the historiography of the subject. A brief list of additional important books on the same subject or on related subjects follows each selection. Each volume contains a brief introduction to the period as a whole that delineates the leading themes by which modern scholarship has illuminated the era.

Almost all of the forty-eight selections in the six volumes were written in the past forty years and the majority since 1940. In recent decades historians of Europe have sought to extrapolate broad movements of historical change from the vast amount of data that modern research has built up. There has been a general tendency in modern scholarship to bridge the conventional compartmentalization of political, economic, social, and intellectual history and to analyze a movement or event which falls primarily in one of these categories within the context of a total view of social and cultural change. Historians more and more attempt to present a picture of the past as rich, as complex, and as full as human experience itself. The intertwining and mutual involvement of many kinds of aspirations and achievements are now seen to be the basic existential facts shaping previous societies just as they shape social conditions in our own time.

We have sought in these six volumes to present to the student and lay reader examples of this comprehensive and total approach to the understanding of European history. In making our selections we have been governed by the criterion of choosing interpretations which view critical movements and trends in the history of Western civilization in as broad and as many-faceted a context as possible. We have also aimed to make selections which are distinguished by a clear and forceful style and which can be easily comprehended by students in a freshman survey course and by the college-educated lay reader.

Most of the selections in each of the six volumes of this series are the original, seminal theses presented by distinguished scholars after many years of research and reflection. In a few instances the criterion of comprehension by the novice student and lay reader has led us to take an extract from a work of synthesis and high vulgarization which in turn is based on very important monographic studies.

N.F.C.
M.S.W.

# Contents

# Introduction

European history in the Middle Ages first began to be seriously and carefully studied about a hundred years ago. The pioneering medieval scholars of the second half of the nineteenth century either worked under the auspices of national governments and sought to find the roots of modern nationhood and the sources of the power of the modern European states in the medieval past, or they were clerical scholars commissioned to discover and portray the organization and doctrine of the medieval Church. These nationalist and clerical scholars did magnificent work. They discovered, collected, and in many instances edited and published the major primary sources for medieval history and by their assiduous labors revealed the complexity and richness of the medieval world. By 1900 the medieval era was no longer the "dark ages" of the eighteenth-century Enlightenment imagination or simply the stage setting for virtuous knights and beautiful maidens, as it had been enthusiastically portrayed by the Romantic poets of the early nineteenth century. By 1900 it was evident that the medieval era was both an age of faith and an age of heathen superstition; it was an age of great intellectual and cultural achievement and also an age of barbaric violence and savagery; it was an age of anarchic disorder and also an age of authoritarianism and absolutism; it was a time that blended intense ruralism and localism with the founding of cities and the emergence of capitalism. By the 1920's it had become evident that the parameters of medieval society

were many, that its structure was intricate. The world of
the Middle Ages could not be defined by facile, one-dimen-
sional categories. It would take enormous learning and
great effort of historical imagination to conceptualize a
holistic and functioning model of medieval society.

The lines of research into medieval civilization opened
up by late nineteenth-century nationalist and clerical scholars have continued to be explored, but they have been
broadened and altered in accord with inevitable change
in historiographical assumptions. With their nineteenth-
century predecessors, twentieth-century medieval scholars
have focused a great deal of their interest on political and
legal institutions. But they have abandoned the rather naive
search for organic "origins" and "roots" of modern nations
and institutions and have instead devoted themselves to
analyzing the functional operation of medieval administration and law. Similarly, the study of medieval thought and
culture no longer needs to be inspired by an ambition to
defend the Roman Catholic Church. The indispensable
contribution of the Church to all aspects of medieval life
can now be accepted as a truism, and scholars are able to
explore the full course of development of medieval
thought, piety, art, and literature without resorting to
either apologetics or condemnation.

On the basis of the researches of flourishing schools of
medieval history in all Western countries including the
United States and Canada, some historians have tried to
develop general interpretations which relate institutional
and intellectual facets; show the interrelationship of religion, power, and wealth; and delineate the structure of
medieval society as a whole. This work is still a long way
from definitive conclusion, but it is possible to bring together in this volume the attempts of eight scholars to de-
fine the nexus of political, economic, and intellectual
change in medieval civilization. The first of these studies
is an introduction to the elements of early medieval society and culture and an evaluation of the so-called Carolingian Renaissance. The second study is the classic sociological interpretation of medieval history, drawing heavily
upon the concepts of the behavioral sciences. The third

selection covers much the same ground but in a more intuitive and less conceptualized way, with great sensitivity to the thought and feeling of medieval men. The fourth essay is an assessment of the pattern of economic change over several centuries of medieval history and an inquiry into the causes of social upheaval. Selection number five demonstrates the impact of Byzantine culture upon European civilization. The sixth selection discusses the relations between church and state in the Middle Ages, with special attention to the struggles caused by opposing notions about the nature of secular and ecclesiastical power. It tries to show the influence of this ideological conflict on the general course of medieval social and political change, and to determine the social and psychological foundations of revolutionary ideals. Essay seven is a detailed account of the scientific and technological accomplishments of the Middle Ages, which also places medieval achievements in the wider context of the history of western science and technology. The final selection analyzes the forms of, and suggests the causes for, the intellectual frustrations and cultural ossification experienced by late medieval society as it slid toward its dissolution.

ROBERT S. LOPEZ

# The Carolingian Prelude

During the fifth and sixth centuries A.D., with the conquest of western Europe by various Germanic peoples, the social structure of the later Roman Empire was faced with a society that was substantially different. It cannot be said, however, that there was very much of a confrontation between two economic systems. The Germans were completely devoted to agricultural, pastoral, and warrior life, and the Romans were on the way toward a similarly rural existence. In economic matters, the German invasions only accelerated a process that was already started. The expansion of Islam in the eighth century, which cut off Europe even more effectively than had the Germanic conquest from trade with the eastern Mediterranean, dealt the death blow to urban and commercial life. But deurbanization was very extensive before the Germans *or* the Muslims arrived on the scene. By the seventh century there were no urban centers of commerce or industry in western Europe. There were only civic centers—centers of government, fortresses where dependents of the government lived, and cathedrals. Even before the German invasions, the merchant was on his way out, production for market was in decline, and markets were disappearing. The villas or fortified estates were already self-sufficient. This villa economy,

FROM Robert S. Lopez, *The Birth of Europe* (New York: M. Evans and Company, Inc., 1967), pp. 82–106. Copyright © 1962 by Max Leclerc et Cie, Proprietors of Librairie Armand Colin; © 1966 translation J. M. Dent & Sons Ltd.

or manorial economy, was intensified by the German invasions but not inaugurated by them. The Roman Empire did not decline and fall economically in response to external pressure, although it may very well have done so politically and intellectually. Economically an active process was simply accelerated.

In social structure, however, there was substantial variance between the German and Roman systems that required accommodation. An amalgamation of the two occurred after the invasions, and nineteenth-century historians debated at enormous length whether the resulting social structure was more markedly Roman or German. French historians say it was more heavily Roman, and German historians naturally say it was predominantly German, but it would be hard to make this determination. One can say that two social systems were brought together and that after about three centuries of experimentation and functional adjustment, a distinctive new society appeared. It can be shown to have continuity with the late Roman system and with the Germanic system, but it should be understood as a new one—the early medieval social structure.

The German social structure was very much like that of the Homeric Greeks; it too typified the Heroic Age described by H. M. Chadwick, the great pioneering comparative historian of the early twentieth century. German society originally was based entirely upon kinship, blood affiliation, and the tribe as an amalgamation of families. The family was gradually replaced as the basic social unit by what was called the war band in the period of the German migrations and conquest in the fourth, fifth, and sixth centuries. If the patriarch of the tribe was not the best possible warrior, the young warriors went to follow some relative who was a better war leader and booty giver. If they could not find a blood relative, they supported a fighter of a different tribe who could provide sustenance and protection. Blood ties remained enormously significant, however, as did devotion to the family, but the war band became central to social life. The relationship between warriors and their leaders was fundamental both to the migrating war bands and to the early medieval Germanic kingdoms established on the remains of the fallen Roman Empire.

It is not very important to decide whether early medieval society was more Roman or more German in its origins and background, but it is important to understand how it functioned. Its essential aspect was the relationship between the lord and his followers. In the sixth century, land became important as a means of reward for service. At first this was significant only in the higher ranks of German society, in the relationship of the king and the great nobles. He rewarded them with land and with appropriate titles, such as duke and count. These titles were recoverable at will, but they tended to become hereditary in great families, and attached to specific lands. In this fashion were created the dukes of Aquitaine, counts of Toulouse, and counts of Paris, to name but three. Theoretically, they ruled vast territories with the king's consent, but in practice, their titles, offices, and land became self-perpetuating and were beyond the king's direct control.

By the eighth century, many lords chose to reward their followers with land instead of booty (or largesse). They gave away pieces of land, complete with serfs to grow crops, to provide the follower enough wealth to support the cost of his military equipment. Horses had become an important part of warfare by then, and a soldier's equipment was expensive. By the ninth century, the follower felt that he could not sustain himself without control of a manor and its income. This system of mutual obligation and reward of contractual service, of rewarding the warrior with land, is known as feudalism. It involved, in the first place, vassalage—the service of one man to another, with mutual obligations and mutual loyalty. The obligation of the vassal was to fight, that of the lord to protect and to provide sustenance. By the eighth century, the grant of land to a follower was called an enfiefment—a fief being equivalent to an estate—and the process of enfiefment became very widespread. So by the year 800, two aspects of bona fide feudalism had come into existence: vassalage and enfiefment. These integral elements of what historians call feudalism operated effectively as methods of providing military service to the leaders and employment and compensation for the soldiers.

The system of rewards in land began at a very high level. The king rewarded the great aristocrats—or actually bribed them against future conduct—as early as the sixth century. By the eighth century, this system of vassalage and enfiefment had become the most common relationship in free society. The manorial serf did not enter into vassalage because he was already bound to the land; he could not bargain and he had no choice. Vassalage is a relationship between free men. It is true that one party may be much poorer than the other, he may need protection, may be frightened or coerced, but he must enter freely into contract with the lord. The manorial serf had no such agreement, no contractual relationship; his father had been a peasant on the land, he was a peasant on the land, and his family was bound to labor for an overlord not of their choosing *ad infinitum*.

Eighth-century society perpetuated the Roman system with its great aristocratic holdings and a servile class to do the work. What was novel was the professional warrior class, whose relationship to the lord was a quite clearly defined contractual affair. The symbolic and legal act that served as a fulcrum for the unique social system of feudalism was that of homage. A vassal appeared before his lord and put his hands between the lord's hands; he promised to love what the lord loved and to shun what the lord shunned. The lord promised to sustain him, protect him, cherish, and honor him—it was a kind of marriage—and then, if the lord was beneficent and wealthy (and by the ninth and tenth centuries, if he was prudent) he enfiefed his vassal. He handed over a stalk of grain or a knife, a symbolic gesture that indicated whether he was thinking about the fruits of land or military service, and drew up a land deed in which the fief was specified.

From a purely structural point of view, the early medieval lords resembled the Roman aristocracy. The difference was that they were very crude. The Roman aristocrats of the late Empire were men of great education and wisdom.

They were often selfish and narrow-minded, but it was not
entirely their fault; when the Empire became feeble and
rather dangerous, they abandoned it and retired to their
estates. When the Germans came in, there was a tremendous
cultural decline which was accelerated by intermarriage.
As a result, the ninth-century lord was a much rougher
person than the Roman aristocrat. Indeed, historians
appear uncomfortable about using the term aristocrat with
reference to the feudal lords of the ninth and tenth centuries, no matter how many castles or estates they had. The
Greek word for *aristocrat* means the "best man," and
*aristocracy* is the rule of the best; but these early medieval
men were extremely crude and violent. Theirs was an un-
civilized, violent, and primitive society. In privilege the
feudal lords were the successors of the Roman aristocracy,
but in their values and behavior they were not far removed
from the barbarian German chieftains who were their
ancestors.

The manorial economic system was not very rational; it
was quite unproductive. In its social aspect, feudalism was
based on violence; robbery and organized mayhem were
in a sense its objects. The system functioned very well for
its purpose, however, and it did establish some form of
social order. Its primary achievement, though, was to bind
the structure of society to the land. When the German
tribes came into Europe, Roman colonization had extended
into only one-third of Gaul, and there were enormous
stretches of empty land and forest in western Germany, the
northern two-thirds of France, and southern England. Land
was central in the operation of feudalism; over the years it
was cleared and cultivated and a whole social structure was
based upon it. Lords owned it; vassals held it; peasants
worked it. Given the limited contemporary technology, the
feudal system had to be one of intensive cultivation which
required that the entire society accommodate itself to the
land. This, of course, was enormously important in the
long-range development of European history.

These observations provide the necessary background
for the following analysis of eighth-century government,
society, and culture by a great American medievalist,

Robert S. Lopez of Yale University. Lopez examines the
Carolingian era, that period during which medieval civilization made its first attempts to fashion a genuine, self-
consciously European community out of its Roman and
Germanic heritage.

◄§౩෨

## FROM MAYOR OF THE PALACE TO MASTER OF EUROPE

'Charles, wise and modest . . . master of the world, beloved
of the people . . . summit of Europe . . . hero, august . . . pious . . . is
tracing out the walls of the Rome of the future.'

Thus an unknown poet describes Charlemagne and his capital (Aix-
la-Chapelle, not Rome) some months before the Christmas of 800
when the Pope placed the imperial crown on the head of the monarch
(in Rome, not at Aix-la-Chapelle).

In 801, as soon as the effects of shock produced by the coronation
had been absorbed, Charlemagne—or his chancellery—adopted another string of titles, half Germanic, half Roman: 'Most serene Augustus, crowned by God, great emperor and peacemaker, governing the
Roman Empire and, likewise by the mercy of God, king of the Franks
and Lombards'. His scholars bestowed still more titles on him: 'King
David', which well became the Anointed of the Lord, or 'the shepherd
Palaemon', which on the other hand was ill-suited to the tastes of this
mighty hunter. History does not record whether he was given other
names by the wife he repudiated, the nephews he dispossessed, or the
Saxons he had hunted down, massacred, forcibly baptised, or deported
if they were 'treacherous' enough to revolt. The empire he established
by force of arms was already beginning to disintegrate before his
death, but the imperial idea which it had nurtured was to dominate
Europe until the end of the Middle Ages and beyond.

THE IMAGE OF CHARLEMAGNE   The image of Charlemagne, embellished
in the biography of Eginhard [Einhard], who had known him, but still
human, was transfigured by legend. An eleventh-century monk was
told by an eyewitness that in the year 1000, when Otto III opened the
tomb of the founder of the Empire, he found Charlemagne 'seated on
a throne as if he still lived . . . none of his members was corrupted'.
The [*chansons de geste,* medieval French epics] attributed to him, with

embellishments, the exploits of his whole dynasty, a life-time of two hundred years, and the flowing white beard that it seems he never wore. In 1165 the Church bowed to tradition (and to the wishes of Frederick Barbarossa) and admitted Charlemagne to the number of her saints. That was enough to drown the discordant voices of certain poets who represented him as a greedy old dotard.

It is not easy to analyse a man who was the embodiment of so many ideals throughout the ages. We know that he was energetic, active and courageous; that he had a firm belief in Christianity according to the Roman formula and in his own mission to uphold and propagate it, by sword and book; that he accepted and sought the collaboration of warriors and learned men of all nations, but held himself to be of Frankish race (which does not mean either German or French) at the most important occasions and public appearances of his life. His other characteristics elude us. The sources, which are fairly full for a time which does not overindulge us, lend themselves to different interpretations.

But whatever the part played by his personality, his successes and failures are best explained by the fact that he came on the scene at the moment when the elite of the West was impatient for restoration of the Empire, but when the political and economic instruments needed to maintain such an Empire were certainly not up to it.

FRANKISH TRUMP-CARDS   The Frankish army was almost ready. From the time of Clovis [ruled 481–511] . . . the Frankish people seemed marked out for the hegemony of the West. They controlled a larger territory and a more numerous population than the other barbarian kingdoms. They had promptly solved the problems of their relations with the Catholic Church and the Gallo-Roman masses, and yet controlled enough Germanic lands not to lose their cohesion among the Roman crowds, or the autonomous character of their clergy. Justinian had halted Frankish expansion, it is true, but nothing could have stopped their taking the offensive again after his death if their monarchy had been able to keep its authority over the nobility.

This had not been the case. The Merovingian aristocracy, anarchistic, greedy for pleasure, indifferent to ideas, profited by dissension or the incompetence of the sovereigns, then by the rivalry of the Mayors of the Palace [chief deputies of the King], to grow powerful at the expense of the State, the Church and the people. At least it kept in good training for war, thanks to internal struggles between Austrasians, Neustrians, Burgundians and Aquitainians [those from the contending regions that constituted the Frankish domain], and though it suffered some defeats at the hands of the Avars, Slavs, Lombards or Bretons, it never allowed any incursion into what was, strictly speaking, Frankish territory.

Moreover, the fundamental unity of the Frankish nation took definite shape in the world of ideas at the very moment when in fact it was falling to pieces; it was the seventh century that shaped the legend of a Trojan origin for the Franks, as for the Romans and Macedonians. A little later, the prologue to the Salic law was a hymn to the *gens Francorum inclita,* valiant in war, unshakable in peace, uncontaminated by heresy. No doubt patriotic expressions of the same kind are to be found at the same date among the Anglo-Saxons, Lombards and Visigoths. But of these only the Visigoths were of stature to rival the Franks, and they fell before the Arabs. As for the Anglo-Saxons and Lombards, they had not even achieved the conquest of the regions where they had settled, Great Britain and Italy, and they were too few to aim higher. The horizons of the other barbarian nations were even more limited.

THE RISE OF THE CAROLINGIANS   So to become masters of the West the Franks needed only to find a leader and learn how to obey him. At the beginning of the seventh century, while the members of the royal line were busy devouring one another in the famous quarrel between Fredegund and Brunhild, an Austrasian family of great landowners put forward its claim: the Arnulfings, ancestors of the Carolingians and perhaps prototypes of the Nibelungen of the epic where they appear in company with Attila, Theodoric, and other heroes of still more remote times. In 656, Grimoald, son of Pepin the Old and all-powerful Mayor of the Palace under king Sigebert, had the audacity to install his own son on the Austrasian throne, having first had him adopted by the king. The time was not yet ripe; father and son were put to death, but the Arnulfingian family soon recovered itself, producing more Mayors of the Palace. Pepin II was victorious over his Neustrian enemies, raised Frankish prestige in Germany, and sent missionaries to complete the work of his soldiers.

There was another set-back at the death of Pepin II, another advance under his illegitimate son Charles Martel. Defeating the Moslem Arabs and their Christian allies north of the Pyrenees, conquering the Frisians, Saxons and other still pagan Germans, Charles managed to

grab Church possessions to reward his knights, without forfeiting the
favour of the missionary clergy, who had need of his support. The
Pope himself offered his alliance to the Mayor of the Palace in return
for help against the Lombard King Liutprand; but Charles Martel gave
preference to Liutprand, who was his ally against the Arabs and
became godfather to his son (Pepin 'the Short') in a Germanic ceremony which 'grafted' the young man on to the royal stock of Lombardy. The Franks themselves were without a king at this moment, the
Merovingian pretender having died in 737. The vacant throne was only
one short step away.

This step was taken by Pepin the Short, in a way that radically
transformed the Frankish kingship by covering its military and Germanic foundations with a sacerdotal and Roman veneer. Other barbarian kingdoms had already gone the same way; the Visigoths had
even adopted the Hebrew rite of consecrating the king with holy oil,
though they did not surrender their right to depose him. In England,
the mystical fervour of some of the kings was not always popular; it is
said that Sigeberht of Essex was killed 'because he was accustomed to
spare his enemies and forgive them the wrongs they had done him'. All
the same, increasing emphasis on a religious symoblism seemed to be
the only corrective for political ferocity.

A symbolism of this kind seemed needed to take the place of the
ghost of the Merovingian king, *fainéant* but legitimate and quasi-
sacred. When Pepin the Short ventured on the usurpation that so many
others had achieved in neighbouring kingdoms, he was anxious to
purify it by the most unassailable form of consecration possible. First,
he made the Pope declare that the royal title ought to fall to the man
who held the real power. Then, after being elected king by the assembly of nobles, he had himself anointed by St. Boniface, the most famous
of the missionaries, in the presence of the Frankish bishops. Finally, in
754, he knelt before the Pope who had come to France, led the Pope's
horse by the bridle, and promised him armed protection. In return he
obtained a new consecration by the head of the Catholic Church in
person, and in addition the title of 'patrician of the Romans' which he
had probably not asked for.

Henceforth the path of the Carolingians lay clear before them; their
triumphal progress in the second half of the eighth century, as well as
their difficulties in the ninth, bound them closely with the papacy.
Patricians, conquerors of Italy and Germany, emperors or competitors
for the Empire, they poured the profits of their arms and their adminis-

tration into the common funds of a company in which the Pope was first a junior partner, then an equal, and finally a claimant for the overall directorship.

## FROM THE ADMINISTRATION OF ROME
## TO THE TUTELAGE OF THE WEST

In fact, the protection Pepin the Short had promised to Pope Stephen II in 754 implied acceptance of the principles contained in a document which the pontifical experts had, it seems, just drawn up to meet the needs of the cause: the *Donation of Constantine*. This put into the mouth of the first Christian Emperor, the founder of Constantinople, these surprising words: 'We deem it proper to move our Empire . . . for in the place where the sacerdotal principality and the capital of the Christian religion have been installed by the Emperor of Heaven, it is not right that the terrestrial emperor should exercise his power . . . We concede and abandon [to the Pope] . . . the town of Rome, together with all the provinces, localities and cities of Italy and the western regions, to be held by him and his successors in their power and tutelage.'

We must resist the temptation to treat this 'donation' as a forgery; its very language, which is certainly anachronistic, betrays the uncouthness of Roman culture in the eighth century, yet its authenticity was not seriously questioned before the Renaissance. Forgery presupposes an intention to deceive; but the clerks who drew up the *Donation* to fill what they felt was a lacuna in the archives were no doubt convinced that the facts had been much as they described them. Since God had willed that the Pope should have the West in his tutelage and Pepin the Frankish monarchy in his power, it was an act of faith to provide an incontestable legal basis for them. But the mutual guarantee which the two protagonists exchanged, against any claim by a third party, made a longstanding but distant friendship into real complicity, first against the Lombards, then against the Byzantine Empire.

The 'donation' transformed the political destiny of the papacy as radically as that of the Frankish state which the papacy was prepared to wed in order to secure Rome and Ravenna as dowry and the West as joint estate. A hasty marriage, all things considered, and fraught with consequences that the popes had probably not clearly foreseen or desired: irreparable separation from the East and the final partition of Italy.

THE POPES BETWEEN ROMANS AND LOMBARDS   Long before the compact
with the Franks Gregory I [pope, 590–604] was, in fact, already the
administrator of Rome. This involved no conflict with the Emperor,
since a law of Justinian conferred on all bishops extensive powers over
the civil authorities. If the papacy subsequently looked more and more
to the barbarian West, yet the spiritual unity of the two Romes had for
long been ensured by the recruitment of popes. Between 606 and 752
there were thirteen popes born in the East or in Byzantine Italy.
Gregory III, the enemy of the iconoclast emperors, was a Syrian.

Nevertheless the political unity of the two Romes was difficult to
maintain. The elder Rome was too far from Constantinople, too close
to the Lombard border; inevitably, Byzantine Italy and barbarian Italy
attracted each other.

In the course of the seventh century the increasing difficulties of the
Empire in the East left its delegates in Italy almost entirely to their
own resources. Exarchs of Ravenna, doges of Venice and Naples,
archons of Sardinia, 'masters of soldiers' and 'tribunes' of the different
districts—some sent from Constantinople, others elected from the local
aristocracy with the express or tacit consent of the Emperor—relied
more and more on the native population, in a disorder not very
different from the anarchy of the Merovingian kingdom. The Pope,
who had fewer military forces than they but was consecrated by his
ecclesiastical office and possessed of vast estates throughout Italy, consolidated his Roman domain and extended his influence through the
rest of the *pars romana* or *Respublica Romanorum* (Byzantine Italy),
of which he gradually became, as it were, president. His frequent
clashes with the Emperors, over religious or practical matters, were no
doubt often serious embarrassments to him, but his own perseverance
and the solidarity of the Italians always enabled him to emerge victorious. At the beginning of the eighth century even Ravenna, the seat
of the chief lieutenant of Byzantium and of a bishop whose autonomy
Byzantium had established by decree, sought the protection of the Pope
against Greek officials and against the Lombards who were closing in
on her. In their turn, a few Lombard dukes appealed to the Pope for
help against their kings' policy of centralization. These were all excellent chances to develop the function of mediator between 'Romans'
and 'Lombards' which Gregory I had so successfully inaugurated.

Despite the quarrels and confusion which prevailed on the surface,
there were signs of a reconciliation between the peoples of Italy. The
Lombards, who dominated most of it, were originally one of the most
backward Germanic peoples. The mark they left on the country was in

brutal contrast with what survived of traditional Italian culture, but was all the more susceptible to the influence of the civilization round about them. Between the end of the sixth and the beginning of the seventh century, the Lombards in fact abandoned their Arian beliefs, their Teutonic tongue, their way of dressing. Their law put up a stronger resistance, but mingled with the other legal currents in Italy, Roman law, canon law, customs born of day-to-day experience. King Liutprand felt it necessary to state categorically that Lombard procedure was just as valid as Roman. To forbid the marriage of a widow with the cousin of her dead husband, he invoked the authority of the Pope 'venerated through the whole world as head of the Church'.

That does not mean that the Lombards were no longer conscious of their individuality, but that the *pars Langobarda* was now identifying itself with the rest of the kingdom, in which all inhabitants were grouped according to their social rank rather than their ethnical origins. Even rank did not weigh with king Aistulf, the son of a duke and a peasantwoman, who in 750 mobilized landowners and merchants side by side, according to wealth and not to birth.

THE DOWNFALL OF THE LOMBARDS    Across the Italian peninsula, a strange indented frontier marked the place where the Lombard conquest had been halted on the death of the last Arian king, in 652. This frontier was not an effective barrier against penetration, whether economic, cultural or religious. On the one hand, Ravenna diluted its Byzantine colouring and became almost barbarian. On the other Pavia, the Lombard capital, increasingly welcomed Byzantine influence. In 725-6, when the *pars romana* revolted, first against a tax for the war against the Arabs and then against the iconoclast measures of Leo III [Byzantine emperor, 717-741], the Lombards, who were on the side of the images, had a chance to present themselves to the rebels as the lesser of two evils.

At that point Liutprand invaded the territories of Ravenna and Rome; but he was undecided, ill supported by his dukes, intimidated by the popes, who had designs on the whole region and used all possible weapons to stop him before he reached his goal. The opportunity was lost and never recurred. When later Aistulf took Ravenna at one fell swoop and claimed that his sovereignty be recognized by Rome (no doubt without prejudice to the rights the Pope had acquired), the agreement of 754 unleashed against him the superior might of the Franks. Once the Lombards were crushed, Pepin the Short gave Pope

Stephen II Ravenna, which, together with Rome, was to be the first nucleus of the pontifical State.

Twenty years later, King Didier lost his crown in an attempt to carry out Aistulf's plans; Charlemagne, King of the Franks, became also King of the Lombards by conquest, and patrician of the Romans by papal nomination (774). For though the popes wanted no sovereign at as close quarters as Didier would have been, they needed a sovereign at a distance, more respectful, capable of defending them against the lordlings who swarmed among the ruins of the Lombard state and the fragments of Byzantine Italy. So they heaped favours on Charlemagne, in a crescendo that led to the 'imperial restoration' of Christmas 800.

THE CORONATION OF CHARLEMAGNE: SEVERAL WILLS COINCIDE   The last act was played in the best Byzantine tradition: coronation by the metropolitan bishop (in Rome, the Pope), acclamation by the people, adoration of the Emperor by all present. It might be objected that these were not really the proper actors or the proper theatre, but at that moment Constantinople had only an empress, who, though she showed due respect for images, had acceded to the throne of Constantine by deposing and blinding her own son. To get rid of her, it was said, Charlemagne had a choice of three methods: to depose her, marry her, or persuade her to recognize him as a colleague (in fact, she was overthrown by her own people before the choice was made; and it took a war to extract provisional acceptance of the third alternative from one of her successors).

Though the official acts were all accomplished by popes, none of them apparently of outstanding intellectual or moral stature, the restoration was the result of several wills coinciding. First of all there were the builders of the Empire, Charlemagne and his noblemen, who were perhaps not bent on the coronation taking the exact form it did, but who no doubt welcomed any formula that might express the superiority of the victorious monarch over all other kings, past or present. Lombards, Bavarians, Saxons, Frisians, all the old enemies of the Franks at last subdued; the Avars of the Danubian plain, only a short time ago a force to be feared even though weakened by their struggle with Byzantium, now reduced to unconditional surrender together with their Slav subjects; the Arabs, in spite of Roncevaux [a defeat of the Franks in 778], thrown back south of the Pyrenees and beyond the glacis of the Spanish marches—these were the tangible titles that made Charlemagne worthy of a special title.

But in the eyes of the Nordic clergy his piety was a still more important merit. By the protection he accorded to the Church in the land of his ancestors, in the provinces won from the pagans, and even in Jerusalem under infidel rule, Charlemagne gave reality to the ideal of St. Augustine, the 'Christian Empire' in which the City of Men prefigured the City of God.

Finally, all who were not resigned to the death of the Roman Empire or its exile in the East, all who idealized ancient Rome as the model of justice or peace, might or intellect, saw in this German 'clad in the skins of beasts' the man destined to give flesh and blood once more to the ghost of the Empire. A ghost indeed, for history never retraces its steps, nor was Rome ever so beautiful as she appeared in dreams; but an all-conquering ghost, who accomplished the miracle of its own resurrection.

## PRELUDE TO EUROPE, OR A FALSE START?

What strikes us most, after so many dormant years, is not the confusion and conflict of intentions behind the momentous decision of Christmas 800, but the re-emergence of a will to experiment and build. The Carolingian restoration is like an early thaw which spends its heat before all the snow has melted: most plants are dead or barren, but some have buds, and there are ephemeral flowers to announce the hardier blossoming of the spring to come. Universalism, Europeanism, feudalism, nationalism: all of these trends found a first expression, more or less rudimentary, in the ninth century. On the almost blank book they had inherited from the earlier age, the Carolingians wrote down many important questions; satisfactory answers were found only at a later period, when the problems themselves had substantially changed.

THE EUROPEAN FRAMEWORK   From a geographical point of view, it is not unwarranted to regard the Carolingian Empire as prelude to Europe. Even if it did not exercise effective power over all Catholic Europe (not to mention Byzantium), it came nearer to doing so than any state in later years, except perhaps Napoleon's Empire. It is true that Catholic Europe, in the time of Charlemagne, did not yet include the Scandinavian countries or the Iberian peninsula (except the Spanish March and the little Visigothic kingdom of the Asturias, whose sovereign recognized the Frankish monarch as his superior). The Slavs, too, were

represented only by a few Slovene tribes, precariously attached to the
Carolingian possessions of Bavaria and Italy. Nevertheless Charlemagne made so deep an impression on the Southern Slavs that his
name (Charles, *kral*) became the title of royalty in their tongue, as
Caesar's name was in many others.

The family of Catholic nations, such as it was at the time, had thus
come almost entirely under the direct or indirect authority of Charlemagne. England was the most important exception; even there, a king
of Northumbria recovered his throne through diplomatic pressure by
the Emperor and the Pope, but the powerful King of Mercia claimed
an equal footing with Charlemagne. Certainly Mercia was puny as
compared with the Carolingian Empire, but King Offa had no map, and
was entitled to be proud of the great earthwork he had built along the
Welsh border. Ireland, further away, was left to anarchy, scarcely
mitigated by the presidency of her *Ard-rí* (high king) over her two
hundred kinglets. She did, however, contribute stars of the first magnitude to the intellectual firmament which was the glory of the Carolingian court, and which included a fair number of English and Spaniards,
besides subjects of the many provinces of the Empire.

Though the European framework of the Empire was never acknowledged in the Carolingian official vocabulary, it did not pass wholly
unnoticed in the literature of the time. The name of Europe, known in
antiquity but seldom mentioned in the barbarian period, dramatically
reappears in one of the earliest accounts of the battle of Poitiers [or
Tours, 732] described by a Spanish chronicler as a triumph of the
*Europeenses* over the Arabs. In the ninth and tenth centuries, literary
references to 'Europe' grew more numerous, then faded away. The
mutual distrust of Rome and Byzantium, both aspiring to universal
predominance, made it impossible for that notion to prevail over the
rivalry between West and East. All this has a familiar ring.

Return to Universality   Had Charlemagne entertained no greater
ambition than that of being the 'summit of Europe', something like an
*ard-rí* or *bretwalda* of the Catholic West, he would have encountered
no obstacles: he was an eminently successful warrior, whose frequent
expeditions brought fresh conquests and booty for distribution to the
largest army in the continent. To be 'Emperor of the Romans', however, meant much more. It entailed an all-embracing responsibility to
ensure the moral and material order of the City of Men and a claim to
universal rule, if not over the entire world (for neither the Roman

Empire nor the Roman Church ever were literally universal), at least over the civilized commonwealth.

On the first score, Charlemagne performed remarkably well, especially if we consider how little most of his predecessors had cared for the responsibility of kingship. Within the limits and forms of his own culture, he was as well aware of his public duties as the most conscentious of the Byzantine emperors. He did his best to order and improve everything, from the morals of the clergy to the alloy of the coinage, from collections of legal texts to popular epics. But he did not perceive as clearly the universal significance of the imperial crown. He tended to the day of his death to govern his state as a simple 'extension of the kingdom', or rather a collection of territories and tribes which his personal talent had brought together and his personal whim could re-distribute among his relatives according to Frankish custom. A few household officials helped the Emperor to take care of general affairs: the 'master of the chamber', a weakened substitute of the Merovingian mayor of the palace; the 'seneschal', a chief steward; the 'count of the stable'; the 'butler', and other officials whose titles remind one of the barbarian notion of the state as a private property. But each of the kingdoms included in the Empire maintained its own administration, institutions and laws.

The Empire would have been partitioned at Charlemagne's death, but for the fact that only one of his sons happened to survive him: Louis 'the Pious'. He had been indoctrinated by the imperial-minded clergy enough to discard at once the titles of King of the Franks and King of the Lombards and style himself Emperor, *tout court*. In 817, Louis proclaimed that any division of the Empire would be contrary to the will of God and the unity of the Church. One of his bishops, applying St. Paul's words to a new context, added that the entire population of the Empire must be 'one body in Christ'. A body with an imperial head: in 824, Louis ordered that no pope should be consecrated before taking an oath of fidelity to the Emperor. Meanwhile, growing Italian and Byzantine influences blew faint whiffs of Roman air into the Germanic atmosphere of the Carolingian court and administration. Charles 'the Bald', one of Louis' sons, was even to shock his Frankish retinue by dressing like a Byzantine Emperor.

It was, however, either too early or too late. Louis may have been more far-sighted than Charlemagne, but lacked his iron will and overwhelming prestige. The anarchical tendencies of the Franks broke the spell cast by the first Emperor; Louis' sons and grandsons tore the

Empire to pieces, before the imperial theory could fully mature. Yet it had developed far enough to survive, independently of the Frankish hegemony, the person of the Emperor and the integrity of the Empire, as the dominant political symbol of the Catholic world.

THE CHRISTIAN REPUBLIC IN THE WEST   Not quite ready when it might have been strong enough, not strong enough when it might have been almost ready, the Carolingian Empire may appear to a modern eye as a most ineffectual body politic, wrapped in mystical haze. But the men of the ninth century saw a *Respublica Christiana* embracing most of Europe and functioning with unprecedented harmony. State and Church were merged within it to the point at which the initiative could come from one or the other, according to the needs of the moment or the talents and energy of their respective heads, without causing conflict or serious divergencies.

Collaboration was particularly fruitful in the lands recently won from the pagans. Here the clergy formed a sort of army of occupation and administration, larger and better organized than the soldiers and lay officials. Just as the appearance of a stipple of towns formerly showed that Rome had tamed some barbarian nation, so the network of parishes and monasteries indicated that some new subjects of the Carolingian Empire had served their apprenticeship in the civilization of the old provinces. Certain usages condemned by Christianity, such as human sacrifices and polygamy, were forbidden; the elementary methods of Frankish or Lombard agriculture were imported, by means of direct colonization or instruction of the natives: native ecclesiastical cadres were formed, reading and speaking Latin after a fashion and teaching as best they could a 'Christian' way of life. Because the Carolingian culture was simpler than Roman culture of the classical age, it was more easily assimilated. Several centuries were needed before provincials proved themselves capable of governing the *Respublica Romana;* a century and a half was enough for the newly converted Saxons to take the helm of the *Respublica Christiana* after the Franks let it slip from their grasp.

State and Church collaborated too in the old provinces, but their work there was done with less enthusiasm and produced no radical changes. The susceptibilities of the two capitals, Rome and Aix-la-Chapelle, had to be reckoned with, and their traditions and aims did not always provide a meeting point. Besides this divergence, there was provincial opposition, ranging from the turbulence of Aquitaine to the rebellions in Brittany and the Lombard principality of Benevento, which had escaped the fate of the Lombard kingdom; incidentally, Benevento and Brittany recovered their independence in the end, and the main body of Lombard Italy had to be granted a large degree of autonomy.

The main enemies were demoralization and ignorance, shared by most of the clergy and nearly all the flocks. But it was possible to believe without understanding every dogma or keeping every commandment. Heresies seem to have found few adherents among the people, though the problem of predestination was a source of quarrels among the learned. Pagan superstitions were more widespread, but superstition does not exclude faith.

The whole population of Carolingian Europe, the humble and obscure as well as the powerful and illustrious, rested on a uniform religious basis. This, and the fundamental similarity of customs, made possible the gradual development of a rudimentary commonwealth. Its memory has long haunted the imagination of historians and politicians; it was evoked recently by Napoleon's courtiers and ultimately by European federalists in our days. Yet it would be improper to carry the comparison too far and call 'the first Europe' what actually should be defined, in the light of the present, a false start. For the word 'Europe' today implies not so much a single body of beliefs or a universal state as the sum of political institutions, secular learning, artistic and literary traditions, economic and social interests, created by many independent nations. From this point of view the Carolingian Empire must seem to us a remarkable effort but, when all is said and done, an irrelevant one.

## BEGINNINGS OF FEUDALISM, GLEAMS OF NATIONALITY

For the discharge of the heavy tasks that fell to him as head of the *Respublica Christiana* the Carolingian sovereign had at his disposal, first and last, the political framework which had served the Merovingians so ill: collective organs, local agents, personal assistants and servants. Collective organs of a 'democratic' kind (that is, assemblies formed by the adult males of the ruling nation) could hardly be used for functions outside local justice. At any rate, the general assembly of free men had been transformed into a council of military and religious notables, who alone still enjoyed complete liberty. As for the local agents, such as counts and their subordinates, they would have found their task hard if they had attempted to carry it out with any measure of zeal. But they almost all had become independent property-owners, ungovernable and irremovable, for in the absence of regular taxes the royal domain of their district was their salary and the price of their loyalty. If loyalty wavered, how could the salary be retracted?

So the main weight of the task fell on the king's intimates and personal servants, who made up a floating group, of differing ranks and with ill-defined functions. A good servant was not content to be 'kept' in the king's palace. He wanted to be bought by the gift of lands where he could live as master rather than servant. Gradually the Merovingians stripped themelves of a vast patrimony of estates, ruining themselves in the vain hope of governing.

THE PROBLEMS OF GOVERNMENT   Of course the first Carolingians were in a much better position than their immediate predecessors. They were the acknowledged leaders of a competent and local clergy, and their military successes and their unequalled energy compelled recognition by laymen. They had at their disposal a fresh supply of estates, lands acquired in the service of the Merovingians, Church property seized by Charles Martel, conquests of Pepin the Short and Charlemagne. Propelled by their vigour, the old wheels of government began to turn again, though they still creaked: the assembly deliberated, counts (and later dukes and marquises) carried out orders, the household servants of the palace exerted themselves in all directions. Then the wheels were greased: everything possible was done to instruct the staff, to explain their duties clearly (in writing, if the recipient could read), and to prepare lodging for them if they had to travel. But in spite of all this feverish and well-directed activity, there was no question of making one ill-conditioned jade do the work of several well trained horses.

To govern as the Byzantine emperors did, the emperors of the West would have had to re-establish the Roman system of taxation and use the proceeds to pay in money a large staff of civil employees whose salary could be withdrawn at the first sign of insubordination. They did not even consider it. A revolution of this kind, even if the economic conditions of the Carolingian Empire had allowed it—and that is doubtful—would have been repugnant to a society which met most of its needs without recourse to money and respected only the land-owning military class. There was no alternative to granting land in order to reward service. Like the Merovingians, the Carolingians would have to squander the royal estates in order to rule.

No doubt; but steps could be taken to prevent the disloyalty of the grantees. While distributing land, the Carolingians endeavoured to tighten the bonds of loyalty. The simplest means, widely used by the Merovingians and other barbarian rulers, was to require an oath of fidelity that would stress the personal bond between sovereign and dependant, and call God as a witness and avenger of broken pledges. Experience, however, had abundantly proved that no promise will create loyalty where loyalty is not present from the start; the path which led the Merovingians to their doom was paved with faithless oaths.

Nonetheless, Charlemagne demanded oaths from all free men, and closer oaths from his closer retainers ('vassals'), with an insistence bordering on obsession; he also encouraged his vassals to demand oaths from their own dependants. At the same time, he groped for devices that could compel obedience. He and his successors endeavoured to preserve loyalty by retaining ownership of lands conceded to dependants, to hallow it by strengthening the religious symbolism of the oath, to stabilize it by playing it off against rival loyalties, and to control it by periodical inspections. Their methods were neither entirely new nor always consistent, but they formed the first nucleus of what was later to be called feudalism.

THE DAWN OF FEUDALISM   For the moment we shall do no more than indicate the chief characteristics which emerged thus before the mid ninth century. Unconditional gifts of free-hold lands were replaced by the concession of 'benefices' in simple possession. The grant implied perpetual obligations of obedience and service. These duties had to be acknowledged by a promise of 'fidelity', impressively staged and including the taking of an oath on relics. Clergymen serving the government received privileges which enabled them, in spite of their military inferiority, to act as counterbalance to the lay vassals. Itinerant officials of high rank, the *missi dominici,* armed with full powers, checked the performance of the vassals at frequent intervals.

These practices, like the imperial theory, needed time to be tested and improved upon. They could not at once make up for the lack of public spirit; their observance still depended upon the personal qualities of the sovereign and the assistance of his family. However, the heirs of Louis the Pious began to quarrel among themselves and attack him even during his lifetime. With the Empire rent by these internal wars, new waves of barbarians broke over it and hastened the collapse of central authority. This resulted in an accelerated development of feudalism, but in a direction which Charlemagne had not foreseen. At first, the holders of benefices sold their loyalty to the highest bidder among the claimants to the throne, and demanded larger grants in return for smaller services. Then, as the paralysis of the central government progressed, they stepped into the vacuum, took over more fully the defence and administration of their land, and governed it with little if any reference to the paramount interests of the sovereign.

Thus, after a first stage during which the sovereign had emphasized the duties of the vassals, there was a second stage during which the vassals affirmed their rights. The third and final stage, that of balanced reciprocal obligations, was still a long way off. But even the chaotic second stage was not entirely negative. It placed an increased responsibility on the shoulders of the vassals and almost forced them to reconstitute to their own profit those local cells of government that had disappeared with the downfall of the Roman network of city-states. [And] the revival of local government and initiative was an essential factor in changing the false start made under the Carolingians into a real beginning of Europe.

NATION COMES FROM 'NASCI', TO BE BORN     Modern Europe, however, does not rest directly on local governments but on nationalities. Ancient Rome had melted primitive nationalisms into a universal patriotism; nationalities were a product of Middle Ages, and the Carolingian period made some contribution, although unconsciously and unwillingly.

There is a great difference between the solidarity of tribe and folk, such as the barbarians undoubtedly had always known, and nationalism based upon the relation of a people to a home land. This feeling had obscurely grown with the long stay of the Lombards in Lombardy, the Bavarians in Bavaria, the Neustrians in Neustria, and, in each region, with the gradual fusion of barbarians and natives. The vague universalism of the Carolingian Empire, however, was not favourable to the development of nations as distinguished from kinship groups. The emperors allowed their subjects to practise the tribal customs of their ancestors. Under their rule a great number of curious formulae appeared in legal documents, in which each of the interested parties declared that he 'lived according to the Frankish law'—or Lombard, Alamanic, Visigothic or Roman, as the case might be—'by virtue of his birth' (*ex natione*). But *nation* in these texts had a meaning quite different from the one we give it; it ignored geographical context, bypassed administrative divisions, and recognized only ties of blood.

But even this criterion allowed of exceptions. We find individuals who professed a different law from their fathers'. Automatically entry into the Church implied adoption of 'Roman' law, which indicates the extent to which the Catholic Church disapproved of any manifestation of nationalism within her bosom. Her insistence on the Latin of the liturgy, in contrast with the more accommodating attitude of the Orthodox Church, is further proof of this. Without going as far towards universalism as the Popes, the first Carolingian Emperors took some steps in the same direction. They promulgated capitularies [ordinances] that were valid throughout the Empire, and though they codified the 'national' laws they left them to decay for lack of fresh ordinances. It is said that Louis the Pious considered imposing Salic 'national' law as the general law of Europe, but never put his plan into execution.

FROM THE COUNCIL OF TOURS TO THE PARTITION OF VERDUN: THE SEPARATION OF LANGUAGES   Several more centuries were to pass before true nationalism was born, but the preliminary conditions that were to transform Europe into a pattern of national states made an early appearance, as a result of struggles for the succession. The repeated partitions of the Carolingian state under the heirs of Louis the Pious were based on lines familiar to us on the maps of modern nationalities, with a persistence that it is difficult to attribute to mere chance. At any rate, they corresponded roughly with the linguistic frontiers for which the Carolingian age provides our first reliable evidence. In 813 the Council of Tours recommended the clergy to translate sermons into the Romance or Teutonic tongue, so that the people might understand them. Twenty-nine years later, the two younger sons of Louis the Pious and their armies took an oath of mutual aid against the elder son, the Emperor Lothar: the soldiers of Charles the Bald took the oath in Romance, those of Louis the German in Teutonic. The Treaty of Verdun in the next year almost translated the Strasburg oaths into a political partition: the entirely French provinces went to Charles the Bald, those entirely German to Louis the German. Lothar kept for himself, besides the Italian and Provençal provinces with particularly marked Romance characteristics, a long strip of intermediate lands, in which even in our own days the languages interlock: the Low Countries, Dutch and Walloon, Lorraine and Alsace which are still bones of contention, and polyglot Switzerland.

Nevertheless it is certain that criteria of nationality played no *conscious* part in the Partition of Verdun, which was brought about by transient and accidental causes. The problem was to make three shares, roughly equivalent from the point of view of their economic and military resources, adding to the regions already under the control of each brother the bordering districts needed to make the parts equal. The younger brothers, the real winners, kept the more compact slices for themselves, though they left to their elder brother the two capitals, Rome and Aix-la-Chapelle, which fell to him with the imperial title. Further, the officials who counted the abbeys and counties assigned to the three brothers were little concerned with linguistics, and as they had no atlas were not even in a position to form a clear mental picture of the mass of states they were carving up.

The fact remains that two of the kingdoms of 843 stood firm against all the currents of the future and provided the framework of modern France and Germany. The third, on the other hand, bisected by the Alps and peopled by races who could not understand each other's speech, disintegrated almost at once. Gradually France and Germany absorbed its northern provinces. The transalpine section, for which the name of 'Italy' was again beginning to be more common than that of 'Lombard kingdom', might still have occupied an honourable place in the triad if it had succeeded in extending its territory south of Rome, where the Lombard and Carolingian conquests had been halted. But the Emperor Louis II, Lothar's successor, failed completely in his military and diplomatic efforts to rally under his authority that other 'Italy' (the wreckage of Lombard Benevento, Byzantine towns that were autonomous but threatened by the Arabs). Too small without its southern part, the 'garden of the Empire' (to borrow Dante's expression) was for the pleasure of others; indeed, a hundred years after the Partition of Verdun it became a dependency of Germany in a lame Empire which did not include France. From the ninth century onwards the inequality of the Italian partner compromised the second political solution open to the Carolingians: failing European unity, a balance of three national kingdoms.


## THE BALANCE-SHEET OF CAROLINGIAN CIVILIZATION

Carolingian culture, a transitional culture, found its lasting formula in the restricted field of handwriting, Latin grammar, and the indispensable classical texts.

The reform of handwriting was its most important success. Formed in the *scriptoria* (copying-centres) of France, the 'Caroline' minuscule ousted, one by one, the 'national' hands: Visigothic, Merovingian, Lombard, Irish, Anglo-Saxon, all of them developed from decadent non-epigraphic Roman scripts (uncial, semi-uncial, cursive). It triumphed in the end, long after the extinction of the Carolingians, as far afield as Spain, England and the Italian south. The Caroline minuscule had not perhaps all the virtues that its success has attributed to it: the national hands were more imaginative, the capitals of classical inscriptions and expensive manuscripts were more harmonious and could have been just as economical of space if their size had been reduced. But the Caroline minuscule is clear and does not tire the eyes; we can speak of it in the present tense, for this book is printed in Caroline minuscules that have hardly been modified, with the addition of capitals that the humanists were to rediscover in the inscriptions of Roman monuments. It is one of the first in the series of standards that simplify international life: the Gregorian calendar, the metric system, a universal postal union.

LITERARY RENAISSANCE: ITS LIMITATIONS  In the same order of ideas comes the work of official Carolingian circles in establishing the elementary rules of classical Latin and the models of language and style as contained in the great books of Christian or pagan literature. There was no time to lose: national languages were already thrusting up through the clumsy jargon of Continental writers, though they had not yet, as in England, achieved the status of literary languages. True Latin was dead, and must be embalmed to serve for the understanding of the Scriptures, the conversation of the learned, and official acts applying to a community speaking different idioms. Also the less futile of profane authors must be preserved before their last manuscripts were lost, or effaced by some industrious monk eager to cover their costly parchment with one of the holy texts of which there could never be too many copies.

We can measure both our great debt to the 'Carolingian renaissance' and the limits of its culture if we draw up a list of the Latin classics which have come down to us (almost invariably, the manuscript tradition goes back to a Carolingian archetype), and compare it with the mass of lost works. A revealing symptom of the spirit of this age is that the pagan poets found favour more often than men of science, in spite of the difficulty of neutralizing the poison of their sensuality or worldliness by allegorical interpretations. Truth, it was said, had not been revealed to the Ancients, but they possessed the secret of style. This style was successfully imitated: there was a sudden outburst of poetry in correct classical meters, and Eginhard took Suetonius as a model.

We have purposely used the word 'renaissance', which some would like to see restricted to the humanist age. No doubt the Carolingian renaissance lighted no more than an altar candle, which shone in surrounding darkness, while the other Renaissance took some of the light of heaven to give it to man. But the intellectual elite of the two ages had in common a feeling of the discontinuity of the past, and the desire to suppress the most recent phases and revive the ideal of an earlier age.

Some poems and drawings of the ninth century are like pages torn from a book of the second or third century—but a book of very modest worth, for though the Carolingian renaissance recruited a number of men of talent, it produced only one thinker of the first rank, the Irish philosopher Johannes Scotus Erigena. It is true that Erigena knew Greek well. As a result, he had more direct access than most of his contemporaries to Byzantine civilization, the source of classical, hellenistic and oriental inspiration.

ARTISTIC RENAISSANCE: ITS COMPLEXITY   As for the arts, which needed no translator, Byzantium freely furnished the Carolingian renaissance with craftsmen, motifs and techniques. We must not think only of Rome, which lay hardly outside the political orbit of the East and where the ninth century produced some of her most beautiful mosaics, or of Ravenna, though her San Vitale supplied the main inspiration for Charlemagne's church at Aix-la-Chapelle, but also of the Asiatic core of the Byzantine Empire. Even in the heart of France, the church of Theodulf at Germigny-les-Prés seems to stem from an Armenian model, the cathedral of Echmiadzin.

Carolingian art was more original and fruitful than literature. It absorbed all kinds of foreign influences, made use of all native themes available in the vast Empire (from Nordic interlace to the palmetto of the Mediterranean), and occasionally recovered aspects of the classic naturalistic tradition at its best. The human figure again became a centre of interest—and that is the first step on the long road of humanism. Some of the Carolingian themes in turn nourished later artistic revivals—the Ottonian and Anglo-Saxon 'renaissances' of the tenth and eleventh centuries—and some had an influence on Romanesque art.

But in its own time, the art of the Carolingians had little impact beyond a few centres.

One feature is common to all the manifestations of the Carolingian renaissance: they were hot-house plants, cultivated by a handful of intellectuals who, in their turn, relied on the encouragement and support of a handful of patrons: the sovereigns, the Court, a very small number of ecclesiastical institutions. Even the reform of handwriting at first concerned a few thousand people at most; the others could not write.

COMMERCE: OF SMALL VALUE, BUT INFLUENTIAL    How many people were affected by the other stimulant of local life, international trade? In the absence of statistical data we may guess at some tens of thousand customers: those who were refined enough to want ornaments, arms, medicines, seasonings, and above all rich enough to buy them; that is to say, a part of the nobility and high ecclesiastics. As for the suppliers, they could not have been more than a few thousand, even if we take into account those who trafficked in slaves, in wood, metals and other products of the West (raw materials for the most part) that could command a sale in Byzantine and Arab markets. It is impossible to estimate the number of merchants engaged in domestic trade, if only because a considerable proportion of this trade was in the hands of people normally employed in other professions: landowners, farmers, moneylenders, fishermen.

Not only in Catholic Europe, but from one end of the Old World to the other, the greatest merchants were Jews. We recall in particular those of whom the ninth-century Arab sources say that they spoke seven languages and operated a shuttle-service between Spain and China over three parallel routes, of which one ran through the whole length of the Carolingian Empire. Purveyors to the Merovingian and then the Carolingian kings, organizers of the slave trade, wholesale dealers in wine and salt, the Jews owed their success chiefly to their intellectual equipment: widespread education, exchange of ideas and techniques between communities in all countries, respect for commercial activities, at a time when the West had little esteem for any but the soldier and the priest. But they were also served by the exceptional treatment which, in so many other respects, was their misfortune: because they had no full citizen's rights in any state, they escaped the restrictions that every country placed on the movement of aliens, especially in time of war.

Less important than the Jews, but destined for a more brilliant career in the centuries to come, the citizens of the autonomous Byzantine ports of Italy—Venice, Amalfi, Naples, Gaeta and yet others—were beginning to enjoy similar advantages without suffering the same inconvenience. Their ambiguous political status allowed them to arrive at all frontiers as friends rather than aliens; their relations with the Byzantine and Arab world opened windows on cultures more advanced than that of Catholic Europe, whose outer wall they skirted. In its turn, the Carolingian Empire possessed a culture more advanced than that of its neighbours to the north, all along a semicircle running from Ireland to Bohemia. The profitable but intermittent trade carried on in these areas swelled the meagre income the Frisians drew from the agriculture practised in their swampy country. Finally, the Scandinavians often deigned to buy products they could quite as well have taken by force, or sell products which they had stolen in one or other of their raids.

Certainly we must not measure economic currents by their volume, and use the scale of our own days to plot them. The few thousand people selling little groups of slaves or thin rolls of material (or, over shorter distances, enough salt to fill a barge or two) did valuable work in keeping open a ventilator in the dark cellar where, but for them, the Carolingian economy would have been locked up. Similarly, the few native traders who still lived in the decayed towns of the interior and drew their resources as much from their landed estates as from local trade and money-lending were not a negligible quantity. Socially, they were the shadow of a middle class inserted between the great and the poor, both fettered to the land. Economically, they prevented money from going out of circulation altogether, and each village from becoming an island abandoned to its own resources. In the northern provinces of the Empire, where urban life had altogether ceased or had never existed, the merchants joined the missionaries and the soldiers in conjuring up small towns, such as Quentovic and Dorestad, which blossomed brightly before disappearing totally in the turmoil of the following centuries. In all probability these merchants, whether foreigners or natives, of whom we know next to nothing (for they had no pretensions to literature, and no commercial document of the ninth century has come down to us), played a part as important as any Erigena or Eginhard. Like them, they ensured for the life of their day the survival of marginal activities, and possibilities for the immediate future.

THE TRUE SCOPE OF THE CAROLINGIAN REVIVAL  Marginal: that is the
word that comes to mind as soon as we move away from the three
pillars of Carolingian civilization: religion, war, agriculture. Even in
these three fields the orders and advice of the active minorities were
stifled by the inertia of the majority.

On a clergy lacking zeal and a people lacking fervour, the religious
learning of Alcuin or the holiness of Benedict of Aniane had little hold.
The severest punishments and the most extravagant rewards were
hardly enough to mobilize recalcitrant and greedy vassals against the
most dangerous enemies. It should have been easier to organize agricultural work: serfs could hardly refuse to co-operate, and in any case
man must plough if he would eat. But hands were few, the little properties lovingly tended by independent peasants had almost all disappeared, and the great estates were only oases in the midst of a
deserted countryside. To make any profit at all, the lord's agents had to
exercise unwearying vigilance. These estates tried to produce everything so as not to have to buy anything; because there was no need to
buy, there was no incentive to produce surpluses for resale. It was
hardly possible to accumulate enough reserves to avoid the famines of
lean years. Even Charlemagne, when he had not the windfall of a
profitable war, went back to supervising his kitchen-gardens, his hen-
runs, the weaving of wool by his maid-servants. In an empire of
farmers he was a model farmer.

Meanwhile under his orders new land was cleared all along the frontiers, in the same spirit that led Rome and her heir, Byzantium, to provide the districts exposed to attack with soldier-farmers. But the
progress of Carolingian agriculture all too often resembled the movements of nomadic tribes: behind the ploughmen who opened up a
clearing, the forest closed in again on the fields they had just left.
Similarly, the roads that the Carolingians strove to repair, just as they
restored the Latin grammar, were soon obliterated again; not enough
people passed to trample the weeds down and keep them open. To
maintain the cohesion of the Empire, to stir up a bureaucracy barely
sufficient to govern it, ceaseless journeys on horseback were needed.

This was, in fact, the beginning of the age of the mounted knight;
but if knights may sometimes conquer vast areas at lightning speed,
they cannot hold them long without the help of the humble farm cart.
The new Europe was almost in sight. It was to be built from the bottom
rather than the top, thanks to better farm carts rather than to more
fiery horses. In the ninth century the Carolingian Empire, that frail

giant, was sinking to its premature grave; in the tenth century struc-
tures that were more viable because smaller and better provided with
manpower would rise in its place, and usher in a thousand years of
almost unbroken economic and intellectual growth.

## Suggestions for Further Reading

BOLGAR, R. R., *The Classical Heritage and Its Beneficiaries*. Cambridge,
England: Cambridge University Press, 1958.

BURNS, C. D., *The First Europe*. London: Allen & Unwin, 1947.

*Cambridge Economic History*, Vol. I, 2d ed. Cambridge, England:
Cambridge University Press, 1967.

DAWSON, CHRISTOPHER, *The Making of Europe*. New York: Sheed and
Ward, 1932.

FICHTENAU, HEINRICH, *The Carolingian Empire*. Oxford: Basil Blackwell,
1957.

GANSHOF, F. L., *Frankish Institutions under Charlemagne*. Providence:
Brown University Press, 1968.

HALPHEN, LOUIS, *Charlemagne et l'empire carolingien*. Paris: A. Michel,
1947.

HINKS, R., *Carolingian Art*, London: Sidgwick & Jackson, 1935.

MOSS, H., *The Birth of the Middle Ages*. London: Oxford University
Press, 1961.

WALLACE-HADDRILL, J. M., *The Barbarian West*. London: Hutchinson,
1952.

# MARC BLOCH

# The Feudal World

۵۶۶۶ In the spring of 1944, shortly before the Allied invasion of Nazi-occupied France, the Gestapo executed a leader of the French Resistance. This Nazi victim and French patriot, a man in his early fifties, was Marc Bloch, professor of economic history at the Sorbonne before the war, and the leading French medievalist of his generation. Bloch's martyrdom and his self-sacrificing heroism—in 1940 he could have escaped from France to easy refuge in England or the United States, but instead chose to join the Resistance—together with the impact of his pioneering adaptation of the concepts of sociology and cultural anthropology to historical methodology, have made him the most revered French scholar of the twentieth century. Every fragment of his unpublished writings was traced down and published after the war, and a new institute was founded under government auspices to pursue the new methods he advocated. His work has therefore been not infrequently evaluated in a spirit somewhat tinged with hagiography, but these pardonable excesses do not detract from the fact that Bloch was indeed a saint, a great man, a master historical craftsman, and a seminal historical thinker. His general interpretation of *Feudal Society*, published in 1940—the most perceptive and illuminating of the host of books on the feudal world—and his unfinished

FROM Marc Bloch, *Feudal Society*, translated by L. A. Manyon. (Chicago: The University of Chicago Press, 1961), pp. 59–87, 109–129, 421–422.

inquiry into the nature of historical thought, *The Historian's Craft*, written while he was hiding from the Gestapo are alike characterized by critical insight and synthetic power rarely attained in the historical literature of
the past hundred years.

Bloch was the scion of a distinguished Parisian Jewish
academic family, fervent in its liberalism and devotion to
the French Republic. He was trained in the positivist,
harshly scientific tradition of early twentieth-century
French scholarship and he was a master of the techniques
of academic historical research. His work shows the impress of this background, exhibiting a primary concern
with the history of French society, a scientific ambition to
get at the reality of history, an austere, unsentimental,
almost harsh tone, and an exhaustive knowledge of the
material. But there is something more in Bloch's work; in
his later writings, French positivist scholarship passes
beyond its earlier exclusive concern with data and detailed
analysis and tries to work out the general structure of
medieval society in accordance with the theories of modern
social science. French positivism had always claimed that
its concentration on dry detail, the heaping up of data,
and close analysis was only the first step; ultimately, a
secure scholarly foundation having been laid, general patterns would become evident.

In Bloch's work, this level was finally attained in medieval scholarship, and a host of disciples have continued
his program in medieval and early modern studies. Yet
Bloch escaped from the naiveté of French positivism, its
simple belief that the accumulation of data would someday
spontaneously show a pattern of change and of general
laws in history. Bloch realized that it was the creative
imagination of the historian that made generalization possible, that the perception of general trends was not a
mechanical process, but was the impress of the synthetic
power of the historian's mind. Bloch believed that primary
sources reveal only "tracks" or traces of human experience
in the past; it was the historian's critical intuition which
recaptured the actual experience. The same view was held
by Lucien Febvre, the Reformation historian who was

Bloch's friend and colleague at the University of Strasbourg, where Bloch began his academic career in the late
1920's. In 1929, Bloch and Febvre together founded the
*Annales*, which became the extremely influential journal
of the new school of French historians that sought to
reinterpret the past in the light of the concepts and
methods of the social and behavioral sciences.

There are five themes or ideas which stand out in
Bloch's work, and they are well illustrated in *Feudal Society*, from which the following selection is taken. First,
Bloch tried to examine a whole society and not just one
part or aspect of it, and to show the functional interaction
of the constituents of that society. For this goal he was
partly indebted to the example of the functional history of
medieval English law, written by the great English scholar
F. W. Maitland in the late nineteenth century, and to the
early twentieth-century French sociologist Emile Durk-
heim, who claimed that a society has a life and destiny of
its own which is separate from the development of its
constituent parts. Second, Bloch was conscious of the
necessity for a social history of thought, rather than the
abstract, elitist history-of-ideas pursued by German
scholars in the 1920's and 30's. He tried to examine the
assumptions, such as the sense of time, that conditioned
ordinary, unintellectual people's daily lives. Third, he realized that the most significant and realistic form of historical periodization is by generations, by men who bear the
"common stamp" of shared experience, and that no two
generations can see the world in quite the same way.
Fourth, Bloch applied the concepts of the new behavioral
science to get behind the abstract, legalistic facade of
social institutions, and tried to get at the meaning of these
institutions for the people whose lives were conditioned by
their operation. His pragmatic sense was always seeking
to find out what the institution was really for, what it
meant in terms of human love and fear. Thus, after
scholars had pointlessly debated for over fifty years about
whether feudalism had a Germanic or Roman origin, Bloch
pointed out that the feudal lord was a father figure who
appeared to replace the leader of the kin when an era of

violence and migration had weakened the family structure.
Feudalism arose out of human need, not out of some hy-
postasized juristic tradition.

Finally, Bloch followed the methodology of the social
sciences in creating a "model" of feudal society. Drawing
upon his vast knowledge of the details of feudal government, law, and economy, he tried to envision a distinct
social system, whose general pattern could be defined
without immediate reference to a particular time and place.
The model he developed has been very useful for understanding the newly liberated underdeveloped societies of
the post-1945 world and for teaching us what to anticipate
in the operation of these underdeveloped, feudal-type societies of our own time.

The framework of institutions which governs a society can in
the last resort be understood only through a knowledge of the whole
human environment. For though the artificial conception of man's
activities which prompts us to carve up the creature of flesh and blood
into the phantoms *homo oeconomicus, philosophicus, juridicus,* is
doubtless necessary, it is tolerable only if we refuse to be deceived by
it. That is why, despite the existence of other works on the various
aspects of medieval civilization, the descriptions thus attempted from
points of view different from ours did not seem to us to obviate the
necessity of recalling at this stage the fundamental characteristics of
the historical climate in which European feudalism flourished. Need I
add that in placing this account near the beginning of the book there
was no thought of claiming any sort of illusory primacy for facts
of this kind? When it is a question of comparing two particular phenomena belonging to separate series—a certain distribution of population, for example, with certain forms of legal groups—the delicate
problem of cause and effect undoubtedly arises. On the other hand,
to contrast two sets of dissimilar phenomena over a period of several
centuries, and then say: 'Here on this side are all the causes; there on
that are all the effects', would be to construct the most pointless of
dichotomies. A society, like a mind, is woven of perpetual interaction.
For other researches, differently oriented, the analysis of the economy

or the mental climate are culminating points; for the historian of the social structure they are a starting-point.

$$* \quad * \quad * \quad * \quad *$$

It would . . . be a grave mistake to treat 'feudal civilization' as being all of one piece chronologically. Engendered no doubt or made possible by the cessation of the last invasions, but first manifesting themselves some generations later, a series of very profound and very widespread changes occurred towards the middle of the eleventh century. No definite break with the past occurred, but the change of direction which, despite inevitable variations in time according to the countries or the phenomena considered, affected in turn all the graphs of social activity. There were, in a word, two successive 'feudal' ages, very different from one another in their essential character. We shall endeavour in the following pages to do justice as much to the contrasts between these two phases as to the characteristics they shared.

It is and always will be impossible for us to calculate, even approximately, the population of Western countries during the first feudal age. Moreover, there undoubtedly existed marked regional variations, constantly intensified by the spasms of social disorder. Compared with the veritable desert of the Iberian plateaux, which gave the frontier regions of Christendom and Islam the desolate appearance of a vast 'no man's land'—desolate even in comparison with early Germany, where the destruction wrought by the migrations of the previous age was being slowly made good—the country districts of Flanders and Lombardy seemed relatively favoured regions. But whatever the importance of these contrasts and whatever their effect on all the aspects of civilization, the fundamental characteristic remains the great and universal decline in population. Over the whole of Europe, the population was immeasurably smaller than it has been since the eighteenth century or even since the twelfth. Even in the provinces formerly under Roman rule, human beings were much scarcer than they had been in the heyday of the Empire. The most important towns had no more than a few thousand inhabitants, and waste land, gardens, even fields and pastures encroached on all sides amongst the houses.

This lack of density was further aggravated by very unequal distribution. Doubtless physical conditions, as well as social habits, conspired to maintain in the country districts profound differences between systems of settlement. In some districts the families, or at least some of them, took up their residence a considerable distance apart, each in the middle of its own farmland, as was the case, for example, in Limousin. In others on the contrary, like the Île-de-France, they mostly crowded together in villages. On the whole, however, both the pressure of the chiefs and, above all, the concern for security militated against too wide dispersal. The disorders of the early Middle Ages had in many cases induced men to draw nearer to each other, but these aggregations in which people lived cheek by jowl were separated by empty spaces. The arable land from which the village derived its sustenance was necessarily much larger in proportion to the number of inhabitants than it is today. For agriculture was a great devourer of space. In the tilled fields, incompletely ploughed and almost always inadequately manured, the ears of corn grew neither very heavy nor very dense. Above all, the harvests never covered the whole area of cultivation at once. The most advanced systems of crop-rotation known to the age required that every year half or a third of the cultivated soil should lie fallow. Often indeed, fallow and crops followed each other in irregular alternation, which always allowed more time for the growth of weeds than for that of the cultivated produce; the fields, in such cases, represented hardly more than a provisional and short-lived conquest of the waste land, and even in the heart of the agricultural regions nature tended constantly to regain the upper hand. Beyond them, enveloping them, thrusting into them, spread forests, scrub and dunes—immense wildernesses, seldom entirely uninhabited by man, though whoever dwelt there as charcoal-burner, shepherd, hermit or outlaw did so only at the cost of a long separation from his fellow men.

Among these sparsely scattered human groups the obstacles to communication were many. The collapse of the Carolingian empire had destroyed the last power sufficiently intelligent to concern itself with public works, sufficiently strong to get some of them carried out. Even the old Roman roads, less solidly constructed than has sometimes been imagined, went to rack and ruin for want of maintenance. Worse still, bridges were no longer kept in repair and were lacking at a great number of river-crossings. Added to this was the general state of insecurity, increased by the depopulation to which it had itself in part contributed. Great was the surprise and relief at the court of Charles the Bald, when in the year 841 that prince witnessed the arrival at Troyes of the messengers bringing him the crown jewels from Aquitaine: how wonderful that such a small number of men, entrusted with such precious baggage, should traverse without accident those vast areas infested on all sides by robbers! The Anglo-Saxon Chronicle shows much less surprise when relating how, in 1061, one of the greatest nobles of England, Earl Tostig, was captured and held to ransom by a handful of bandits at the gates of Rome.

Compared with what the world offers us today, the speed of travel in that age seems extremely slow. It was not, however, appreciably slower than it was at the end of the Middle Ages, or even the beginning of the eighteenth century. By contrast with today, travel was much faster by sea than by land. From 60 to 90 miles a day was not an exceptional record for a ship: provided (it goes without saying) that the winds were not too unfavourable. On land, the normal distance covered in one day amounted, it seems, to between nineteen and twenty-five miles—for travellers who were in no hurry, that is: say a caravan of merchants, a great nobleman moving round from castle to castle or from abbey to abbey, or an army with its baggage. A courier or a handful of resolute men could by making a special effort travel at least twice as fast. A letter written by Gregory VII at Rome on the 8th December 1075 arrived at Goslar, at the foot of the Harz, on the 1st of January following; its bearer had covered about 29 miles a day as the crow flies—in reality, of course, much more. To travel without too much fatigue and not too slowly it was necessary to be mounted or in a carriage. Horses and mules not only go faster than men; they adapt themselves better to boggy ground. This explains the seasonal interruption of many communications; it was due less to bad weather than to lack of forage. The Carolingian *missi* had earlier made a point of not beginning their tours till the grass had grown. However, as at present in Africa, an experienced foot-traveller could cover astoundingly long distances in a few days and he could doubtless overcome certain obstacles more quickly than a horseman. When Charles the Bald organized his second Italian expedition he arranged to keep in touch with Gaul across the Alps partly by means of runners.

Though poor and unsafe, the roads or tracks were in constant use. Where transport is difficult, man goes to something he wants more easily than he makes it come to him. In particular, no institution or method could take the place of personal contact between human beings. It would have been impossible to govern the state from inside a palace: to control a country, there was no other means than to ride through it incessantly in all directions. The kings of the first feudal age positively killed themselves by travel. For example, in the course of a year which was in no way exceptional, the emperor Conrad II in

1033 is known to have journeyed in turn from Burgundy to the Polish frontier and thence to Champagne, to return eventually to Lusatia. The nobleman with his entourage moved round constantly from one of his estates to another; and not only in order to supervise them more effectively. It was necessary for him to consume the produce on the spot, for to transport it to a common centre would have been both inconvenient and expensive. Similarly with the merchant. Without representatives to whom he could delegate the task of buying and selling, fairly certain in any case of never finding enough customers assembled in one place to assure him a profit, every merchant was a pedlar, a 'dusty foot' (*pied poudreux*), plying his trade up hill and down dale. The cleric, eager for learning or the ascetic life, was obliged to wander over Europe in search of the master of his choice: Gerbert of Aurillac studied mathematics in Spain and philosophy at Rheims; the Englishman Stephen Harding, the ideal monarchism in the Burgundian abbey of Molesmes. Before him, St. Odo, the future abbot of Cluny, had travelled through France in the hope of finding a monastery whose members lived strictly according to the rule.

Moreover, in spite of the old hostility of the Benedictine rule to the *gyrovagi*, the bad monks who ceaselessly 'vagabonded about', everything in contemporary clerical life favoured this nomadism: the international character of the Church; the use of Latin as a common language among educated priests and monks; the affiliations between monasteries; the wide dispersal of their territorial patrimonies; and finally the 'reforms' which periodically convulsed this great ecclesiastical body and made the places first affected by the new spirit at once courts of appeal (to which people came from all parts to seek the good rule) and mission centres whence the zealots were despatched for the conquest of the Catholic world. How many foreign visitors came to Cluny in this way! How many Cluniacs journeyed forth to foreign lands! Under William the Conqueror almost all of the dioceses and great abbeys of Normandy, which the first waves of the 'Gregorian' revival were beginning to reach, had at their head Italians or Lorrainers; the archbishop of Rouen, Maurille, was a man from Rheims who, before occupying his Neustrian see, had studied at Liège, taught in Saxony and lived as a hermit in Tuscany.

Humble folk, too, passed along the highways of the West: refugees, driven by war or famine; adventurers, half-soldiers, half-bandits; peasants seeking a more prosperous life and hoping to find, far from their native land, a few fields to cultivate. Finally, there were pilgrims.

For religious devotion itself fostered travel and more than one good Christian, rich or poor, cleric or layman, believed that he could purchase salvation of body and soul only at the price of a long journey.

As has often been remarked, it is in the nature of good roads to create a vacuum around them—to their own profit. In the feudal age, when all roads were bad, scarcely any of them was capable of monopolizing the traffic in this way. Undoubtedly such factors as the restrictions of the terrain, tradition, the presence of a market here or a sanctuary there, worked to the advantage of certain routes, although far less decisively than the historians of literary or artistic influences have sometimes believed. A fortuitous event—a physical accident, the exactions of a lord in need of money—sufficed to divert the flow, sometimes permanently. The building of a castle on the old Roman road, occupied by a race of robber knights—the lords of Méréville—and the establishment some distance away of the St. Denis priory of Toury, where merchants and pilgrims found by contrast a pleasant reception, were sufficient to divert the traffic from the Beauce section of the road from Paris to Orleans permanently westward, so that the ancient roadway was abandoned from that time on. Moreover from the beginning of his journey to the end, the traveller had almost always the choice of several itineraries, of which none was absolutely obligatory. Traffic, in short, was not canalized in a few great arteries; it spread capriciously through a multitude of little blood-vessels. There was no castle, burg, or monastery, however far from the beaten track, that could not expect to be visited occasionally by wanderers, living links with the outer world, although the places where such visits were of regular occurrence were few.

Thus the obstacles and dangers of the road in no way prevented travel. But they made each journey an expedition, almost an adventure. If men, under pressure of need, did not fear to undertake fairly long journeys (they feared it less, perhaps, than in centuries nearer to our own) they shrank from those repeated comings and goings within a narrow radius which in other civilizations form the texture of daily life; and this was especially so in the case of humble folk of settled occupations. The result was an ordering of the scheme of human relations quite different from anything we know today. There was scarcely any remote little place which had not some contacts intermittently through that sort of continuous yet irregular 'Brownian movement' which affected the whole of society. On the other hand, between two inhabited centres quite close to each other the connections were much rarer, the isolation of their inhabitants infinitely greater than would be the case in our own day. If, according to the angle from which it is viewed, the civilization of feudal Europe appears sometimes remarkably universalist, sometimes particularist in the extreme, the principal source of this contradiction lay in the conditions of communication: conditions which favoured the distant propagation of very general currents of influence as much as they discouraged, in any particular place, the standardizing effects of neighbourly intercourse.

The only more or less regular letter-mail service which functioned during the whole of the feudal era was that which linked Venice to Constantinople. Such a thing was practically unknown in the West. The last attempts to maintain a royal posting-service, on the model left by the Roman government, had disappeared with the Carolingian empire. It is significant of the general disorganization that the German monarchs themselves, the true heirs of that empire and its ambitions, should have lacked either the authority or the intelligence necessary to secure the revival of an institution clearly so indispensable to the control of vast territories. Sovereigns, nobles, prelates were obliged to entrust their correspondence to special couriers, otherwise—as was usual among persons of lesser rank—the transport of letters was simply left to the kindness of passing travellers; as, for instance, the pilgrims on their way to St. James of Galicia. The relative slowness of the messengers, the mishaps that at every stage threatened their progress, meant that the only effective authority was the one on the spot. Forced constantly to take the gravest steps—the history of the papal legates is in this respect very instructive—every local representative of a great potentate tended only too naturally to act for his personal advantage and thus finally to transform himself into an independent ruler.

As for knowledge of distant events, everyone, whatever his rank, was obliged to rely on chance encounters. The picture of the contemporary world which the best-informed men carried in their minds presented many lacunae; we can form an idea of them from the unavoidable omissions even from the best of those monastic annals which are as it were the written reports of medieval news-hawks. Moreover, it was seldom exact as to time. It is, for example, remarkable to find a person so well placed for acquiring information as Bishop Fulbert of Chartres showing astonishment on receiving gifts for his church from Cnut the Great: for he admits that he believed this prince to be still a heathen, although in fact he had been baptized in infancy. The monk

Lambert of Hersfeld is quite well-informed about German affairs, but when he goes on to describe the grave events which occurred in his time in Flanders (a region bordering on the Empire and in part an imperial fief), he soon makes a series of the strangest blunders. Such an imperfect state of knowledge was a poor foundation for any large political designs.

The life of the Europe of the first feudal age was not entirely self-contained. There was more than one current of exchange between it and the neighbouring civilizations, and probably the most active was that which linked it to Moslem Spain, as witnessed by the numerous Arab gold pieces which, by this route, penetrated north of the Pyrenees and were there sufficiently sought after to become the object of frequent imitations. In the western Mediterranean, on the other hand, long-distance navigation was now practically unknown. The principal lines of communication with the East were elsewhere. One of them, a sea-route, passed through the Adriatic, at the head of which lay Venice, to all appearance a fragment of Byzantium, set in a world apart. On land the Danube route, for a long time severed by the Hungarians, was almost deserted. But farther north, on the trails which joined Bavaria to the great market of Prague and thence, by the terraces on the northern flank of the Carpathians, continued to the Dnieper, caravans passed back and forth, laden on the return journey with products of Constantinople or of Asia. At Kiev they met the great transversal which, running across the plains and from river to river, linked the riparian countries of the Baltic with the Black Sea, the Caspian or the oases of Turkestan. For the West had missed its chance of being the intermediary between the north or north-east of the continent and the eastern Mediterranean, and had nothing to offer on its own soil to compare with the mighty comings and goings of merchandise which made the prosperity of Kievian Russia.

Not only was this trade restricted to very few routes; it was also extremely small in volume. What is worse, the balance of trade seems to have been distinctly unfavourable—at any rate with the East. From the eastern countries the West received almost nothing except a few luxury articles whose value—very high in relation to their weight—was such as to take no account of the expense and risks of transport. In exchange it had scarcely anything to offer except slaves. Moreover, it seems that most of the human cattle rounded up on the Slav and Lettish territories beyond the Elbe or acquired from the slave-traders of Britain took the road to Islamic Spain; the eastern Mediterranean was too abundantly provided with this commodity from its own sources to have any need to import it on a large scale. The profits of the slave-trade, in general fairly small, were not sufficient to pay for the purchase of precious goods and spices in the markets of the Byzantine world, of Egypt or of nearer Asia. The result was a slow drain of silver and above all gold. If a few merchants unquestionably owed their prosperity to these remote transactions, society as a whole owed scarcely anything to them except one more reason for being short of specie.

However, money was never wholly absent from business transactions in feudal Europe, even among the peasant classes, and it never ceased to be employed as a standard of exchange. Payments were often made in produce; but the produce was normally valued item by item in such a way that the total of these reckonings corresponded with a stipulated price in pounds, shillings and pence. Let us therefore avoid the expression 'natural economy', which is too summary and too vague. It is better to speak simply of shortage of currency. This shortage was further aggravated by the anarchic state of minting, another result of the subdivision of political authority and the difficulty of communication: for each important market, faced with the threat of shortage, had to have its local mint. Except for the imitation of exotic coinages and apart from certain insignificant little pieces, the only coins now produced were *denarii*, which were rather debased silver pieces. Gold circulated only in the shape of Arab and Byzantine coins or imitations of them. The *libra* and the *solidus* were only arithmetical multiples of the *denarius*, without a material base of their own. But the various coins called *denarii* had a different metallic value according to their origin. Worse still, even in one and the same area almost every issue involved variations in the weight or the alloy. Not only was money generally scarce, and inconvenient on account of its unreliability, but it circulated too slowly and too irregularly for people ever to feel certain of being able to procure it in case of need. That was the situation, in the absence of a sufficiently active commerce.

But here again, let us beware of too facile a formula—the 'closed economy'. It would not even apply exactly to the small farming operations of the peasants. We know that markets existed where the rustics certainly sold some of the produce of their fields or their farmyards to the townsfolk, to the clergy, to the men-at-arms. It was thus that they procured the *denarii* to pay their dues. And poor indeed was the man who never bought a few ounces of salt or a bit of iron. As to the 'autarky' of the great manors, this would have meant that their masters had gone without arms or jewels, had never drunk wine (unless their estates produced it), and for clothes had been content with crude materials woven by the wives of tenants. Moreover, even the inadequacies of agricultural technique, the disturbed state of society, and finally the inclemency of the weather contributed to maintain a certain amount of internal commerce: for when the harvest failed, although many people literally died of starvation, the whole population was not reduced to this extremity, and we know that there was a traffic in corn from the more favoured districts to those afflicted by dearth, which lent itself readily to speculation. Trade, therefore, was not non-existent, but it was irregular in the extreme. The society of this age was certainly not unacquainted with either buying or selling. But it did not, like our own, live by buying and selling.

Moreover, commerce, even in the form of barter, was not the only or perhaps even the most important channel by which at that time goods circulated through the various classes of society. A great number of products passed from hand to hand as dues paid to a chief in return for his protection or simply in recognition of his power. It was the same in the case of that other commodity, human labour: the *corvée* furnished more labourers than hire. In short, exchange, in the strict sense, certainly played a smaller part in economic life than payment in kind; and because exchange was thus a rare thing, while at the same time only the poorest could resign themselves to living wholly on their own produce, wealth and well-being seemed inseparable from authority.

Nevertheless, in an economy so constituted the means of acquisition at the disposal even of the powerful were, on the whole, singularly restricted. When we speak of money we mean the possibility of laying by reserves, the ability to wait, the 'anticipation of future values'—everything that, conversely, the shortage of money particularly impedes. It is true that people tried to hoard wealth in other forms.

The nobles and kings accumulated in their coffers gold or silver vessels and precious stones; the churches amassed liturgical plate. Should the need arise for an unexpected disbursement, you sold or pawned the crown, the goblet or the crucifix; or you even sent them to be melted down at the local mint. But such liquidation of assets, from the very fact of the slowing down of exchange which made it necessary, was never easy nor was it always profitable; and the hoarded treasure itself did not after all constitute a very large amount. The great as well as the humble lived from hand to mouth, obliged to be content with

the resources of the moment and mostly compelled to spend them at
once.

The weakness of trade and of monetary circulation had a further
consequence of the gravest kind. It reduced to insignificance the social
function of wages. The latter requires that the employer should have
at his disposal an adequate currency, the source of which is not in danger of drying up at any moment; on the side of the wage-earner it
requires the certainty of being able to employ the money thus received
in procuring for himself the necessities of life. Both these conditions
were absent in the first feudal age. In all grades of the hierarchy,
whether it was a question of the king's making sure of the services of
a great official, or of the small landlord's retaining those of an armed
follower or a farm-hand, it was necessary to have recourse to a method
of remuneration which was not based on the periodic payment of a
sum of money. Two alternatives offered: one was to take the man into
one's household, to feed and clothe him, to provide him with 'prebend',
as the phrase went; the other was to grant him in return for his services an estate which, if exploited directly or in the form of dues levied
on the cultivators of the soil, would enable him to provide for himself.

Now both these methods tended, though in opposite ways, to create
human ties very different from those based on wages. Between the
prebendholder and the master under whose roof he lived the bond
must surely have been much more intimate than that between an employer and a wage-earner, who is free, once his job is finished, to go
off with his money in his pocket. On the other hand, the bond was
almost inevitably loosened as soon as the subordinate was settled on
a piece of land, which by a natural process he tended increasingly to
regard as his own, while trying to reduce the burden of service. Moreover, in a time when the inadequacy of communications and the in-
sufficiency of trade rendered it difficult to maintain large households
in relative abundance, the 'prebend' system was on the whole capable
of a much smaller extension than the system of remuneration based on
land. If feudal society perpetually oscillated between these two poles,
the narrow relationship of man and man and the looser tie of land
tenure, the responsibility for this belongs in large part to the economic
regime which, to begin with at least, made wage-earning impracticable.

We shall endeavour, in another work, to describe the intensive
movement of repopulation which, from approximately 1050 to 1250,
transformed the face of Europe: on the confines of the Western world,
the colonization of the Iberian plateaux and of the great plain beyond

the Elbe; in the heart of the old territories, the incessant gnawing of the plough at forest and wasteland; in the glades opened amidst the trees or the brushwood, completely new villages clutching at the virgin soil; elsewhere, round sites inhabited for centuries, the extension of the agricultural lands through the exertions of the assarters. It will be advisable then to distinguish between the stages of the process and to describe the regional variations. For the moment, we are concerned only with the phenomenon itself and its principal effects.

The most immediately apparent of these was undoubtedly the closer association of the human groups. Between the different settlements, except in some particularly neglected regions, the vast empty spaces thenceforth disappeared. Such distances as still separated the settlements became, in any case, easier to traverse. For powers now arose or were consolidated—their rise being favoured by current demographic trends—whose enlarged horizons brought them new responsibilities. Such were the urban middle classes, which owed everything to trade. Such also were the kings and princes; they too were interested in the prosperity of commerce because they derived large sums of money from it in the form of duties and tolls; moreover they were aware—much more so than in the past—of the vital importance to them of the free transmission of orders and the free movement of armies. The activity of the Capetians towards that decisive turning-point marked by the reign of Louis VI, their aggressions, their domanial policy, their part in the organization of the movement of repopulation, were in large measure the reflection of considerations of this kind—the need to retain control of communications between the two capitals, Paris and Orleans, and beyond the Loire or the Seine to maintain contact with Berry or with the valleys of the Oise and the Aisne. It would seem that while the security of the roads had increased, there was no very notable improvement in their condition; but at least the provision of the bridges had been carried much farther. In the course of the twelfth century, how many were thrown over all the rivers of Europe! Finally, a fortunate advance in harnessing methods had the effect, about the same time, of increasing very substantially the efficiency of horse-transport.

The links with neighbouring civilizations underwent a similar transformation. Ships in ever greater numbers ploughed the Tyrrhenian Sea, and its ports, from the rock of Amalfi to Catalonia, rose to the rank of great commercial centres; the sphere of Venetian trade continually expanded; the heavy wagons of the merchant caravans now followed the route of the Danubian plains. These advances were important enough. But relations with the East had not only become easier and more intimate. The most important fact is that they had changed their character. Formerly almost exclusively an importer, the West had become a great supplier of manufactured goods. The merchandise which it thus shipped in quantity to the Byzantine world, to the Latin or Islamic Levant and even—though in smaller amounts—to the Maghreb, belonged to very diverse categories. One commodity, however, easily dominated all the rest. In the expansion of the European economy in the Middle Ages, cloth played the same vital rôle as did metal and cotton goods in that of nineteenth-century England. If in Flanders, in Picardy, at Bourges, in Languedoc, in Lombardy, and yet other places—for the cloth centres were to be found almost everywhere—the noise of the looms and the throbbing of the fullers' mills resounded, it was at least as much for the sake of foreign markets as for local requirements. And undoubtedly this revolution, which saw our Western countries embarking on the economic conquest of the world by way of the East, is to be explained by a multiplicity of causes and by looking—as far as possible—towards the East as well as towards the West. It is none the less true that it could not have occurred without the demographic changes mentioned above. If the population had not been more numerous than before and the cultivated area more extensive; if the fields—their quality improved by augmented manpower and in particular by more intensive ploughing—had not become capable of yielding bigger and more frequent harvests, how could so many weavers, dyers or cloth-shearers have been brought together in the towns and provided with a livelihood?

The North was conquered, like the East. From the end of the eleventh century Flemish cloth was sold at Novgorod. Little by little, the route of the Russian plains became hazardous and was finally closed. Thenceforward Scandinavia and the Baltic countries turned towards the West. The process of change which was thus set in motion was completed when, in the course of the twelfth century, German merchants took over the Baltic. From that time onwards the ports of the Low Countries, especially Bruges, became the centres where northern products were exchanged not only for those of the West itself but also for merchandise from the East. Strong international links united the two frontiers of feudal Europe by way of Germany and especially through the fairs of Champagne.

Such a well-balanced external trade could not fail to bring a flow of coin and precious metals into Europe and so add substantially to its monetary resources. This relative easing of the currency situation was reinforced—and its effects multiplied—by the accelerated rhythm of circulation. For in the very heart of the West the progress of repopulation, the greater ease of communications, the cessation of the invasions which had spread such an atmosphere of confusion and panic over the Western world, and still other causes which it would take too long to examine here, had led to a revival of commerce.

Let us avoid exaggeration, however. The picture would have to be carefully shaded—by regions and by classes. To live on their own resources remained for long centuries the ideal—though one that was rarely attained—of many peasants and most villages. Moreover, the profound transformations of the economy took place only very gradually. It is significant that of the two essential developments in the sphere of currency, one, the minting of larger pieces of silver much heavier than the *denarius*, appeared only at the beginning of the thirteenth century (and even at that date in Italy alone) and the other, the resumption of the minting of gold coins of an indigenous type, was delayed till the second half of the same century. In many respects, what the second feudal age witnessed was less the disappearance of earlier conditions than their modification. This observation applies to the part played by distance as well as commerce. But the fact that the kings, the great nobles, and the manorial lords should have been able to begin once more to amass substantial wealth, that wage-earning, sometimes under legal forms clumsily adapted from ancient practices, should have increasingly supplanted other methods of remunerating services—these signs of an economy in process of revival affected in their turn, from the twelfth century onwards, the whole fabric of human relations.

Furthermore, the evolution of the economy involved a genuine revision of social values. There had always been artisans and merchants; individuals belonging to the latter class had even been able, here and there, to play an important rôle, though collectively neither group counted for much. But from the end of the eleventh century the artisan class and the merchant class, having become much more numerous and much more indispensable to the life of the community, made themselves felt more and more vigorously in the urban setting. This applies especially to the merchant class, for the medieval economy, after the

great revival of these decisive years, was always dominated, not by
the producer, but by the trader. It was not for the latter class that the
legal machinery of the previous age—founded on an economic system
in which they occupied only an inferior place—had been set up. But
now their practical needs and their mental attitude were bound to
imbue it with a new spirit. Born in the midst of a very loosely-knit society, in which commerce was insignificant and money a rarity, European feudalism underwent a fundamental change as soon as the meshes
of the human network had been drawn closer together and the circulation of goods and coin intensified.

The men of the two feudal ages were close to nature—much closer
than we are; and nature as they knew it was much less tamed and
softened than we see it today. The rural landscape, of which the waste
formed so large a part, bore fewer traces of human influence. The wild
animals that now only haunt our nursery tales—bears and, above all,
wolves—prowled in every wilderness, and even amongst the cultivated
fields. So much was this the case that the sport of hunting was indispensable for ordinary security, and almost equally so as a method of
supplementing the food supply. People continued to pick wild fruit and
to gather honey as in the first ages of mankind. In the construction of
implements and tools, wood played a predominant part. The nights,
owing to the wretched lighting, were darker; the cold, even in the
living quarters of the castles, was more intense. In short, behind all
social life there was a background of the primitive, of submission to
uncontrollable forces, of unrelieved physical contrasts. There is no
means of measuring the influence which such an environment was
capable of exerting on the minds of men, but it could hardly have failed
to contribute to their uncouthness.

A history more worthy of the name than the diffident speculations
to which we are reduced by the paucity of our material would give
space to the vicissitudes of the human organism. It is very naive to
claim to understand men without knowing what sort of health they enjoyed. But in this field the state of the evidence, and still more the inadequacy of our methods of research, are inhibitive. Infant mortality
was undoubtedly very high in feudal Europe and tended to make people somewhat callous towards bereavements that were almost a normal
occurrence. As to the life of adults, even apart from the hazards of
war it was usually short by our standards, at least to judge from the
records of princely personages which (inexact though they must often
be) constitute our only source of information on this point. Robert the

Pious died at about the age of 60; Henry I at 52; Philip I and Louis VI at 56. In Germany the first four emperors of the Saxon dynasty attained respectively the ages of 60 (or thereabouts), 28, 22 and 52. Old age seemed to begin very early, as early as mature adult life with us. This world, which, as we shall see, considered itself very old, was in fact governed by young men.

Among so many premature deaths, a large number were due to the great epidemics which descended frequently upon a humanity ill-equipped to combat them; among the poor another cause was famine. Added to the constant acts of violence these disasters gave life a quality of perpetual insecurity. This was probably one of the principal reasons for the emotional instability so characteristic of the feudal era, especially during its first age. A low standard of hygiene doubtless also contributed to this nervous sensibility. A great deal of effort has been expended, in our own day, in proving that baths were not unknown to seignorial society. It is rather puerile, for the sake of making this point, to overlook so many unhealthy conditions of life: notably under-nourishment among the poor and overeating among the rich. Finally, we must not leave out of account the effects of an astonishing sensibility to what were believed to be supernatural manifestations. It made people's minds constantly and almost morbidly attentive to all manner of signs, dreams, or hallucinations. This characteristic was especially marked in monastic circles where the influence of mortifications of the flesh and the repression of natural instincts was joined to that of a mental attitude vocationally centred on the problems of the unseen. No psychoanalyst has ever examined dreams more earnestly than the monks of the tenth or the eleventh century. Yet the laity also shared the emotionalism of a civilization in which moral or social convention did not yet require well-bred people to repress their tears and their raptures. The despairs, the rages, the impulsive acts, the sudden revulsions of feeling present great difficulties to historians, who are instinctively disposed to reconstruct the past in terms of the rational. But the irrational is an important element in all history and only a sort of false shame could allow its effects on the course of political events in feudal Europe to be passed over in silence.

These men, subjected both externally and internally to so many ungovernable forces, lived in a world in which the passage of time escaped their grasp all the more because they were so ill-equipped to measure it. Water-clocks, which were costly and cumbersome, were very rare. Hour-glasses were little used. The inadequacy of sundials, especially under skies quickly clouded over, was notorious. This resulted in the use of curious devices. In his concern to regulate the course of a notably nomadic life, King Alfred had conceived the idea of carrying with him everywhere a supply of candles of equal length, which he had lit in turn, to mark the passing of the hours, but such concern for uniformity in the division of the day was exceptional in that age. Reckoning ordinarily—after the example of Antiquity—twelve hours of day and twelve of night, whatever the season, people of the highest education became used to seeing each of these fractions, taken one by one, grow and diminish incessantly, according to the annual revolution of the sun. This was to continue till the moment when —towards the beginning of the fourteenth century—counterpoise clocks brought with them at last, not only the mechanization of the instrument, but, so to speak, of time itself.

An anecdote related in a chronicle of Hainault illustrates admirably the sort of perpetual fluctuation of time in those days. At Mons a judicial duel is due to take place. Only one champion puts in an appearance—at dawn; at the ninth hour, which marks the end of the waiting period prescribed by custom, he requests that the failure of his adversary be placed on record. On the point of law, there is no doubt. But has the specified period really elapsed? The county judges deliberate, look at the sun, and question the clerics in whom the practice of the liturgy has induced a more exact knowledge of the rhythm of the hours than their own, and by whose bells it is measured, more or less accurately, to the common benefit of men. Eventually the court pronounces firmly that the hour of 'none' is past. To us, accustomed to live with our eyes turning constantly to the clock, how remote from our civilization seems this society in which a court of law could not ascertain the time of day without discussion and inquiry!

Now the imperfection of hourly reckoning was but one of the symptoms, among many others, of a vast indifference to time. Nothing would have been easier or more useful than to keep an accurate record of such important legal dates as those of the births of rulers; yet in 1284 a full investigation was necessary to determine, as far as possible, the age of one of the greatest heiresses of the Capetian realm, the young countess of Champagne. In the tenth and eleventh centuries, innumerable charters and memoranda were undated, although their only purpose was to serve as records. There are exceptional documents which are better in this respect, yet the notary, who employed several systems of reference simultaneously, was often not successful in making his various calculations agree. What is more, it was not the notion of time only, it was the domain of number as a whole which suffered from this haziness. The extravagant figures of the chroniclers are not merely literary exaggeration; they are evidence of the lack of all awareness of statistical realities. Although William the Conqueror certainly did not establish in England more than 5,000 knights' fees, the historians of a somewhat later time, and even certain administrators (though it would certainly not have been very difficult for them to obtain the right information), did not hesitate to attribute to him the creation of from thirty-two to sixty thousand of these military tenements. The period had, especially from the end of the eleventh century, its mathematicians who groped their way courageously in the wake of the Greeks and Arabs; the architects and sculptors were capable of using a fairly simple geometry. But among the computations that have come down to us—and this was true till the end of the Middle Ages—there are scarcely any that do not reveal astonishing errors. The inconveniences of the Roman numerical system, ingeniously corrected as they were by the use of the abacus, do not suffice to explain these mistakes. The truth is that the regard for accuracy, with its firmest buttress, the respect for figures, remained profoundly alien to the minds even of the leading men of that age.

On the one hand, the language of the educated, which was almost uniformly Latin; on the other, the variety of tongues in everyday use: such is the singular dualism which prevailed almost throughout the feudal era. It was peculiar to Western civilization properly so called and helped to distinguish it sharply from its neighbours—from the Celtic and Scandinavian worlds with their rich poetic and didactic literatures in the national languages; from the Greek East; and, at least in the really Arabized zones, from the world of Islam.

In the West itself, it is true, one society long remained an exception. This was Anglo-Saxon Britain. Not that Latin was not written there and written very well, but it was by no means the only language written. The old English tongue was elevated at an early date to the dignity of a literary and legal language. It was King Alfred's wish that young people should learn it in the schools before the more gifted passed on to Latin. The poets employed it in their songs, which were set down in writing as well as recited. It was also used by the kings in their laws; by the chanceries in the legal documents drawn up for kings or magnates; and even by the monks in their chronicles. This was something unique in that age, a culture that was able to keep in touch

on its highest levels with the medium of expression employed by the
mass of the population. The Norman Conquest cut short this development. Between William's letter to the people of London, written soon
after the battle of Hastings, and a few occasional administrative instructions in the late twelfth century, there was not a single royal deed
that was not drawn up in Latin. With virtually only one exception, the
Anglo-Saxon chronicles are silent from the middle of the eleventh
century. As for those writings which may, by stretching a point, be
called 'literature', they were not to reappear till shortly before the year
1200 and then at first only in the form of a few minor works of
edification.

On the continent the fine cultural effort of the Carolingian renaissance had not wholly neglected the national languages. True it occurred to no one in that age to consider the Romance tongues as
worthy of being put into writing; they were regarded merely as a
highly corrupt form of Latin. The German dialects, on the other hand,
invited the attention of many men, at court or in the ranks of the
higher clergy, whose mother-tongue they were. Old poems, hitherto
purely oral, were transcribed and new ones, mainly on religious
themes, were composed; manuscripts in *lingua theotisca* (Germanic)
figured in the libraries of the great. But here again political events—
this time the dismemberment of the Carolingian empire, with the
troubles which followed—interrupted the trend. From the end of the
ninth century to the end of the eleventh, a few pious poems and some
translations comprise the meagre treasure which the historians of
German literature must be content to record. In comparison with the
Latin writings composed on the same soil and during the same period,
we may as well admit that both in quantity and in intellectual quality
it is negligible.

We must be careful, moreover, not to think of this Latin of the
feudal era as a 'dead language', with all that the epithet implies of the
stereotyped and uniform. In spite of the taste for correctness and
purism re-established by the Carolingian renaissance, there was much
which tended to produce to a greater or lesser extent, according to the
environments and the persons concerned, new words and new turns of
phrase. One of these circumstances was the need to describe facts
unknown to the Ancients or to express thoughts which, in the sphere
of religion especially, had been foreign to their ideas; another was the
infectious influence of the logical process (very different from that
embodied in the traditional grammar) to which people's minds grew

accustomed through the use of the vernacular; finally, there were the effects of ignorance or half-knowledge. Moreover, if books tend to impede change, does not speech always favour it? Now men did not confine themselves to writing Latin. They sang it—witness the abandonment by poetry (at least in those forms of it most imbued with true feeling) of the classical prosody of long and short syllables in favour of accented rhythm, the only music henceforth perceptible to the ear. They also spoke it. It was for a solecism committed in conversation that a cultivated Italian, summoned to the court of Otto I, found himself cruelly mocked by a little monk of St. Gall. In preaching, Bishop Notker of Liège, if he was addressing laymen, used Walloon; on the other hand, if he was preaching to his clergy he used Latin. Undoubtedly many ecclesiastics, especially among the parish priests, would have been incapable of imitating him, or even of understanding him. But for educated priests and monks the old χοινή of the Church retained its function for oral communication. Without Latin, how would it have been possible, at the Curia, in the great councils or in the course of their wanderings from abbey to abbey, for these men from different countries to communicate with each other?

Of course, in almost every society, the modes of expression vary, sometimes very considerably, according to the use which it is desired to make of them or the class to which the people concerned belong. But the contrast is limited, as a rule, to slight variations in grammatical exactitude or quality of vocabulary. In feudal society it was incomparably more profound. In a great part of Europe, the common languages, which were connected with the Germanic group, belonged to quite another family from the language of the educated. The Romance tongues themselves were so far removed from their common ancestor that to pass from them to Latin involved long training at school.

Thus the linguistic separation was reduced, in the long run, to the division between two human groups. On the one hand there was the immense majority of uneducated people, each one imprisoned in his regional dialect, limited, so far as literary culture was concerned, to a few secular poems transmitted almost exclusively by word of mouth, and to those pious cantilenas which well-meaning clerics composed in the vulgar tongue for the benefit of simple folk and which they sometimes committed to parchment. On the other hand, there was the little handful of educated people who, constantly alternating between the local everyday speech and the universal language of learning, were in the true sense bilingual. To them belonged the works of theology and history, invariably written in Latin; the knowledge of the liturgy; even the understanding of business documents.

Latin was not only the language in which teaching was done, it was the only language taught. To be able to read was simply to be able to read Latin. Though there were exceptional cases, in legal documents, of a lapse into the vernacular, this anomaly, where it occurs, must be simply regarded as a sign of ignorance. If, from the tenth century, certain charters of southern Aquitaine are full of Provençal terms, in the midst of a more or less incorrect Latin, it is because the monasteries of Rouergue or Quercy, situated away from the great centres of the Carolingian renaissance, could count very few literate monks. Because Sardinia was a poor country whose inhabitants, after their flight from the coastal region ravaged by pirates, lived in quasi-isolation, the first documents written in Sardinian are much older than the earliest Italian texts of the Peninsula.

The most immediately perceptible result of this hierarchic division of languages is that the picture of itself left by the first feudal age is exasperatingly blurred. Acts of sale or donation, of bondage or en-franchisement, judgments of the courts, royal privileges, written records of homage—the legal documents of everyday life—are the most valuable sources for the historian of society. If they are not always honest, they have at least, unlike the narrative texts intended for posterity, the merit of having been at worst designed to deceive only contemporaries, whose credulity had other limits than ours. Now, with very few exceptions which have just been explained, they were, till the thirteenth century, invariably drawn up in Latin. But this was not the way in which the realities they were intended to record were first expressed. When two lords debated the price of an estate or the clauses of a contract of subjection they certainly did not talk to each other in the language of Cicero. It was the notary's business later to provide, as best he could, a classical vestment for their agreement. Thus every Latin charter or notarial record is the result of a work of translation, which the historian today, if he wishes to grasp the under-lying truth, must put back, as it were, into the original.

This would be well enough if the process had always followed the same rules. But this was by no means the case. From the schoolboy exercise, clumsily reproducing an outline mentally projected in the vernacular, to the Latin oration, carefully polished by a learned clerk, all stages are to be found. Sometimes—and it is incontestably the most favourable case—the current word is simply disguised, as well as may be, by the addition of a pseudo-Latin termination: for example, *hom-mage* is scarcely concealed as *homagium*. In other cases, there was an endeavour to use only strictly classical terms, to the point of writing—by an almost blasphemous *jeu d'esprit* assimilating the priest of the Living God to the priest of Jupiter—*archiflamen* for archbishop. The worst of it was that, in the search for parallelisms, the purists did not hesitate to be guided by the analogy of sounds rather than of meanings. Because, in French, the nominative case of *comte* was *cuens*, it was translated as *consul*; or *fief* might be rendered as *fiscus*. It is true that general systems of translation were gradually established, some of which shared the universalist character of the learned language: *fief*, which was called *Lehn* in German, had as regular equivalents, in the Latin charters of Germany, words coined from French. But nothing was ever translated into notarial Latin, even when most skilfully handled, without being slightly deformed.

Thus, the technical language of law itself was handicapped by a vocabulary that was at once too archaic and too unstable to come really close to reality. As for the vulgar tongue, it had all the want of precision and the instability of a purely oral and popular vocabulary. As regards social institutions, confusion in words inevitably involved confusion of things. If only by reason of the imperfection of their terminology, a great uncertainty beset the classification of human relations. But this was not all. To whatever purposes it was applied, Latin had the advantage of providing the intellectuals of the age with an international medium of communication. On the other hand, to most of the men who made use of it, it presented the grave inconvenience of being radically divorced from the inner word—the term that stood naturally, in their minds, for the concept—so that they were forced to resort to perpetual approximations in the expression of their thoughts. Among the multiple causes that doubtless combine to explain the absence of mental precision, which was, as we have seen, one of the characteristics of those times, should we not include this incessant movement to and fro between the two planes of language?

To what extent was the language of the educated, medieval Latin, also the language of the aristocracy? To what extent, in other words, can the group of *literati* be identified with the ruling class? So far as the Church is concerned, the answer is clear. It is of no great consequence that the pernicious system of nominations had resulted, here and there, in the appointment of ignorant men to the highest posts. The episcopal courts, the great monasteries, the chapels royal, in a word, all the headquarters of the ecclesiastical army, never lacked educated clergy who, while often of noble or knightly origin, had been brought up in the monastic and especially the cathedral schools. But as soon as we come to the lay world, the problem becomes more complex.

Let us not imagine that, even in the darkest times, this society was positively hostile to all learning. That it was commonly deemed proper that a leader of men should have access to the treasure-house of thoughts and memories to which the written word, that is to say Latin, alone provided the key is most clearly shown by the importance attached by many sovereigns to the education of their heirs. Robert the Pious, 'king learned in God', had been the pupil of the illustrious Gerbert at Rheims; William the Conqueror gave his son Robert a cleric as tutor. Among the great of the earth, there were to be found genuine book-lovers: Otto III, brought up, it is true, by his mother who, as a Byzantine princess, had brought from her native country the customs of a much more refined civilization, spoke Greek and Latin fluently; William III of Aquitaine had assembled a fine library where he was sometimes to be found reading far into the night. To these examples may be added the cases, by no means exceptional, of those princes who, intended originally for the Church, had retained some of the learning and some of the tastes proper to the clerical world; such a one was Baldwin of Boulogne—a rough soldier, nevertheless—who became king of Jerusalem.

But an education of this type was possible only in the atmosphere of a great dynasty, already firmly based on their hereditary power. Nothing is more significant in this respect than the almost regular contrast in Germany between the founders of dynasties and their successors. Both Otto II, the third Saxon king, and Henry III, the second of the Salians, were carefully educated, in contrast with their fathers— Otto the Great, who learned to read at the age of thirty, and Conrad II, whose chaplain avows that he 'knew not his letters'. As often happened, both the fathers were thrown too young into a life of adventure and peril to have had time to prepare themselves, otherwise than by practical experience or oral tradition, for their profession as rulers. Still more was this true of the lower ranks of the nobility. The relatively brilliant culture of a few great royal or noble families should not deceive us; nor should the exceptional fidelity with which the knightly classes of Italy and Spain held to pedagogic traditions, somewhat rudimentary though these were: the Cid and Ximenes, if their knowledge perhaps did not extend much farther, at least knew how to sign their names. But north of the Alps and the Pyrenees at least the majority of the small or medium lords who exercised most authority at this time were illiterates in the full sense of the word. So much was this the case that in the monasteries into which some of them precipitately retreated in the evening of their days, the terms *conversus*, that is to say one who comes late to the monk's vocation, and *idiota*, which designated the monk incapable of reading the Holy Scriptures, were treated as synonymous.

This neglect of education among the laity explains the rôle of the clergy both as interpreters of the ideas of the great and as depositaries of political traditions. The princes were obliged to rely on the clerical element among their servants for services that the rest of their entourage would have been incapable of rendering. About the middle of the eighth century the last lay referendaries of the Merovingian kings had disappeared; in April 1298, Philip the Fair handed over the seals to the knight Pierre Flotte. Between these two dates more than five centuries elapsed, during which the chancelleries of the sovereigns who reigned over France had at their head churchmen exclusively. It was the same elsewhere, on the whole. It is important to realize that the decisions of the powerful of this world were sometimes suggested and always expressed by men who, whatever their national or class allegiances, none the less belonged by their whole training to a society by nature universalist and founded on spiritual things. Beyond question they helped to maintain, above the confusion of petty local strife, a concern for certain wider issues. When required, however, to give written form to acts of policy, they felt impelled to justify them officially by reasons drawn from their own moral code. Thus there came to be diffused over the documents of almost the entire feudal era that veneer of disingenuousness the evidence of which is to be seen in particular in the preambles of so many enfranchisements masquerading as pure gifts, though they were in fact purchased for money, or in so many royal grants of privileges, invariably made to appear as inspired by simple piety. Since for a long period the writing of history itself, with accompanying value-judgments, was also in the hands of the clergy, the conventions of thought as much as the conventions of literature combined to hide the cynical reality of human motives behind a sort of veil which was only to be finally torn asunder, on the threshold of modern times, by the harsh hands of a Commynes and a Machiavelli.

The laity, however, remained in many respects the active element in secular society. Undoubtedly the most illiterate of them were not on that account ignorant men. Apart from the fact that they were in a position, when necessary, to have translated for them what they could not read themselves, we shall see presently to what an extent tales told in the vernacular could transmit both memories and ideas. Still, we must never forget that the majority of lords and many great barons were administrators incapable of studying personally a report or an account, judges whose decisions were recorded (if at all) in a language unknown to the court. Is it surprising that these leaders, who were ordinarily obliged to reconstitute their past decisions from memory, should often have totally lacked the sense of continuity which, quite erroneously, some historians of today are at great pains to ascribe to them?

Almost strangers to writing, they tended to be indifferent to it. After Otto the Great had received the imperial crown in 962, he allowed a privilege to be issued in his name which was inspired by the 'pacts' of the Carolingian emperors and perhaps by certain historical writings, granting to the popes, 'till the end of time', the possession of an immense territory. By thus denuding himself of territory, the king-emperor would have abandoned to the Patrimony of St. Peter the greater part of Italy and even the control of some of the most important Alpine routes. Certainly Otto never dreamed for one moment that these dispositions, though very precise, would in fact be carried out. It would be less surprising if it were a question of one of those dishonest agreements which at all times, under pressure of circumstances, have been signed without the least intention of executing them. But absolutely nothing, save perhaps an imperfectly understood historical tradition, obliged the Saxon prince to make such a pretence. On the one hand, there is the parchment with the ink on it; on the other—quite unconnected with it—what was actually done; such was one particularly flagrant example of a typical dichotomy. A great many people in a position to direct human affairs did not understand the only language deemed worthy to record, not only the knowledge most useful to man and his salvation, but even the results of all social activity.

'Ages of faith', we say glibly, to describe the religious attitude of feudal Europe. If by that phrase we mean that any conception of the world from which the supernatural was excluded was profoundly alien to the minds of that age, that in fact the picture which they formed of the destinies of man and the universe was in almost every case a projection of the pattern traced by a Westernized Christian theology and eschatology, nothing could be more true. That here and there doubts might be expressed with regard to the 'fables' of Scripture is of small

significance; lacking any rational basis, this crude scepticism, which
was not a moral characteristic of educated people, melted in the face
of danger like snow in the sun. It is even permissible to say that never
was faith more completely worthy of its name. For the attempts of the
learned to provide the Christian mysteries with the prop of logical
speculation, which had been interrupted on the extinction of ancient
Christian philosophy and revived only temporarily and with difficulty
during the Carolingian renaissance, were not fully resumed before the
end of the eleventh century. On the other hand, it would be wrong to
ascribe to these believers a rigidly uniform creed.

Catholicism was still very far from having completely defined its
dogmatic system, so that the strictest orthodoxy was then much more
flexible than was to be the case later on, after scholastic philosophy
and the Counter-Reformation had in turn exercised their influence.
Moreover, in the ill-defined border land where Christian heresy de-
generated into a religion actively opposed to Christianity, the old
Manichaeanism retained a number of votaries in various places. Of
these it is not precisely known whether they had inherited their
religion from groups who had remained obstinately faithful to this
persecuted sect since the first centuries of the Middle Ages, or had
received it, after a long interval, from Eastern Europe. But the most
notable fact was that Catholicism had incompletely penetrated among
the common people. The parish clergy, taken as a whole, were intellectually as well as morally unfit for their task. Recruited with insufficient care, they were also inadequately trained; most commonly instruction consisted in casual lessons given by some priest, himself
poorly educated, to a youth who was preparing himself for orders
while serving the mass. Preaching, the only effective means of making
accessible to the people the mysteries locked up in the Scriptures, was
but irregularly practised. In 1031 the Council of Limoges was obliged
to denounce the error which claimed that preaching was the preroga-
tive of the bishops, for obviously no bishop would have been capable
by himself of preaching the Gospel to the whole of his diocese.

The Catholic mass was recited more or less correctly in all parishes,
though sometimes the standard was rather low. The frescoes and bas-
reliefs on the walls or the capitals of the principal churches—'the
books of the unlettered'—abounded in moving but inaccurate lessons.
No doubt the faithful nearly all had a superficial acquaintance with the
features most apt to strike the imagination in Christian representations
of the past, the present, and the future of the world. But their religious

life was also nourished on a multitude of beliefs and practices which, whether the legacy of age-old magic or the more recent products of a civilization still extremely fertile in myths, exerted a constant influence upon official doctrine. In stormy skies people still saw phantom armies passing by: armies of the dead, said the populace; armies of deceitful demons, declared the learned, much less inclined to deny these visions than to find for them a quasi-orthodox interpretation. Innumerable nature-rites, among which poetry has especially familiarized us with the May-day festivals, were celebrated in country districts. In short, never was theology less identified with the popular religion as it was felt and lived.

Despite infinite variations according to environment and regional traditions, some common characteristics of this religious mentality can be discerned. Although it will mean passing over various deep and moving features and some fascinating problems of permanent human interest, we shall be obliged to confine ourselves here to recalling those trends in thought and feeling whose influence on social behavior seems to have been particularly strong.

In the eyes of all who were capable of reflection the material world was scarcely more than a sort of mask, behind which took place all the really important things; it seemed to them also a language, intended to express by signs a more profound reality. Since a tissue of appearances can offer but little interest in itself, the result of this view was that observation was generally neglected in favour of interpretation. In a little treatise on the universe, which was written in the ninth century and enjoyed a very long popularity, Rabanus Maurus explained how he followed his plan: 'I conceived the idea of composing a little work . . . which should treat, not only of the nature of things and the properties of words . . . , but still more of their mystic meanings.' This attitude explains, in large part, the inadequacy of men's knowledge of nature—of a nature which, after all, was not regarded as greatly deserving of attention. Technical progress—sometimes considerable—was mere empiricism.

Further, this discredited nature could scarcely have seemed fitted to provide its own interpretation, for in the infinite detail of its illusory manifestations it was conceived above all as the work of hidden wills —wills in the plural, in the opinion of simple folk and even of many of the learned. Below the One God and subordinated to his Almighty Power—though the exact significance of this subjection was not, as a rule, very clearly pictured—the generality of mankind imagined the

opposing wills of a host of beings good and bad in a state of perpetual
strife; saints, angels, and especially devils. 'Who does not know,' wrote
the priest Helmold, 'that the wars, the mighty tempests, the pesti-
lences, all the ills, indeed, which afflict the human race, occur through
the agency of demons?' Wars, we notice, are mentioned indiscriminately along with tempests; social catastrophes, therefore, are placed
in the same class as those which we should nowadays describe as
natural. The result was a mental attitude which the history of the
invasions has already brought to notice: not exactly renunciation, but
rather reliance upon means of action considered more efficacious than
human effort. Though the instinctive reactions of a vigorous realism
were never lacking, a Robert the Pious or an Otto III could nevertheless attach as much importance to a pilgrimage as to a battle or a law,
and historians who are either scandalized by this fact or who persist
in discovering subtle political manœuvres in these pious journeys
merely prove thereby their own inability to lay aside the spectacles of
men of the nineteenth and twentieth centuries. It was not merely the
selfish quest of personal salvation that inspired these royal pilgrims.
From the patron saints whose aid they went to invoke, they expected
for their subjects as well as for themselves, not only the promise of
rewards in heaven, but the riches of the earth as well. In the sanctuary,
as much as on the field of battle or in the court of law, they were
concerned to fulfil their function as leaders of their people.

The world of appearances was also a transitory world. Though in
itself inseparable from any Christian representation of the Universe,
the image of the final catastrophe had seldom impinged so strongly
on the consciousness of men as at this time. They meditated on it; they
assessed its premonitory signs. The chronicle of Bishop Otto of Frei-
sing, the most universal of all universal histories, began with Creation
and ended with the picture of the Last Judgment. But, needless to say,
it had an inevitable *lacuna*: from 1146—the date when the author
ceased to write—to the day of the great catastrophe. Otto, certainly,
expected this gap to be of short duration: 'We who have been placed
at the end of time . . .' he remarks on several occasions. This was the
general conviction among his contemporaries as it had been in earlier
times, and it was by no means confined to the clergy; to suppose so
would be to forget the profound interpenetration of the two groups,
clerical and lay. Even among those who did not, like St. Norbert, go so
far as to declare that the event was so close that the present generation
would witness it no one doubted of its imminence. In every wicked

prince, pious souls believed that they recognized the mark of Anti-christ, whose dreadful empire would precede the coming of the King-dom of God.

But when in fact would it strike—this hour so close at hand? The Apocalypse seemed to supply an answer: 'and when the thousand years are expired . . .' Was this to be taken as meaning a thousand years after the death of Christ? Some thought so, thus putting back the great day of reckoning—according to the normal calculation—to the year 1033. Or was it rather to be reckoned from his birth? This latter interpretation appears to have been the most general. It is certain at any rate that on the eve of the year one thousand a preacher in the churches of Paris announced this date for the End of Time. If, in spite of all this, the masses at that time were not visibly affected by the universal terror which historians of the romantic school have mis-takenly depicted, the reason is above all that the people of that age, though mindful of the passage of the seasons and the annual cycle of the liturgy, did not think ordinarily in terms of the numbers of the years, still less in figures precisely computed on a uniform basis. How many charters lack any trace of a date! Even among the rest, what diversity there is in the systems of reference, which are mostly un-connected with the life of the Saviour—years of reigns or pontificates, astronomical indications of every kind, or even the fifteen-year cycle of the indiction, a relic of Roman fiscal practices! One entire country, Spain, while using more generally than elsewhere the concept of a definite era, assigned to it—for reasons that are somewhat obscure—an initial date absolutely unrelated to the Gospel, namely the year 38 B.C. It is true that legal documents occasionally and chronicles more frequently adhered to the era of the Incarnation; but it was still neces-sary to take into account the variations in the beginning of the year. For the Church excluded the first of January as a pagan festival. Thus, according to the province or the chancellery, the year designated the thousandth began at one or other of six or seven different dates, which ranged, according to our calendar, from 25th March 999 to 31st March 1000. What is worse, some of these initial dates, being essentially moveable since they were linked with a particular liturgical moment of the Easter period, could not be anticipated without tables, which only the learned possessed; they were also very apt to lead to perma-nent confusion in men's minds by making some years longer than others. Thus it was not unusual for the same day of the month, in March or April, or the feast of the same saint to occur twice in the same year. Indeed, for the majority of Western men this expression, 'the year 1000', which we have been led to believe was charged with anguish, could not be identified with any precise moment in the sequence of days.

Yet the notion of the shadow cast over men's minds at that time by the supposed imminence of the Day of Wrath is not altogether wrong. All Europe, it is true, did not tremble with fear towards the end of the first millennium, to compose itself suddenly as soon as this supposedly fateful date was past. But, what was even worse perhaps, waves of fear swept almost incessantly over this region or that, subsiding at one point only to rise again elsewhere. Sometimes a vision started the panic, or perhaps a great historic calamity like the destruction of the Holy Sepulchre in 1009, or again perhaps merely a violent tempest. Another time, it was caused by some computation of the liturgists, which spread from educated circles to the common people. 'The rumour spread through almost the whole world that the End would come when the Annunciation coincided with Good Friday,' wrote the abbot of Fleury a little before the year 1000. Many theologians, however, re-membering that St. Paul had said: 'the day of the Lord cometh like a thief in the night', condemned these indiscreet attempts to pierce the mystery in which the Divinity chose to veil his dread purpose. But is the period of waiting made less anxious by ignorance of when the blow will fall? In the prevailing disorders, which we should unhesitatingly describe as the ebullience of adolescence, contemporaries were unani-mous in seeing only the last convulsions of an 'aged' humanity. In spite of everything, an irresistible vitality fermented in men, but as soon as they gave themselves up to meditation, nothing was farther from their thoughts than the prospect of a long future for a young and vigorous human race.

If humanity as a whole seemed to be moving rapidly towards its end, so much the more did this sensation of being 'on the way' apply to each individual life. According to the metaphor dear to so many religious writers, the true believer was in his earthly existence like a pilgrim, to whom the end of the road is naturally of more importance than the hazards of the journey. Of course, the thoughts of the major-ity of men did not dwell constantly on their salvation. But when they did, it was with deep intensity and above all with the aid of vivid and very concrete images, which were apt to come to them by fits and starts; for their fundamentally unstable minds were subject to sudden revulsions. Joined to the penitent mood of a world on the verge of dissolution, the desire for the eternal rewards cut short more than one leader's career by voluntary withdrawal to the cloister. And it ended for good and all the propagation of more than one noble line, as in the case of the six sons of the lord of Fontaines-lès-Dijon who eagerly embraced the monastic life under the leadership of the most illustrious of their number, Bernard of Clairvaux. Thus, in its way, the religious mentality favoured the mixing of the social classes.

Many Christians, nevertheless, could not bring themselves to submit to these austere practices. Moreover, they considered themselves (and perhaps not without reason) to be incapable of reaching heaven through their own merits. They therefore reposed their hopes in the prayers of pious souls, in the merits accumulated for the benefit of all the faithful by a few groups of ascetics, and in the intercession of the saints, materialized by means of their relics and represented by the monks, their servants. In this Christian society, no function exercised in the collective interest appeared more important than that of the spiritual organizations, precisely in so far—let us make no mistake about this—as they were spiritual. The charitable, cultural and economic rôle of the great cathedral chapters and of the monasteries may have been considerable: in the eyes of contemporaries it was merely accessory. The notion of a terrestrial world completely imbued with supernatural significance combined in this with the obsession of the beyond. The happiness of the king and the realm in the present; the salvation of the royal ancestors and of the king himself throughout Eternity: such was the double benefit which Louis the Fat declared that he expected from his foundation when he established a community of Canons Regular at the abbey of St. Victor in Paris. 'We believe', said Otto I, 'that the protection of our Empire is bound up with the rising fortunes of Christian worship.' Thus we find a powerful and wealthy Church, capable of creating novel legal institutions, and a host of problems raised by the delicate task of relating this religious 'city' to the temporal 'city'; problems ardently debated and destined to influence profoundly the general evolution of the West. These features are an essential part of any accurate picture of the feudal world, and in face of them who can fail to recognize in the fear of hell one of the great social forces of the age?

*     *     *     *     *

Fundamentally traditionalist, as was the whole of civilization in that period, the legal system of the first feudal age rested on the idea that

what has been has *ipso facto* the right to be—though not indeed without some reservations inspired by a higher morality. Faced with a
temporal society whose heritage was far from according completely
with their ideals, the clergy in particular had good reasons for refusing
to identify justice invariably with precedent. Already Hincmar of
Rheims had declared that the king will not judge according to custom
if this is seen to be more cruel than 'Christian righteousness'. Interpreting the Gregorian spirit, which among the zealots was inspired by
a truly revolutionary fervour, and appropriating as a natural heritage
a remark of Tertullian, who had also been in his day a breaker of traditions, Pope Urban II wrote in 1092 to the count of Flanders: 'Dost thou
claim to have done hitherto only what is in conformity with the
ancient custom of the land? Thou shouldst know, notwithstanding, thy
Creator hath said: My name is Truth. He hath not said: My name is
Custom.' There could be, in consequences, 'bad customs'. In fact, the
legal documents quite frequently use these words, but almost invariably they are applied to rules actually or supposedly of recent origin—
'those detestable innovations', 'those unheard-of-exactions', denounced
by so many monastic texts. A custom, in other words, might seem
especially to deserve condemnation when it was too new. Whether it
was a question of Church reform or of a law-suit between two neighbouring lords, the prestige of the past could scarcely be contested save
by setting against it a past more venerable still.

The strange thing is that this law in whose eyes any change seemed
an evil, far from being unchangeable, was in fact one of the most
flexible ever known. This was due above all to the fact that it was not
firmly fixed in writing—either in legal documents or in the form of
statutes. The majority of the courts contented themselves with purely
oral decisions. What if it was desired to restate them later? Inquiry
was made of the judges, if they were still alive. In contracts, the intentions of the parties were made binding by means of gestures and sometimes the repetition of conventional formulas, in fact by a whole series
of formalities well calculated to impress imaginations little susceptible
to the abstract. Italy was an exception in that writing played a part in
the exchange of agreements and was itself a recognized element in the
ritual. To indicate the cession of an estate, the deed was passed from
hand to hand, as elsewhere a lump of earth or a straw would have
been. North of the Alps, the parchment, even if it were produced,
served as little more than a memento; it had no authentic value, and
was intended chiefly to provide a list of witnesses. For in the last

analysis everything depended on personal testimony—even if 'black
ink' had been used, still more so in the undoubtedly more numerous
cases where it had not. Since memory was obviously likely to be the
more enduring the longer its possessors were destined to remain on
this earth, the contracting parties often brought children with them.
Did they fear the heedlessness of childhood? Various methods could
be used to overcome it: a box on the ear, a trifling gift, or even an
enforced bath.

Whether it was a question of particular transactions or of the general
rules of customary law, memory was almost the sole guardian of tradition. Now the human memory, the fluid, the *escoulourjante* memory,
as Beaumanoir calls it, is a marvellous instrument of elimination and
transformation—especially what we call collective memory. Since this
is in fact merely a transmission of material from generation to generation, it is not only liable, if not committed to writing, to the errors to
which each individual brain is liable in the recording of facts but also
suffers through misunderstandings of what is said. This would not
have been serious had there existed in feudal Europe a class of professional keepers of the legal memory such as other societies—the
Scandinavian, for example—employed. But, in feudal Europe and
amongst the laity, few of the men to whom it fell to declare the law
did so regularly. Not having undergone a systematic training, they
were reduced more often than not, as one of them complained, to following 'any course that seemed open to them or was suggested by their
whims'. Jurisprudence, in short, was the expression of needs rather
than of knowledge. Because its efforts to imitate the past were inevitably based only on an inaccurate picture of it, the first feudal age
changed very quickly and very profoundly while believing itself to be
unchanging.

In one sense, moreover, the very authority that was ascribed to tradition favoured the change. For every act, especially if it was repeated
three or four times, was likely to be transformed into a precedent—
even if in the first instance it had been exceptional or even frankly un-
lawful. In the ninth century, when one day there was a shortage of
wine in the royal cellars at Ver, the monks of Saint-Denis were asked
to supply the two hundred hogsheads required. This contribution was
thenceforward claimed from them as of right every year, and it required an imperial charter to abolish it. At Ardres, we are told, there
was once a bear, the property of the local lord. The inhabitants, who
loved to watch it fight with dogs, undertook to feed it. The beast even-

tually died, but the lord continued to exact the loaves of bread. The authenticity of this story may perhaps be disputed, but its symbolic significance is beyond doubt. Many dues originated in this way as benevolent gifts and for a long time continued to be so described. Conversely a rent which ceased to be paid for a certain number of years, or a ceremony of submission once omitted, almost inevitably fell into desuetude by prescription. Thus the practice was introduced of drawing up, in growing numbers, those curious documents which students of diplomatic call 'charters of non-prejudice'. A baron or a bishop seeks lodgings from an abbot; a king, in need of money, appeals to the generosity of a subject. Agreed, replies the person thus approached, but on one condition: that it shall be specified, in black and white, that my compliance shall not create a right at my expense. These precautions, however, were seldom allowed except to men of a certain rank and were only effective when the balance of power was not too unequal. A too common consequence of the notion of custom was that brutality was legalized and encouraged by being made profitable. It was the practice in Catalonia, when an estate was alienated, to state, in a singularly cynical formula, that it was handed over with all the advantages that its possessor enjoyed 'by grace or by violence'.

This respect for what had been done in the past operated with peculiar force on the system of real property rights. It is very rare, during the whole of the feudal era, for anyone to speak of ownership, either of an estate or of an office; much rarer still—never perhaps, except in Italy—for a lawsuit to turn on such ownership. What the parties claim is almost invariably 'seisin' (in German, *Gewere*). Even in the thirteenth century, the *Parlement* of the Capetian kings, responsive to Roman influences, vainly took the precaution, in every judgment on seisin, of reserving the 'petitory', that is to say the action claiming ownership. It does not appear that in fact the procedure envisaged was ever employed. What then was this famous seisin? It was not exactly possession, which the mere seizure of the land or the right would have sufficed to create. It was possession made venerable by the lapse of time. Two litigants go to law about a field or a right to administer justice. No matter which of them is the present holder, that one will succeed who is able to prove that he ploughed the land or administered justice during previous years or, better still, that his ancestors before him did so. For this purpose, in so far as the case is not remitted to the ordeal or to trial by battle, he will invoke as a rule 'the memory of men, as far as it extends'. Title-deeds were hardly ever produced save to assist memory, and if they proved that a transfer had taken place it was merely a transfer of seisin. Once the proof of long usage had been adduced, no one considered it worth while to prove anything else.

Moreover, for yet other reasons, the word 'ownership', as applied to landed property, would have been almost meaningless. Or at least it would have been necessary to say—as was frequently done later on, when a more developed legal vocabulary was in use—ownership or seisin of such and such a right over the ground. For nearly all land and a great many human beings were burdened at this time with a multiplicity of obligations differing in their nature, but all apparently of equal importance. None implied that fixed proprietary exclusiveness which belonged to the conception of ownership in Roman law. The tenant who—from father to son, as a rule—ploughs the land and gathers in the crop; his immediate lord, to whom he pays dues and who, in certain circumstances, can resume possession of the land; the lord of the lord, and so on, right up the feudal scale—how many persons there are who can say, each with as much justification as the other, 'That is my field!' Even this is an understatement. For the ramifications extended horizontally as well as vertically and account should be taken of the village community, which normally recovered the use of the whole of its agricultural land as soon as it was cleared of crops; of the tenant's family, without whose consent the property could not be alienated; and of the families of the successive lords.

This hierarchical complex of bonds between the man and the soil derived its sanction, no doubt, from very remote origins. (In a great part of the Roman world itself, Quiritarian ownership had been little more than a façade.) In feudal times, however, the system blossomed out as never before. To minds not much alive to logical contradictions there was nothing disturbing in this interpenetration of 'seisins' on the same thing, and perhaps this attitude to legal rights could not be better defined than by borrowing a familiar formula from sociology and calling it the mentality of legal 'participation'.

As we have noted, the study of Roman law had never ceased in the schools of Italy. But from about the end of the eleventh century, according to a monk of Marseilles, students were to be seen literally 'in crowds' attending the lectures given by teams of masters, now more numerous and better organized—especially at Bologna, rendered illustrious by the great Irnerius, 'the torch of the law'. Simultaneously, the subject-matter of the teaching was undergoing profound changes.

The original sources, in the past too often neglected in favour of poor summaries, once again took first place; the *Digest*, in particular, which had almost fallen into oblivion, thenceforward opened the way to Latin legal reflection in its most refined form. The links between this revival and the other intellectual movements of the age are obvious. The crisis of the Gregorian reform had inspired among all parties a speculative effort that was as much legal as political; it was no coincidence that the composition of the great canonical collections which it directly inspired was exactly contemporaneous with the appearance of the first works of the school of Bologna. In the latter we cannot fail to recognize the marks of that return to antiquity and that taste for logical analysis which were about to blossom in the new Latin literature, as well as in the revival of philosophy.

Similar developments were occurring at much the same time in the rest of Europe. There also, especially among the great nobles, there was a growing desire to secure the advice of professional jurists. After about 1096 there were to be found, among the assessors at the court of the count of Blois, persons who, not without pride, styled themselves 'learned in the laws'. Possibly they had derived their education from some of the texts of ancient law that were still preserved in the monastic libraries north of the Alps. But these elements were too poor to furnish by themselves the material for an indigenous renaissance. The impulse came from Italy. Favoured by closer and more frequent social contacts than before, the influence of the Bolognese group was disseminated by its lectures (to which foreign students were admitted), by its writings, and finally by the emigration of several of its teachers. Frederick Barbarossa, ruler of the Italian kingdom as well as of the Germanies, welcomed Lombard legists into his retinue during his Italian expeditions. A former student of Bologna, Placentinus, established himself shortly after 1160 at Montpellier; another, Vacarius, had been called some years before to Canterbury. Everywhere, in the course of the twelfth century, Roman law penetrated into the schools. It was taught, for example, about 1170, side by side with canon law, in the shadow of the cathedral of Sens.

Yet the revival of interest in Roman law provoked lively opposition. Fundamentally secular, it disturbed many churchmen by its latent paganism. The guardians of monastic virtue accused it of having turned the monks away from prayer. The theologians reproached it with supplanting the only forms of speculative activity that seemed to them worthy of clerics. The kings of France themselves or their counsellors, at least from Philip Augustus on, seem to have taken umbrage at the too easy justifications which it provided for the theorists of Imperial hegemony. Far from arresting the movement, however, this opposition did little more than attest its strength.

In the south of France, where customary law had retained a strongly Roman stamp, the work of the jurists, by providing access to the original texts, had the effect of elevating the 'written' law to the status of a sort of common law, which was applied in the absence of expressly contrary usages. It was thus too in Provence where, from the middle of the twelfth century, the knowledge of Justinian's Code seemed so important to the laity themselves that they were provided with a summary of it in the vernacular. Elsewhere the influence was less direct. Even where it found a particularly favourable soil, the ancestral rules were too firmly rotted in the 'memory of men' and too closely bound up with a whole system of social organization very different from that of ancient Rome to be overthrown at the mere pleasure of a few teachers of law. But in all regions the hostility henceforth manifested to the old methods of proof, notably trial by battle, and the development, in public law, of the notion of treason owed something to the examples of the *Corpus Juris* and of the gloss. Here again the imitation of the ancient models received powerful support from quite other influences. There was the Church's horror of blood, as of every practice which might seem designed to 'tempt God'. There was the attraction—especially felt by the merchants—of more convenient and more rational procedures. And there was the renewed prestige of monarchy. If we find certain notaries of the twelfth and thirteenth centuries trying to express the realities of their age in the vocabulary of the Codes, these clumsy efforts scarcely affected fundamental human relations. It was by another route that Roman jurisprudence at that time exercised its true influence on living law, namely, by teaching it to acquire a clearer conception of itself.

Looking with a new objectivity at the purely traditional precepts which had hitherto governed society after a fashion, men trained in the school of Roman law must inevitably have been inspired to remove their contradictions and uncertainties. It is in the nature of such attitudes to spread and it was not long before they passed beyond the relatively restricted circles which had a direct acquaintance with the marvellous instruments of intellectual analysis bequeathed by ancient jurisprudence. Here again, moreover, they were in harmony with more than one independent movement. Society was less uneducated than it had been and was filled with a great desire for the written word. More powerful groups—above all, the towns—demanded a more precise definition of rules whose uncertainty had lent itself to so much abuse. The consolidation of societies into great states or principalities favoured not only the revival of legislation but also the extension of a unifying jurisprudence over vast territories. It was not without justification that the author of the *Treatise on the Laws of England*, in the continuation of the passage cited above, emphasized the contrast between the discouraging multiplicity of local usages and the much more methodical practice of the royal court. A characteristic feature of the Capetian kingdom is that about the year 1200, side by side with the old references to local custom in the narrowest sense of the word, there appear the names of much larger areas of customary law, such as France around Paris, Normandy, and Champagne. All these were signs that a work of crystallization was in progress, of which the closing years of the twelfth century witnessed at least the preliminaries, if not the completion.

In Italy, beginning with the charter of Pisa in 1142, the urban statutes steadily increased in number. North of the Alps, the charters of enfranchisement granted to the townsmen tended more and more to become detailed statements of customs. In England, Henry II, the jurist king 'learned in the making and amending of laws, subtle inventor of unwonted judgments', put out a mass of legislation. Under cover of the peace movement, the practice of legislation was reintroduced even in Germany. In France, Philip Augustus, prone in all things to imitate his English rivals, regulated a variety of feudal issues by ordinance. Finally, we come across writers who, without official authorization and simply for the convenience of the practising lawyers, undertook the task of systematizing the rules in force around them. The initiative came, as was natural, from circles which had long ceased to rely upon a purely oral tradition. In northern Italy, for example, about 1150, a compiler brought together in a sort of *corpus* the opinions on the law of fiefs suggested to the lawyers of his country by the laws which the emperors had promulgated in their Lombard kingdom. In England, about 1187, in the circle of the justiciar Ranulf de Glanville, the *Treatise* . . . was compiled. Next we have (*c.* 1200) the oldest Norman customary; and (*c.* 1221) the *Sachsenspiegel*, which was written in the vernacular by a knight; double testimony to the far-reaching conquests of the new spirit.

The work was to be actively pursued during the following generations, and for this reason it is often necessary to make cautious use of relatively late works to understand a social structure which was never adequately described before the thirteenth century and which, in many of its features, survived in the Europe of the great monarchies. These later works reflect the organizing ability belonging to the great age of the cathedrals and the *Summae*. What historian of feudalism could ignore that admirable analyst of medieval society, Philippe de Beaumanoir, knightly poet and jurist, *bailli* to two kings of France (Philip III and Philip IV) and author, in 1283, of the *Coutumes* of Beauvaisis?

Since customary law was now taught and set down in writing and was in part fixed by legislation, it inevitably lost much of its variety and flexibility. There was certainly nothing to prevent it from developing, and it continued to do so, but change was less unconscious and consequently less frequent, for if one deliberates beforehand one may always decide not to make the contemplated change after all. A period of exceptional movement, an age of obscure and profound gestation, is therefore succeeded, from the second half of the twelfth century, by an era in which society tends to organize human relations more strictly, to establish more clear-cut divisions between the classes, to obliterate a great many local variations, and finally to allow change only at a slower rate. For this decisive metamorphosis of about the year 1200, the transformation of legal thought, closely linked as it was with other developments, was not solely responsible. There is no doubt, however, that it was a very important contributory factor.

The ties based on blood relationship existed long before, and were by their very nature foreign to, the human relations characteristic of feudalism; but they continued to exert such an important influence within the new structure that we cannot exclude them from our picture. Unfortunately this is not an easy subject for study. It was not without reason that in old France the family community of the country districts was commonly described as the 'silent' (*taisible*) community. Intercourse between close relatives naturally dispenses with writing. Though it was resorted to in exceptional cases, these specimens of family correspondence, which come almost exclusively from the upper classes, have for the most part perished—at least, those earlier than the thirteenth century. For the ecclesiastical archives are practically the only ones preserved up to that date. But that is not the only difficulty. A comprehensive picture of feudal institutions can be legitimately attempted because, originating at the very time when a real Europe was taking shape, they spread without fundamental differences to the whole European world. But the institutions of blood-relationship were, on the contrary, the legacy—and a singularly tenacious one—of

the particular past of each of the groups of diverse origins whose destiny had brought them to live side by side. Compare for example the
almost uniform character of the rules relating to the inheritance of the
military fief with the almost infinite variety of those which regulated
the transmission of other forms of property. In the following account,
it will be more than ever necessary to concentrate upon a few major
currents.

In the whole of feudal Europe, then, there existed groups founded
on blood-relationship. The terms which served to describe them were
rather indefinite—in France, most commonly, *parenté* or *lignage*. Yet the
ties thus created were regarded as extremely strong. One word is characteristic. In France, in speaking of kinsfolk, one commonly called them
simply 'friends' (*amis*) and in Germany, *Freunde*. A legal document
of the eleventh century originating from the Île de France enumerates
them thus: 'His friends, that is to say his mother, his brothers, his
sisters and his other relatives by blood or by marriage.' Only with a
regard for accuracy that was somewhat rare did people occasionally
say expressly 'friends by blood' (*amis charnels*). The general assumption seems to have been that there was no real friendship save between
persons united by blood.

The best-served hero was he whose warriors were all joined to him
either by the new, feudal relationship of vassalage, or by the ancient
tie of kinship—two equally binding ties which were ordinarily put on
the same plane because they seemed to take precedence of all others.
*Magen und mannen*—this alliteration is almost proverbial in the German epic. But poetry is not our only authority on the point, and the
sagacious Joinville, even in the thirteenth century, knew well that if
Guy de Mauvoisin's force did wonderfully well at Mansurah it was because it was composed entirely either of liegemen of the leader or of
knights of his kin. Devotion reached its highest fervour when the two
solidarities were mingled, as happened, according to the *geste*, to Duke
Bègue whose thousand vassals were *trestous d'une parenté*—'everyone
of the same kin'. Whence did a feudal noble, whether of Normandy
or Flanders, derive his power, according to the chroniclers? From his
castles, no doubt, from his handsome revenues in silver coin, and from
the number of his vassals; but also from the number of his kinsmen.
And the same thing was true at the lower levels, right down the social
scale. It was true of merchants, as for example the burghers of Ghent
of whom a writer who knew them well said that they possessed two
great sources of strength: 'their towers'—patrician towers whose stone

walls, in the towns, cast a huge shadow over the humble wooden dwell-
ings of the people—and 'their kinsfolk'. It was true also of the members of those kindred groups—many of them peasants or at any rate
simple freemen, with the modest wergild of 200 shillings—against
whom, in the second half of the tenth century, the men of London
were ready to go to war 'if they prevent us from exercising our rights,
by giving shelter to robbers'.

The man who was brought before a court found in his kinsmen his
natural helpers. Where the old Germanic procedure of compurgation
or oath-helping remained in force, in which a collective oath sufficed
to clear the accused of any charge or to confirm the complaint brought
by a plaintiff, it was among the 'friends by blood' that either by law
or by custom the oath-helpers must be found. A case in point was
that of the four kinsmen who, at Usagre in Castile, were required to
swear with a woman who declared that she had been the victim of rape.
What if trial by battle were preferred, as a means of proof? In theory,
Beaumanoir explains, it could be claimed only by one of the parties.
There were, however, two exceptions to this rule: it was lawful for the
liege vassal to demand battle on behalf of his lord, and any man could
do so, if a member of his own kin was involved. Once more, the two
relationships appear on the same footing. Thus we see, in the *Chanson
de Roland*, Ganelon's kinsmen delegating one of their members to enter
the lists against the traitor's accuser. In the *Chanson*, moreover, the
solidarity of the kindred extends much farther still. After the defeat of
their champion, the thirty kinsmen, who have 'stood surety' for him,
are hanged all together on the tree of the Accursed Wood. A poet's
exaggeration, beyond any doubt. The epic was a magnifying glass.
But the poet's inventions could hope to find little response unless they
conformed to the common sentiment. About 1200, the seneschal of
Normandy, a representative of a more advanced stage of legal development, had difficulty in preventing his agents from including in the punishment of a criminal all his kinsfolk as well. To such a degree did
the individual and the group appear inseparable.

While the kinship group was a source of strength to the individual,
it was also in its way a judge. To it, if we are to believe the *gestes*, the
thoughts of the knight went out in the hour of peril. 'Come to my aid,
that I may not play the poltroon and thereby bring shame upon my
kindred'—was the simple prayer of Guillaume d'Orange to Our Lady;
and if Roland refuses to call to his aid the army of Charlemagne, it is
for fear lest his kinsmen should incur reproach on his account. The

honour or dishonour of one of the members of the little group reflected upon them all.

It was, however, especially in the vendetta that the ties of kinship showed themselves at their strongest.

The Middle Ages, from beginning to end, and particularly the feudal era, lived under the sign of private vengeance. The onus, of course, lay above all on the wronged individual; vengeance was imposed on him as the most sacred of duties—to be pursued even beyond the grave. A rich Florentine, Velluto di Buonchristiano, was a member of one of those citizen communities whose very independence of the great states bred a deep-rooted regard for traditional point of honour. Having been mortally wounded by one of his enemies, in 1310 he made his will. Now a will, in the eyes of that age, was a work of piety as much as of wise provision and was intended above all to ensure the salvation of the soul by devout bequests. Yet even in such a document Velluto was not afraid to set down a legacy in favour of his avenger, if one were to be found.

The solitary individual, however, could do but little. Moreover, it was most commonly a death that had to be avenged. In this case the family group went into action and the *faide* (feud) came into being, to use the old Germanic word which spread little by little through the whole of Europe—'the vengeance of the kinsmen which we call *faida*', as a German canonist expressed it. No moral obligation seemed more sacred than this. In Flanders, about the end of the twelfth century, there lived a noble lady whose husband and two children had been killed by enemies; from that time, the blood-feud disturbed the surrounding countryside. A saintly man, Bishop Arnulf of Soissons, came to preach reconciliation, and to avoid listening to him the widow had the drawbridge raised. Among the Frisians, the very corpse cried out for vengeance; it hung withering in the house till the day when, the vengeance accomplished, the kinsmen had at last the right to bury it. Even in the last decades of the thirteenth century, why did the wise Beaumanoir, the servant of French kings pre-eminent in the maintenance of peace, deem it desirable that everyone should be able to determine the degrees of relationship? In order, he says, that in private wars a man might be able to call upon 'the aid of his kinsman'.

The whole kindred, therefore, placed as a rule under the command of a 'chieftain', took up arms to punish the murder of one of its members or merely a wrong that he had suffered. But vengeance was not directed solely against the author of the wrong himself, for active solidarity was matched by a passive solidarity equally strong. In Frisia, the death of the murderer was not necessary in order that the corpse, its wrong requited, should be laid in the grave; the death of a member of the murderer's family was enough. And if, as we are told, twenty-four years after making his will Velluto found at last in one of his kinsmen the desired avenger, the vengeance, in its turn, fell not on the guilty man himself but on a kinsman. There is no better proof of the power and endurance of these ideas than a decree—a relatively late one—of the Parlement of Paris. In 1260, a knight, Louis Defeux, was wounded by a certain Thomas d'Ouzouer and proceeded against his assailant in court. The accused did not deny the fact, but he explained that he had himself been attacked some time before by a nephew of his victim. What offence, then, had he committed? Had he not, in conformity with the royal ordinances, waited forty days before taking his revenge—the time held to be necessary to warn one's kindred of the danger? Agreed, replied the knight; but what my nephew has done is no concern of mine. The argument availed him nothing, for the act of an individual involved all his kinsfolk. Such, at any rate, was the decision of the judges of the pious and peace-loving St. Louis. Blood thus called for blood, and interminable quarrels arising from often futile causes set the hostile houses at each other's throats. In the eleventh century a dispute between two noble houses of Burgundy, begun one day during the vintage season, went on for thirty years, and in the course of it one of the parties had lost more than eleven men.

Among these feuds, the chronicles have recorded especially the conflicts of the great noble families, as for example the 'perdurable hatred', mixed with abominable treacheries, which in twelfth-century Normandy embroiled the Giroys with the Talvas. In the tales chanted by the minstrels, the nobility found the echo of their passions, elevated to epic grandeur. The blood-feuds of the *Lorrains* against the *Bordelais*, of the kindred of Raoul de Cambrai against those of Herbert de Vermandois, make up some of the finest of the *gestes*. The mortal blow dealt on a feast day by one of the children of Lara to one of the kinsmen of his aunt engendered the series of murders which, linked one to another, constitute the thread of a celebrated Spanish *cantar*. But at every level of society the same customs prevailed. It is true that when in the thirteenth century the nobility had finally become a hereditary body, it tended to reserve for itself as a mark of honour any form of recourse to arms. Legal doctrine and the public authorities—such as the count's court of Hainault in 1275—readily followed suit, partly from sympathy with the prejudices of the noble class, but also partly from a more or less obscure desire on the part of princes or jurists pre-occupied with keeping the peace, to prevent the fire from spreading. To impose on a military caste the renunciation of all private vengeance was neither possible in practice nor conceivable in principle; but at any rate a big step forward would have been taken if it could be imposed on the rest of the population. Thus violence became a class privilege— at least in theory. For even authors who, like Beaumanoir, consider that 'it is not permissible for others than noblemen to wage war' scarcely leave us in doubt as to the restricted implications of that rule. Arezzo was not the only city from which St. Francis could have exorcised the demons of discord, as in the paintings on the walls of the basilica at Assisi. The first urban constitutions had as their principal concern the maintenance of peace and appeared essentially—according to the very name they sometimes adopted—as acts of 'peace'. The main reason for this was that, among many other causes of strife, the rising bourgeoisie was torn, as again Beaumanoir says, 'by the strife and hatred which set one family against another'. The little that we know about the obscure life of the country districts shows that there too a similar state of things prevailed.

Such aggressive sentiments did not, however, hold undivided sway in men's minds. They were countered by other forces—the horror of bloodshed inculcated by the Church, the traditional notion of the public peace, and, above all, the need for that peace. The history of the painful efforts throughout the feudal era to establish internal order—of which more hereunder—provides striking evidence of the evils that it sought to combat.

The 'mortal hatreds'—the phrase had assumed an almost technical meaning—which the ties of kinship engendered ranked undoubtedly among the principal causes of the general disorder. But since they were an integral part of a moral code to which in their heart of hearts the most ardent champions of peace undoubtedly remained faithful, only a few utopians could believe it feasible to abolish them altogether. While fixing penalties, or naming places where violence of any sort was prohibited, many of the peace pacts still recognized the legality of the blood-feud. The authorities for the most part adopted a similar policy. They sought to protect innocent people against the most flagrant abuses of family solidarity, and they fixed the period of grace. They also strove to draw a distinction between lawful reprisals and plain brigandage car-ried out under the pretext of justifiable vengeance. They tried sometimes to limit the number and nature of the wrongs which could be expiated in blood; in the Norman ordinances of William the Conqueror only the murder of a father or a son was so classified. They ventured increasingly, as they grew stronger, to forestall private vengeance by the repression of flagrant offences or of crimes which came under the heading of violations of the peace. Above all, they laboured to bring the hostile groups to reason, and sometimes to compel them to conclude treaties of armistice or reconciliation under the arbitration of the courts. In short, except in England where, after the Conquest, the disappearance of any legal right of vengeance was one of the aspects of the royal 'tyranny', they confined themselves to moderating the more extreme manifestations of practices which they were unable and perhaps unwilling to stop altogether. The judicial procedures themselves, when by chance the injured party preferred them to direct action, were hardly more than regularized vendettas. A significant illustration, in the case of wilful murder, is the allocation of rights and responsibilities laid down in 1232 by the municipal charter of Arques, in Artois. To the lord is assigned the property of the guilty man; to the kinsmen of his victim his person, so that they may put him to death. The right of lodging a complaint belonged almost invariably to the relatives alone; and even in the thirteenth century in the best governed cities and principalities, in Flanders for example or in Normandy, the murderer could not receive his pardon from the sovereign or the judges unless he had first reached an agreement with the kinsmen of the victim.

For, important as might seem 'those old, well-nourished hatreds', of which the Spanish poets speak complacently, they could hardly be expected to go on for ever. Sooner or later, it was necessary to renounce —as the poet of *Girart de Roussillon* expressed it—'the vengeance of dead men'. According to a very ancient custom the reconciliation was normally effected by means of an indemnity. 'Buy off the spear aimed at your breast, if you do not wish to feel its point'—this old Anglo-Saxon saying was still wise counsel.

The regular tariffs of composition which in the past the barbarian laws had set forth in such detail and, in particular, the meticulous gradation of wergilds now survived only in a few places—in Frisia, in Flanders, and in some regions of Spain—and then only in a much modified form. In Saxony, which was on the whole conservative, the system of tariffs was indeed mentioned in the *Sachsenspiegel*, compiled in the early thirteenth century; but it scarcely figures there save as a rather meaningless archaism. And the *relief de l'homme*, which under St.

Louis certain texts from the Loire valley continued to fix at 100 *solidi*, was applied only in exceptional circumstances. How should it have been otherwise? The old barbarian codes had been replaced by local customs which were thenceforth common to populations with very different penal traditions. The governing powers, which formerly took an interest in the strict payment of the prescribed sums because they obtained a share of them, had, during the anarchy of the tenth and eleventh centuries, lost the strength to claim anything at all. Finally and above all, the class distinctions on which the ancient assessments were based had been profoundly modified.

But the disappearance of the fixed scales did not affect the practice of compensation itself. This continued till the end of the Middle Ages to compete with the physical penalties advocated by the supporters of the peace movement as being more effective deterrents. But the compensation for injury or murder—to which was sometimes added a pious foundation on behalf of the departed soul—was henceforth determined in each particular case by agreement, arbitration, or judicial decision. . . .

In the course of the second feudal age political authority, which up to that time was much subdivided, began everywhere to be concentrated in larger organisms. (These were not new, of course, but their effective powers were genuinely revived.) The apparent exceptions, like Germany, disappear as soon as one ceases to envisage the State exclusively in terms of kingship. So general a phenomenon could only have been the result of causes common to the entire West; and a list of these causes could almost be compiled by taking the opposites of those which earlier had led to disintegration.

The cessation of the invasions had relieved the royal and princely powers of a task which exhausted their strength. At the same time it made possible the enormous growth of population to which, from the eleventh century onwards, the progress of land clearance bore witness. The increased density of population not only facilitated the maintenance of order, but also favoured the revival of towns, of the artisan class, and of trade. As a result of a more active and abundant circulation of money taxation reappeared, and with it salaried officials; and the payment of troops began to be substituted for the inefficient system of hereditary contractual services. True, the small or medial lord also profited by the transformations of the economy; he had, as we have seen, his 'tallages'. But the king or the prince almost always possessed more lands and more vassals than anyone else. Moreover, the very nature of his authority provided him with many opportunities to levy taxes, particularly on the churches and the towns. The daily revenue of Philip Augustus at the time of his death was equal in amount to about half the annual revenue returned, a little later, by a monastic lordship which, while not accounted one of the richest, nevertheless owned very extensive properties in a particularly prosperous province. Thus the State from this time onward began to acquire that essential element of its supremacy—financial resources incomparably greater than those of any private person or community.

Corresponding changes took place in the mentality of men. The cultural 'renaissance', from the end of the eleventh century, had made it easier for them to understand the social bond—always a somewhat abstract conception—which is implicit in the subordination of the individual to the government. It had also revived the memory of the great well-ordered monarchic states of the past: the Roman Empire, whose greatness and majesty under absolute rulers were proclaimed by its Codes and its books of history; the Carolingian Empire, embellished by legend. It is true that men sufficiently educated to be influenced by such memories continued to be relatively very few; but in an absolute sense this *élite* had become much more numerous. Above all, education had spread among the laity—not merely the greater aristocracy, but also the knightly class. At a time when every administrator had to be also a military leader, these noblemen of modest fortune were more useful than the clergy; they were also less liable to be diverted by interests alien to the temporal authorities, and they had long been experienced in the practice of law. Hence it was this class which, well in advance of the bourgeoisie, came to form the general staff of the revived monarchies—the England of Henry Plantagenet, the France of Philip Augustus and St. Louis. The practice of writing and the growing interest in its potentialities enabled states to form those archives without which there could be no real continuity of government. Lists of feudal services due from fiefs, periodic accounts, registers of documents dispatched or received—innumerable memoranda of various kinds made their appearance, from the middle of the twelfth century, in the Anglo-Norman state and the Norman kingdom of Sicily and, towards the end of the same century or in the course of the thirteenth, in the kingdom of France and most of its great principalities. Their emergence was the premonitory sign that there was arising a new power, or at least one that had hitherto been confined to the great churches and the papal court, namely the bureaucracy.

## Suggestions for Further Reading

BENNETT, H. S., *Life on the English Manor*. Cambridge, England: Cambridge University Press, 1938.

BLOCH, MARC, *French Rural History*. Berkeley: University of California Press, 1966.

COLBOURN, R. ed., *Feudalism in History*. Hamden, Conn.: Shoe String Press, 1956.

FAWTIER, ROBERT, *The Capetian Kings of France*. London: Macmillan & Co., Ltd.; New York: St. Martin's Press, 1960.

FICHTENAU, HEINRICH, *The Carolingian Empire*. Oxford: Basil Blackwell, 1957.

GANSHOF, F. L., *Feudalism*. London and New York: Longmans, Green & Co., 1952.

HASKINS, C. H., *Norman Institutions*. Cambridge, Mass.: Harvard University Press, 1918.

HOMANS, GEORGE, *English Villagers of the Thirteenth Century*. Cambridge, Mass.: Harvard University Press, 1942.

LYON, BRYCE, *From Fief to Indenture*. Cambridge, Mass.: Harvard University Press, 1957.

# R. W. SOUTHERN

# The Bonds of Christian Society

᪇ᣖᣖ᪇ At the same time that Marc Bloch and his disciples
were developing a sociology of the medieval world in the
1930's and 40's, a parallel, but significantly different, work
of synthesis was undertaken by the rising school of English medievalists. F. M. Powicke, the head of the history
faculty at Oxford, and David Knowles, a Benedictine monk
who came to occupy the senior chair of European history
at Cambridge in the late 1940's, were the founders of this
school. The book which summed up the results of twenty
years of research and reflection by the new English medieval school and presented its view of the structure of medieval society in a marvelously eloquent and compelling
manner was *The Making of the Middle Ages*, published in
1953, by the Oxford scholar R. W. Southern, Powicke's
most brilliant student.

Powicke's main interest lay in the development of government in twelfth- and thirteenth-century England, and
Knowles's major scholarly contribution was a four-volume
history of the various religious orders in England from
the tenth to the early sixteenth century. Both Powicke and
Knowles, however, examined their particular subjects
within the broad context of medieval society and culture,
and Southern's book extrapolates their assumptions and
conclusions to provide a general view of western European

FROM R. W. Southern, *The Making of the Middle Ages*
(New Haven and London: Yale University Press, 1953), pp. 74–
117.

civilization from the tenth to the early thirteenth century.

Southern's interpretation of the framework of medieval society agrees in most respects with Bloch's exposition. But there are two distinctive themes and assumptions that illuminate his work. In Southern's view the primary theme of medieval history is the impress of Christian culture upon an agrarian society dominated by the aristocracy and peasantry. The great forces for change in the medieval world, he believes, are not the altering of the economic and material environment, but rather subtle shifts in religious values and the impact of ecclesiastical thought and learning on the life of agrarian society.

The first of these movements in Christian thought and values scholars have commonly termed the "new piety." In the eleventh and twelfth centuries medieval Christianity experienced a radical change in its nature. In addition to the old formal hierarchical institutional framework, there was now a widespread tendency to make the Christian religion a personal, profoundly emotional experience in the lives of all groups and classes in the medieval world. This new piety not only engendered tremendous achievements in art and literature; it also profoundly affected political action and social relationships. The other revolutionary aspect of Christian culture in the high Middle Ages historians have termed the "new learning." Thought and education broke out of the narrow confines of the monastic schools that had hitherto exclusively controlled intellectual life and in the new universities attained a creative level in philosophy, theology, science, and law that Western civilization had not experienced since the Athenian triumphs of the fifth century B.C. As in the case of the new piety with which it was intimately related, the new learning brought about an enormous advance in the complexity and sophistication of religious doctrine, but it also opened up hitherto unsuspected horizons for medieval monarchy and made possible the transformation of early medieval theocratic kingship into the protomodern bureaucratic states of the twelfth and thirteenth centuries.

The impact of the new piety and the new learning on the old feudal world is analyzed by Southern with a subtlety and sophistication achieved by no other treatment of the subject. Running through his whole book is the *leitmotif* that this was above all a Christian society and that the aspirations and attainments of medieval men in all areas of endeavor can be clearly understood only in the context of these upheavals in religious values and Church-directed education.

The other distinctive quality of Southern's book is his method of assessing the significance of these broad movements of social change by focusing on the ideals and conduct of individual men and women of the eleventh and twelfth centuries. For the most part he portrays members of the ecclesiastical and feudal elite because they are the ones whose personalities are clearly illuminated in the highly class-biased sources, but wherever possible, by the exercise of an unusually powerful historical imagination he describes members of the lower orders of society as well. In trying to evoke the characteristics of actual individual personalities of the medieval world, Southern follows Powicke and Knowles and reflects the hostility to abstract sociological categorizing that has marked English academic thought in the twentieth century. Bloch and the French sociological school view individuals in the context of sociological types which conditioned and determined social action in the medieval world. Southern is concerned to avoid this sociological determinism and, within the broad framework of definable change in cultural values, to give to the leaders of Christian society in the Middle Ages the freedom to make the choices among alternative ideals and modes of action that led to political and intellectual progress.

We turn now from the description of the relations between Latin Christendom and its neighbours to consider the state of the lands which owed obedience to Rome. It is necessary to bear the broad picture of external relations in mind, because in some ways these relations controlled the course of internal development. In particular, the enclosure of Western Europe at a critical moment in the development of social and political institutions, the practical exclusion from the Baltic, and very limited access to the Mediterranean, meant that the land was the unique source of political power, and almost the only source of wealth. Even at the end of our period, when there were in Europe some centres of intense commercial and industrial activity, Europe was still overwhelmingly a peasant society. The annals of village life are short, yet no more substantial work was accomplished in our period than the building up of a village life which, though full of hardships and short-ages, was not without dignity, colour, and the independence which comes from a well-established routine. So much depended on the establishment of this routine, and so little can be said about it. We can dimly see throughout our period the filling up of the countryside, the waste receding, slow improvements in equipment, regular three-year rotation of crops emerging from more primitive arrangements. More clearly we can see that village churches, which were rare at the beginning of our period, are common by its end. Yet it was not until the thirteenth century that village life, both in its material and spiritual aspects, is illuminated by any large mass of documents. As so often happens, the period of growth is one of silence.

By the thirteenth century, however, the main features of village life were established as they were to exist for another five hundred years. Materially, there was probably remarkably little difference between the life of the peasant in the thirteenth century and in the village be-fore it was transformed by modern mechanisms: the produce of the land had increased six fold or ten fold during these centuries, but very little of this increase went into the pocket or stomach of the individual peasant. Compared with the rest of the community, he remained im-mune from new wants, or the means of satisfying them. Everywhere the peasant kept himself alive on a diet whose scarcity and monotony was broken only by intermittent feastings, at harvest time, at pig-killing time, and when people got married or died. There were great differences in the fortunes of individual peasants: families rose and fell, holdings grew and withered away again, following laws similar to those which governed the rise and fall of kingdoms. Over the for-tunes of all, high and low, there presided the unpredictable factors of marriage and childbirth. The rules of succession, infinitely various and complicated, often modified, but with the general authority of cen-turies of growth behind them, were the framework within which the pattern of village—as of national—life was woven.

The continuity of village life goes back visibly to the thirteenth century. For an earlier period, the records for the most part simply fail us. There are no farming accounts, no court rolls, no treatises on agricultural method, little clear information about the land or its crops. The six hundred years which lie on the other side of the thirteenth century are in these matters a time of great darkness. There are a few surveys of great estates from the landlord's point of view for the eighth, ninth and tenth centuries. After that we must rely on scattered documents: the passing remarks of chroniclers on famines, murrains, droughts, storms and years of plenty; charters which throw light on the most deceptive of all standards of a people's well-being—their legal status; miracle stories and crime stories which show that there was plenty of ready violence—murders committed and houses broken into on small pretexts; men maimed, blinded or emasculated judicially for small offences. The village, from these accounts, seems to have had for its narrow means a strange capacity for supporting men cruelly afflicted in the course either of nature or of law. But to extract a coherent story from these records is beyond our power. Yet the village communicated to society at large in all its activities the rhythm and standards of workmanship of a peasant community. The patient, elaborate skill of the arts, the intricate complexity of law and custom, the slow, remorseless procedure of the courts, the heavy, annually revolving routine of monastic life, the respect for ancient authority in the sciences and for solidity as opposed to novelty in scholarship—all these familiar features of medieval life betray the impulse of an agrarian society. Trade might come to quicken the responses of the community and to create those accumulations of wealth which made possible the art and learning of the later Middle Ages; but at least until the thirteenth century, village life is the basis of every activity, and scholars and artists carry into the world of the spirit the qualities learnt in the stubborn struggle with the land.

But if the society with which we are concerned was predominantly a peasant society, it was also everywhere an aristocratic one; and the aristocracy imposed a unity of a different kind on the face of things. By the end of our period we may picture this unity as one of knightly and political ideals in which the aristocracy of the greater part of Europe concurred. But the way for this diffusion of rules of conduct and guides to statesmanship was prepared by something less intangible than ideals—it was prepared by the bond of marriage. Nothing was

more effective in giving men the sense of belonging to a society beyond
the horizon of their ordinary interests than the recollection of their
distant kinsmen. Women were less rooted in the soil than men; they
brought new influences from distant parts and established bonds between men of little or no identity of purpose or of interest. These new
influences were often, both in the Middle Ages and later, greeted with
cries of distrust and suspicion. The marriage of Henry III of Germany
to Agnes of Poitou in 1043, was viewed by solid German churchmen
with about as much enthusiasm as English puritans showed for
Charles I's marriage to Henrietta Maria: "now we see the shameful
habits of French folly introduced into our kingdom" wrote an indignant
abbot. These suspicions were not without foundation: a great lady had
her own clerks, her own household staff, a large say in the dispensing
of religious endowments, and circumstances might easily make her a
ruler among unknown people. There was a moment in the eleventh
century when the regent in Germany was the French Agnes, and in
France the Russian widow of King Henry I.

The career of Agnes illustrates the way in which a woman in a great
secular position could overcome the local limitations, which pressed
more hardly on a man, and could absorb more easily than a man, with
his more exacting political responsibilities, the disturbing ideas of the
time. She was the daughter of William V of Aquitaine, who died in
1030 when Agnes was about five years old. Her mother was a masterful
woman, also called Agnes, who later married the Count of Anjou, and
made a name for herself for ruthless activity and strong piety. For thirteen years after her father's death, the life of the young Agnes was one
of utter obscurity. Then, in 1043, the greatest ruler in Europe sought
her hand. She became the wife of the German King, who was soon
to become the Emperor, Henry III, and her world shifted to Goslar,
Aachen, Kaiserswerth and Speyer. Thirteen years later, at the age of
about thirty, she was left a widow, and regent of Germany for her
infant son. After six years' rule, a sudden revolution ousted her in
1062, and for the remainder of her life she was one of the small band
of devoted adherents of the reforming Popes. She became known
throughout Italy for her religious generosity, and she was the chief
ambassador between the Papal court and her son Henry IV. It would be
hard to imagine a more cruel position: her affection for her family appears to have been strong, but she had to labour in a thankless task of
reconciliation in which no permanent success could be achieved, and

finally she had to acquiesce in the deposition of her son pronounced by Gregory VII in 1076. It was fortunate for her that she died in the next year, in the false after-glow of Canossa when the reconciliation seemed at last to have been effected, however drastically. Yet it was in these hard years that she found herself. Her friends and spiritual advisers were the French and Italian churchmen who were discovering new forms for the expression of Christian piety—Peter Damian and John of Fécamp; and, in the practical life, Hugh of Cluny, and later, with over-mastering influence, Gregory VII. She was in the inner counsels of a group of men of stern and uncompromising purpose, who watched themselves and others for any sign of weakening in the spiritual cause to which they were committed, and yet relied on the encouragement of the woman who had given up everything in serving their ideal:

Return (wrote Peter Damian to Agnes during one of her missions abroad, using words of Jeremiah with innocent enthusiasm) *turn again, O virgin of Israel to these thy cities. How long wilt thou go about hither and thither?* Although thy journey is not to be ascribed to wandering, but rather to obedience and solid reason, yet I will say to thee in the voice of the Roman Church: Return, return, O Shulamite, return, that we may look upon thy face . . . and that our lord pope may see his desire, and that his great staff and stay Hildebrand, and this broken reed, myself, may all—like Jacob at the coming of Joseph—be strengthened by thy sight.

It could not often happen that a woman by marriage was brought into the centre of such a massive conflict as that between the claims of Empire and Papacy, or that her background and personal preferences were so widely at variance with the traditions and interests of the society into which she was transported by marriage. The gap was too great for her mediation to be of any avail. But less dramatic and less tragic cases than that of Agnes are not uncommon. At a time when the spread of ideas was achieved more through the movement of people than through the impersonal circulation of books, the migrations of ladies of noble birth and the small company of advisers who surrounded them were a potent factor in drawing together remote parts of Christendom. The picture at the front of this book* is an illustration of the point. For nearly seven centuries, from 1094 to 1805, it formed part of one of the most treasured manuscripts of the monastery of Wein-

* Crucifixion from the Gospels of Countess Judith—Eds.

garten not far from Lake Constance, and there is evidence that it served as one of the models for the important school of artists connected with that monastery in the twelfth century. But it was far from its original home, for it was a product of England. It had been made, probably at Winchester, for a Flemish lady, Judith, the sister of the Count of Flanders, who came to England about 1051 as the wife of one of the sons of Earl Godwin. Her husband, Tostig, Earl of Northumbria, was killed at the battle of Stamford Bridge in 1066, and she returned to her native land. In 1072 she married Duke Welf of Bavaria and took with her to southern Germany manuscripts and relics which she had collected in England. When she died she left these treasures to the monastery of Weingarten, which thus unexpectedly became in a small way an agent in the dissemination of Anglo-Saxon artistic influence in a distant land.

The wide net cast by the prohibited degrees of marriage often forced a very great man to look far afield for a wife, unless he would make a disparaging match or fall under ecclesiastical censure. These prohibitions continued to be very comprehensive until the end of our period. There was a generally accepted belief drawn from a variety of sources —Biblical, Roman and Germanic—that the prohibited degrees of marriage were seven in number, and throughout the tenth, eleventh and twelfth centuries these degrees were interpreted in their greatest amplitude: that is to say, a man and woman were considered to be within the prohibited degrees if they had had a common ancestor during the last seven generations. There were many reasons why this very comprehensive rule could not have been strictly observed, and the simplest of these reasons was that even so late as the twelfth century only a few of the greatest families could trace their ancestors back through seven generations. Yet the rule was not a dead letter, as we may see from the experience of King Henry I of England.

Henry I had many illegitimate daughters, and he forwarded his intricate policies by marrying them to members of the Norman and French baronage. Two of the marriages which he projected for them were with William of Warenne, earl of Surrey, and a certain Hugh fitz Gervase. But before proceeding to the first of these marriages he found it necessary to submit a genealogical tree to Archbishop Anselm; and some hostile or scrupulous relatives of Hugh fitz Gervase performed a similar office in sending a family tree to Bishop Ivo of Chartres. The result of these two communications was as follows:—

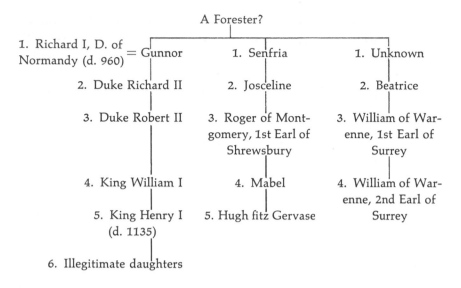

On this showing, King Henry's daughters were clearly well within the prohibited degrees in regard to both their proposed husbands, and the marriages were forbidden by ecclesiastical authority. The common ancestor who was responsible for the legal barrier had lived two hundred years earlier, and his name seems to have been as unknown to the parties concerned as it is to us. The capacious memory of family genealogists had been able to retain no more than the fact of his existence. The case took men back to the days when the greatest of feudal families were just emerging from obscurity, but even so it did not reach to the limit of the prohibited degrees.

It would seem that these very wide restrictions were founded on a misunderstanding of ancient civil and canonical texts which had the intention of prohibiting marriage only within the third and fourth degrees. Already in the eleventh century, the renewed study of Roman law caused some voices in Italy to be raised in favour of the narrower restrictions of earlier days. But these advocates of reform were defeated for the time being by the allegorical and Scriptural reasoning of Peter Damian confirmed by Papal authority, and it was not until 1215 that the Fourth Lateran Council limited the prohibited degrees to the first four generations from the common ancestor. From this time onwards, therefore, both the marriages projected by Henry I would have been lawful.

But if the law did something, dynastic interest did more to make the marriage connexions of any great family very extensive. These connexions were the foundation of public policies and they affected men's ideas in many subtle and unpredictable ways. It is to these public policies that we now turn.

Politically, the great question in the tenth century, outside Germany, was how far the disintegration of authority would go. The immediate cause of the disintegration was lack of loyalty, and with lack of loyalty to persons went a decay and confusion of the ideas for which the persons stood. It was a time when claims of allegiance and duty, however well founded in law or in history, counted for nothing when they went beyond the bounds of effective personal power. It was easy for the Count of Anjou to throw off his obligations to the King of France. Would it prove equally possible for the lord of Loches or of any of the castles of the Loire to throw off the authority of the Count of Anjou? How far would the process go? The answer depended partly on the range of those small bodies of armoured, mounted soldiers who were growing up round the strong points of government. Partly it depended on the extent of the sacrifices people would be prepared to make for peace and security. It was no accident that after the confusion of the tenth century the strongest governmental units appeared where there was least in the way of marsh, mountain or forest to separate one community from another—in the open plains where the competition for power was most intense, and where the need for organization was consequently most keenly felt. But even in the most favourable geographical conditions, man's technical equipment was so primitive that this helplessness before Nature—which added to his misery in one way—saved him from the misery of organized tyranny. There was a mercifully large gap between the will to rule and the power to do so, and it may be that bad roads and an intractable soil contributed more to the fashioning of familiar liberties than any other factor at this time.

Perhaps more simply than anywhere else in Europe, the shaping of a new political order may be seen in the valley of the river Loire. There was here so clean a sweep of ancient institutions, title deeds and boundaries, that the emergence of new forms of loyalty and authority was facilitated. Elsewhere the same processes are to be observed, men have the same objects in view, but they work towards them less directly and less swiftly. We shall observe the ambitions, and the restraints imposed on the wills, of some of the most powerful personalities of their time, in studying the emergence of one of the strongest new political units of the eleventh century in the Loire valley.

THE COUNTY OF ANJOU    The history of this county from the late tenth
to the mid-twelfth century provides a rich portrait gallery of the
makers of a medieval 'state'. Like other families, the counts took a
great interest in their past; they were proud of it, and in the course of
years they left a large collection of documents, which illuminate their
history. Towards the end of the eleventh century, there was a his-
torically minded Count, Fulk Rechin, who set himself to record the
traditions of the family and his own recollections of his predecessors.
Looking back from the eminence which the family had attained in his
time, he could dimly perceive the origins of their good fortune in the
career of an ancestor two hundred years earlier. Nothing was clearly
reported about this ancestor except that his name was Ingelgarius, nor
was much known about his descendants for nearly another hundred
years; but the later panegyrists of the family were able to fill this gap
by proclaiming that Ingelgarius was descended from an ancient Roman-
British family of high rank. No amount of research or invention could
discover how the family had lived in the intervening period since the
fall of Rome, but it was concluded that "the matter is unimportant for
we often read that senators have lived on the land and emperors have
been snatched from the plough". This classical background was a
twelfth-century addition to the history of the family—it reveals the
romantic prejudices of that period—but in essentials the historians of
the family were right. They saw that the effective origins of the family
were to be sought in the later years of the ninth century—a time when,
as one of them remarked, "the men in established positions relied on
the merits of their ancestors and not on their own", and allowed themselves to be elbowed out of the way by new men pushing their way to
the front by superior energy and military effectiveness.

The family of Ingelgarius were among these new men. War made
them conspicuous, grants of land established their position, marriage
consolidated it, and the acquisition of ancient titles of honour cloaked
their usurpations. Ingelgarius gained the first foothold in the valley of
the Loire, but it was his son Fulk the Red—with a name and physical
characteristic which kept reappearing in his descendants—who made
the family a power to be reckoned with in the neighbourhood: marriage added to his possessions, force held them together, and the
comital rights (for what they were worth), which had previously been
shared, were now acquired outright. Two more generations, covering
the period from 941 to 987, gave the family a place in legend and in
general repute, establishing them in a subtle way in men's minds as

well as in their physical experience. The time of Fulk the Good (941 to c. 960) was looked back to as a period of growth, though it was not a time of territorial expansion: it was now that the unnatural fertility of the soil—the fruit of long years of depopulation—was discovered, and prodigious crops rewarded the labours of new settlers. The prize of the Loire valley, the capital city of Tours, still lay outside the range of the count's authority, but the family had great claims to the gratitude of the church in that city. It was said that Ingelgarius had restored to it by force of arms the relics of its patron saint, thus starting the family tradition of goodwill towards the church of Tours. Fulk's reputation in this respect was of a more scholarly kind. It was reported that he delighted to take part in the choir services with the canons and that he was the author of a famous rebuke to a king who ridiculed his clerical tastes. The story is exceedingly improbable, but it illustrates the way in which the family was adding to itself fame of a more than military kind. Fulk's son, Geoffrey Greymantle, who was Count from about 960 to 987, added to this legendary reputation: he was one of the select band of tenth-century heroes whose names were handed down to form part of the stock-in-trade of twelfth-century poetic memory. He was pictured as the standard bearer of Charlemagne in the *Song of Roland*, and in his own right he was the hero of various stories, in which his prowess and counsel saved the kingdom from its enemies.

By 987 the family was ready to emerge from its legendary and epic age on to the stage of history. At this moment there appeared one of those powerful figures, who combined all the qualities and ferocity of his race and consolidated the achievements of the last four generations: Fulk Nerra, the Black, Count of Anjou from 987 to 1040. We cannot do better than look at him through the eyes of his grandson, Count Fulk Rechin. This is what he records of Fulk Nerra:

1. He built thirteen castles, which he can name, and many more besides.
2. He won two pitched battles, against his neighbours to East and West.
3. He built two abbeys, one at Angers and the other near Loches, the great outpost of his power in the South East.
4. He went twice to Jerusalem (this is an understatement: it is almost certain that he went three times); and he died on his way home during his last journey.

Each one of these items, properly considered, stamps him as a man of note: taken together they convey a vivid impression of a pioneer in

the art of feudal government. In the first place, the castles: they were
the guarantee of the stability of the régime. Fulk was a pioneer in the
building of stone keeps, and one formidable example of his handiwork
still survives at Langeais. The inexpugnable fortresses solved at once
the problem of defence and of government—they made loyalty easy.
The battles were more speculative—brilliant gambles based on the
solid capital of defensive positions. It was a time when he who committed himself to open battle, committed his fortune to the winds. But
the reward of successful enterprise was great, as befitted the uncertainty of the outcome; and the battle of Conquereuil in 992 against
the Count of Brittany was one of the foundations of Angevin greatness.

We pass to the expressions of Fulk Nerra's religious zeal. He and
his contemporary Duke of Normandy were the greatest of the pilgrims
who set on foot the movement to Jerusalem. In them the alternation
of headlong violence with abrupt acts of remorse and atonement, which
characterises the early feudal age, has its full play. Perhaps more than
in anything else, the nature of the man is revealed in the documents
which recount his religious benefactions. They breathe a vigorous and
autocratic spirit, unencumbered by any feeling after intangible things,
yet accessible to a sense of guilt and stirred by a sense of littleness
before the miraculous disturbances of nature. These documents deal
with stark facts:

I give them (says Fulk's charter to Beaulieu) the blood, the thieves
and all evil deeds, of whatsoever kind they are (that is to say, jurisdiction over, and the profits arising from the punishment of, mur-
derers, thieves and other criminals), between the rivulet *de Concere*
and the oak of St. Hilary, and between the vegetable garden and the
elm on which men are hanged. And wheresoever, on my land, the
abbot does battle for anything, if his champion is beaten, he shall go
free and pay no fine to my reeve or any official.

So far as Fulk speaks to us at all, he speaks to us in words like these.
Yet, when all is said, we are very far from understanding a man like
Fulk Nerra. It is only occasionally that we are allowed to see behind
the façade of ruthlessness and activity to the not overconfident humanity which guided arm and hand. It takes some extraordinary event to
reveal these men in their more domestic moods. They must often have
sat with their wives at the upper windows of their newly built castles,
but it is not until a meteor falls into the garden below that we have a
picture of Fulk's formidable son Geoffrey Martel and his wife Agnes

(the mother of the Empress) racing down to the spot where it fell and vowing to found an abbey dedicated to the Holy Trinity, in memory of the three glowing fragments which had flashed before their awe-struck eyes. It was in the face of the miraculous that they became most human. When the Duke of Aquitaine heard that a rain of blood had fallen in his duchy, he did not reflect that he was hostile to the royal pretensions—he humbly wrote and asked the king if he had any learned men who could explain the event. And their answers were such as to make any man pause in a career of wrongdoing. But, on the whole, the secular leaders of the early eleventh century must be judged by what they did, and not by what they thought or intended. Judged by this standard Fulk Nerra is the founder of the greatness of the County of Anjou.

His life-time brings us to an age of serious, expansive wars waged by well-organized and strongly fortified territorial lords. The confused warfare, haphazard battles and obscure acts of force of the first hundred years of the family's history had turned scattered and precarious rights into a complex, but geographically compact and militarily impregnable association, dependent on the Count. The process was directed by an instinctive feeling for strategic advantage, which perhaps lends to the history of these years an appearance of consistency greater than in fact it possessed. The methods were not refined, but they were practised with a consistency of purpose which inspires a certain respect. The swallowing of an important strong point might be preceded by many years of steady encroachment. It was necessary, first, to get established at some point within the territory to be threatened—an operation carried out by a careful marriage, a purchase which the documents represent as a gift, or an act of force or fraud. Then a castle was built as a base of operations. After that, watchfulness: a minority, the chance offered by the enemy's engagement elsewhere, or a lucky battle, might complete the circle. The town of Tours, for instance, was not swallowed until 1044, but in a sense the whole history of the family was a preparation for this event: the good relations with the church of the city seem to go back to the founder of the dynasty; the encircling of the town by a ring of castles at Langeais, Montbazon, Montrichard and Montboyan had been begun by Fulk Nerra fifty years before the final victory. How much was design and how much a kind of inspired opportunism it would be useless to enquire. Once started, the process went on as relentlessly as the operations of the Stock Exchange.

But by the middle of the eleventh century, easy progress by these familiar methods was no longer possible. The weak had been made dependent, the strongholds of intruding neighbours had been taken and, by the same token, distant claims of the Counts outside their own territory had been abandoned. To the west stood Brittany, to the east Blois, to the north—across the still debatable land of Maine—Normandy, to the south Poitou. They faced each other as equals. Although the armed peace was often broken, the chief interest of the next hundred and fifty years lies in the emergence of stable political institutions and the elaboration of a new system of law. The swashbuckling days were over, and the régimes which had emerged began to clothe themselves in habits of respectability. Up to this point, St. Augustine's dictum that secular governments are nothing but large-scale robbery seemed to be abundantly justified by the facts: but slowly something more complex, more sensitive to the positive merits of organized society, seemed to be required. Government became something more than a system of exactions from a conquered countryside, and there developed a routine for the peaceful exploitation of resources and for the administering of justice. For this, an expert and literate staff was needed, in addition to the menials and military leaders who had satisfied the requirements of a more primitive age. Government by means of the written word returned after a long silence. Until the time of Fulk Rechin, the Count seems not to have felt the need for having someone at hand who could write his letters. All the known comital documents were written by an outsider. It was quite natural that this should be so. The most frequent occasion for writing a document was to make a record of some act of generosity, by which the Count had endowed a religious house: it was the beneficiary who was interested in making the record, and to him fell the labour of making it. If on the other hand, as might sometimes happen, the Count wished to correspond with the Pope or the King of France, he called in some notable scholar for the occasion to write his letters for him. But slowly his needs outgrew this primitive expedient. The necessity for transmitting orders and preserving information became more pressing, and by the end of the eleventh century the Count was not only sealing or witnessing documents which had been written for him by those with whom he was in casual contact; he had men about him who could conduct his correspondence and were eager to manage his affairs. It is an important moment in history, not peculiar to Anjou but common to the governments of northwestern Europe. The continuity of government was re-established. The work required trained men, and the presence of trained men—by a process with which we are familiar—made more work for more trained men.

The rise of the great schools of Northern France and Norman England coincided with and forwarded this movement in government. Slowly the ruling households of Europe, at all levels from the Papal Court to the household of a minor baron, were penetrated by men calling themselves 'Masters', men who had studied in the Schools—or as we should say university men. The flow of university men into the Civil Service and into technical positions from the 1870's to our own day is not more significant of the new part played by government in daily affairs, than the similar flow of 'Masters' into official positions which began in the early twelfth century and, by the end of our period, had transformed the operations and outlook of secular government. The revolutions in thought which transformed the mainly monastic learning of the eleventh century on the one hand, and the mainly clerical education of the early nineteenth century on the other, had, both of them, wide repercussions in the sphere of government. The 'Masters' of the twelfth century brought to government a training, a method and a breadth of vision which had been unknown in the previous century; they were only the instruments of government, but they were finer instruments than had been known before.

With the refinement of the instruments of government, the range of effective government became greater. The intense localism of the eleventh century, in government as in other spheres of activity, gave place to a greater spaciousness. Anjou was as much affected by this extension of range as any other part of Europe. But the extension did not come by the old piecemeal method of encroachment—a castle here and a town there. It came in the first place as a result of a series of remarkable marriages which made Anjou part of a wide Empire: in 1128, Geoffrey Count of Anjou married Matilda the heiress of Normandy and England. It took nearly twenty years of war and uncertainty to make good her claim to these lands, but in the end it was made good in the person of Henry II, *Rex Anglorum, Dux Normannorum, Comes Andegavorum*; and—by his marriage with Eleanor of Aquitaine—*Dux Aquitanorum*, then finally (although the title was not officially used until the reign of his son, John) *Dominus Hiberniae*, Lord of Ireland by Papal authority. Henry II's complex association of lands and titles symbolizes the extension of vision of a late twelfth-century ruler. Events quickly demonstrated the insecurity of this great territorial combination, which was broken asunder by a few vigorous strokes of the French King Philip Augustus in the years 1203 to 1205. Anjou henceforth moved in the family orbit of the kings of France. During the remainder of the Middle Ages, it formed part of more than one political combination; but whether it was part of the French royal demesne, or was joined in uneasy association with the Kingdom of Naples, its days of independent local development were over.

No single pattern of political development holds good for the whole of Europe. There was not everywhere the clean sweep of ancient institutions, title-deeds and boundaries which facilitated the emergence of a new order in Anjou. It would be quite wrong to take Anjou as a typical case. Yet what happened there is unusually instructive for we can point to Anjou and say: this is what happened where the control exercised by the past was least effective, and where the disturbing elements of trade, large towns and active commercial oligarchies were not conspicuous. Where these elements are present, the pattern of events is greatly complicated. For example, if we compare the history of the Counts of Tuscany with that of the Counts of Anjou, we find a broad similarity of development shot through with some remarkable differences of detail. Like the Angevins, the Counts of Tuscany could not in the twelfth century trace their ancestry further back than the late ninth century. They also began as an obscure family of vassals who rapidly made their way forward in the tenth century. Their fortunes also were founded on royal favour, and it was their aim to form their scattered possessions into a compact territorial lordship. But the methods they had to employ were more tortuous than those of the Counts of Anjou, and their success was more limited. The royal, or Imperial, power counted for more in Northern Italy than in Northern France, and the Tuscan counts made their way more peacefully and less boldly on that account. They owed much of their land to grants made by churches, on conditions which were already obscure and no doubt ignored in the eleventh century. And, of course, marriage contributed its share to the accumulation.

When the great Countess Matilda died in 1115 she left, by her will, her lands to the Roman Church. It was a donation which had been in the wind for thirty or forty years: Gregory VII had negotiated it, and the friends of the Roman Church attached great importance to the expected event. The document of Gregory VII's time was lost—perhaps in the troubles of his later years—but in 1102 a new one was drawn up to make the gift as unambiguous and absolute as possible. To prevent a repetition of its loss it was carved on a marble slab and preserved in the crypt of St. Peter's, where fragments of it have come to light during the last century. Yet all these careful preparations and high expectations foundered because the diverse origin of the lands which made up the Countess's heritage had not been forgotten. The Emperor claimed his own. But here endless difficulties arose. The past was remembered sufficiently well to confuse the issue, not sufficiently well to clarify it. The question of distribution was never solved, and the problem added another cause of confusion to the tangled relations of Popes and Emperors for the next two generations. Like Anjou, but as a result of a quite different chain of events, the county of Tuscany from scattered origins in the tenth century achieved a limited cohesion and territorial compactness in the eleventh, and in the twelfth century was drawn into the field of wider politics and became part of the complicated sum of imperial rights and possessions. In law, no doubt, the territories should have been torn apart and returned to their original sources: in practice, the force of cohesion was enough to prevent this, and the lands continued to be treated as a whole, though not in the way that the Countess Matilda had sought to bring about.

It was the misfortune of Northern Italy generally that the past was remembered sufficiently well to suggest problems and to raise claims, which could neither be settled nor adequately defined; Imperial rights and Roman Law were never quite forgotten, but their application was doubtful in the extreme, as Frederick Barbarossa discovered to his cost. The county of Anjou was happier in that, in the tenth century, it had no history, and having no history, it produced new forms of organization unencumbered and uncontrolled by the theories which had guided men in the past.

There was indeed, at the time when Anjou was emerging as a recognizable unit of government, a great deal of theory about the duties and position of the secular ruler, but it contained nothing to help—and men of the stamp of Fulk Nerra saw to it that it did little to hinder—the activity of the Counts. The weightiest part of political theory was enshrined in the coronation rites used in the hallowing of kings. And if the words used in these rites are to be trusted, the majesty of kingship had reached a height to which even the Tudors could not aspire. But this majesty of kingship only emphasized the nothingness of countship, unless (which was far from the truth) the count would be satisfied with the reflected glory of a royal official. The position of the count was based on violence, with the covering of such respectability as it could gather around it in the course of time. By contrast, the position of a king rested on eternal foundations: he was in the strictest sense God's anointed, endowed by God with powers which combined important aspects of the powers of bishops and priests, as well as the sanctions of secular rule. He was anointed with the holy oil used in the consecration of priests; he was invested with the ring and staff conferred on bishops, with the power to destroy heresies and to unite his subjects in the Catholic faith; and he received the sword and sceptre with words which gave the highest authority to his use of violence. It was by virtue of this consecration that kings could call themselves— as they could without impropriety in the tenth century—*Vicars of Christ;* and it was by this same virtue that an extreme advocate of old-fashioned views in the late eleventh century could write:

Kings and Priests have a common unction of holy oil, a common spirit of sanctification, a common quality of benediction, the name and power (*rem*) of God and Christ in common. . . Both Kings and Priests are deified and sanctified by the grace of unction and by the consecration of their benediction . . . If therefore the King and the Priest are both, by grace, Gods and Christs of the Lord, whatever they do by virtue of this grace is not done by a man but by a God and a Christ of the Lord. And when the King gives a bishopric or a Priest a kingdom, it is not a man who gives them but a God and a Christ of the Lord.

This is a strange language to our ears, but it would have been less strange in the tenth than it was in the eleventh, and less strange in the eleventh than it became in the twelfth century. The man who wrote these words was struggling against a rising tide, against a new spirit of definition which would rigidly sever the powers and nature of a king from those of a priest, but the attitude he expressed never quite lost its hold. In the time of Henry II and Archbishop Becket, John of Salisbury could still complain of ignorant people who believed that the dignity of priesthood belonged to the royal office, and it is possible that Henry II did something to encourage this belief. There were important political conclusions to be drawn from the meaning of the king's anointing, and what is remarkable is not that very generous conclusions were drawn therefrom in the early part of our period, but that they made so little impression on either the thought or the practice of the twelfth and thirteenth centuries.

This collapse of a long-established habit of thought was the more remarkable because it took place at the very moment when the Kings of France and England were successfully claiming a new addition to their supernatural powers in the form of a miraculous gift of healing, which (it was said) descended from king to king as part of the royal office. The origins of the belief in this miraculous power are very obscure: all that is certain is that the claim was being made in both France and England in the early twelfth century, and that it had developed in some way from miracles reputed to have been performed by Robert the Pious in France and Edward the Confessor in England in the first half of the eleventh century. Once established the belief proved to be astonishingly tenacious, and it might have seemed to a far-sighted observer in the late eleventh century that the novel claim of miraculous power combined with the ancient semi-priestly character of the king heralded a very extreme form of royal ascendancy in the political sphere. This union of supernatural powers in a temporal ruler, so contrary to the political temper of western Europe as we know it, is one of the might-have-beens of history. There were many forces working against it, but it did not seem so remote a possibility in the time of Gregory VII.

The most important force working against this theocratic conception of secular authority was the real power of men like the Counts of Anjou, whose rule owed nothing to theory or to religion. Their power belonged to a world of crude fact, shockingly unconsecrated and dumb. But if the counts found no words to justify themselves, and took refuge from their secular misdeeds in works of pilgrimage and pious benefaction, there were others who began to find words for them. In about the year 1131, Hildebert, Archbishop of Tours, wrote to the Count of Anjou of that day—a young man, recently married to the sole legitimate daughter of Henry I, and the begetter of a long line of English kings—who had recently laid himself under a vow of pilgrimage:

You have laid yourself under a vow, but God has laid on you an office. Your vow demands a journey, but God requires obedience. Your journey will bring you to the memorials of the saints, but your obedience will make the saints themselves mindful of you. Consider well whether the fruit of this journey can compensate a breach of that obedience. If so, lay down your shield without delay, exchange your sword for a staff, go off at once and join the pleasant companions who, as Solomon says, are as good as a carriage on a journey. But if the fruit of government (*administrationis*) is much greater and more desirable than this—which no one will dare to deny—stay in your palace, help the afflicted, live for all, that all may live for you: live for the State (*reipublicae*); work for it day and night. Let equity not acceptance of persons be the rule of your court. Rule yourself by law, and your subjects by love.

Words like this would certainly have surprised a Count of the old school of Fulk Nerra; he would scarcely have believed that his administration could be so respectable. But Hildebert, and scholars who came after him—men who knew what Cicero and Seneca had said about the office of a ruler—were opening up a new vein of political theory, based on human rights and needs, and the innate dignity of the secular order of society. The view expressed in a few words by Hildebert was developed in great detail in the next generation by John of Salisbury in his *Policraticus*, and afterwards by a long series of distinguished writers. These writers gave new standards of conduct to secular rulers and taught them, or at least the clerks in their service, the dignity of just authority. They defined the limits of the ruler's power, and distinguished the qualities of the just ruler from those of the tyrant: in their hands the idea of a tyrant again became a political concept to be feared and fought over. They raised secular government from the dust of violence and self interest while they divested it of the cloak of a semi-priestly authority. In doing this they spoke not only as advocates of a new view of secular rule, but also as members of a Church which had lately come through a great crisis: churchmen who two centuries earlier would have emphasized the powers which the king received in his religious consecration, now shrank from the dangers which they saw lurking there; and kings, despite their consecration, were placed on the same footing as other secular rulers who derived no dignity from any holy unction.

This change of attitude was the greatest contribution of our period to the science of ordinary life. It affected government at every level. At the beginning of the period, the appeal to the supernatural was the most common of all the expedients of government. From the ninth century onwards we have a large number of liturgical forms designed to elicit a divine judgment in all kinds of doubtful cases, whether of crime or disputed ownership. Churches were repositories for the instruments by which the divine judgment was conveyed—the cauldron for the hot water, the brazier for heating the iron, and so on—and one of the commonest functions of the priest must have been the blessing of these instruments to their purpose. The disappearance of these instruments together with the religious ceremonies which surrounded their use was a slow process. Throughout the eleventh century we can mark

no decline, and many curious cases can be cited of the use to which
they were put: they decided the paternity of two children of Robert,
Duke of Normandy; they convicted a bishop of Florence of simony;
and the greatest church council of the century seems to have contemplated the use of the ordeal as a means of testing the orthodoxy of
Berengar of Tours. These were unusual cases but they illustrate the
tendency to fly to the ordeal in any matter of doubt whatsoever.

During the twelfth century this habit of mind underwent a rapid
change. The change took place at the same time as the change in the
attitude to secular government, and some of the same causes were
operating in both cases. The study of Roman Law opened men's eyes
to the existence of an elaborate system of purely human proof; and
the growth of a uniform Canon Law, which applied the methods of
Roman Law, carried the lessons of the lawyers far and wide. Moreover, with the greater abundance of written evidence supplied by the
growing activity of clerks in government, disputed facts about ownership, which had been one of the most fertile sources of appeal to the
ordeal, became amenable to the test of human testimony. Above all,
men came more and more to doubt the efficiency of judgment by
ordeal. William Rufus appeared a monster when he sneered at the
system; but his great-nephew Henry II could punish those who succeeded in the ordeal, without a murmur. When the Lateran Council of
1215 forbade priests to take part in the administration of the ordeal, it
was here, as in so much else that it did, expressing a change of attitude
which had been developing for a long time. The effect, so far as the
regular administration of justice was concerned, was immediate. Men
were forced to prefer the probability arrived at by human agencies to
the certainties of divine judgment. In many cases they did so unwillingly. Roger Bacon tells us that, half a century after the Lateran
Council, there were still many men in various places saying prayers
over hot iron and cold water and such-like things, by which the innocent were approved and the guilty condemned; and ordeal by battle
lingered on as an instrument of justice for many centuries. But, despite
these exceptions, by 1215 the essential steps had been taken in making
human justice and government an affair subject to human rules and
dependent on the efficacy of human agents.

This process of limiting the scope of the appeal to the supernatural
in human affairs had, as its counterpart, a process of limiting the inter-
ferences of secular persons in spiritual affairs. . . . It is perhaps scarcely
necessary to add that it had nothing to do with any lack of belief in the

existence of a supernatural order: on the contrary, it was a symptom of a more refined spirituality which found something crude in the constant and automatic appeal to the supernatural in earthly matters. The same generation which laid bare the human basis of secular government, was also disclosing a new intensity of spiritual life in the study of the individual soul.

There were two great and universal divisions in the society which emerged from the changes and innovations of the eleventh century: between freemen and serfs, and between freemen and noblemen. How sharp were these divisions? What benefits did the higher status confer, and what disabilities did the lower inflict? To answer these questions fully would require a more technical and complex treatment than can be attempted here. We can only try to seize the meaning of serfdom, liberty and nobility in some critical instances.

Once more it will be convenient to turn to the valley of the Loire, where social no less than political ties were specially open to the transforming influence of present necessity.

SERFDOM    The monks of the important monastery of Marmoutier, on the outskirts of Tours, kept a book in which they recorded the details of transactions by which men came under their lordship during a large part of the eleventh century. The following document of about the middle of the century is typical of many:

Be it known to all who come after us, that a certain man in our service called William, the brother of Reginald, born of free parents, being moved by the love of God and to the end that God—with whom is no acceptance of persons but regard only for the merits of each—might look favourably on him, gave himself up as a serf to St. Martin of Marmoutier; and he gave not only himself but all his descendants, so that they should for ever serve the abbot and monks of this place in a servile condition. And in order that this gift might be made more certain and apparent, he put the bell-rope round his neck and placed four pennies from his own head on the altar of St. Martin in recognition of serfdom, and so offered himself to almighty God. The following are the witnesses who saw and heard what was done. . . .

What was being done here? Let us notice the points on which the document dwells: the original freedom of William, which he inherited from his parents, the religious motive behind the surrender, the perpetuity of the new status, and finally the outward and symbolic acts which accompanied the transaction—the bell-rope and the pennies on the head.

It is hard to say which of the elements in the transaction seems strangest to our eyes—the pretence of a religious motive, the expectation of perpetuity, or the symbolic acts. As for the motive, we may in many cases consider that this was a mere form of words, and that the real impulse was quite different from the pretended one. But we shall see that serfdom *had* a religious side to it, and the appeal to religion in our document—though formal and therefore meaningless as a guide to individual motives—is not meaningless as a guide to the social theory of the time. Nor shall we understand the expectation of perpetuity without some reference to religion. There is indeed something awe-inspiring about this once-and-for-all attitude in social relationships. A man's freedom was hereditary and could not (in theory) be invaded arbitrarily: yet a single act on his part could destroy it for his whole family to the end of time. The consequences of this act would descend as a taint in the blood, like original sin itself. As, by man's first sin, all mankind was delivered to the slavery of sin, so by the action of men in the eleventh century the liberty of their descendants was lost beyond the power of recall. No doubt, during the course of our period, many came to be bound in the chains of serfdom, whose condition could be traced back to no definite act of surrender. But by the beginning of the thirteenth century, almost the only thing which could make a man a serf was the fact that his forefathers had been serfs before him. They were the victims of the Fall of some long forgotten ancestor.

The symbolic acts seem at first sight to add a macabre element to the proceedings which brought about this Fall, but they are an essential part—perhaps *the* essential part—of the business. What was being done was something very serious: it was intended to change the whole future of a man and his descendants. This was not to be done in a corner; it must have publicity—publicity of the only kind which the age recognized. There must be witnesses to some singular act which impressed the occasion and its significance on the memory. The act moreover must be appropriate to the thing it signified. Just as, when a man was freed from serfdom by an act of manumission, primitive law decreed that the owner of the serf should show him the open door and the open road, and place in his hands the weapons of a freeman, so, in the act of submission to serfdom, we have the bell-rope and the head

money. The bell-rope round the neck served both as a means of publicity—for it seems from one document that the bell was tolled by the
new serf—and as a means of emphasizing his abject dependence on his
new lord. The head money was the first-fruit of the man's servile condition, placed on the head—or, as we sometimes find, hung round the
neck—as a sign of submission, not tendered by hand like a freeman's
rent.

In many places the payment of this head money became, in the
twelfth and thirteenth centuries, the determining factor in deciding
whether a man was a serf or not. In itself it was little—an annual payment of a few pence only—but it made a clear line of distinction between free and unfree. It was good to have a simple rule: the gradations of society were infinite and there was no close relation between
status and wealth; it might not always be possible to say whether a
man was a sokeman or a sergeant, but at least he should know if he
was free or unfree.

Yet the necessity for some superficial, straightforward rule like this
prompts the question: if such a small indication can decide such a
weighty matter, can it really have been so important as it seems to us
whether a man was free or unfree? The outward appearance and the
name—which in the Latin documents before us is the same as the word
for slave—are as bad as man can make them. But what did it all amount
to? In many of these documents we read of men of some consequence
who made themselves and their children serfs for one reason or another; but except for the small annual payment which symbolized
their servitude their property was not affected. No new or burdensome
services followed in the wake of their new status—at least not immediately; and, conversely, a man who held land by the most onerous
services might yet be by status a free man. That the serfs of Marmoutier were often men of property is clear on every page of these
records. We hear of one freeman, the feoffee of a vineyard, who became
a serf in return for an additional vineyard of equal extent: and this
new vineyard was to be so much his own property that he might sell
it, provided he gave the monastery the first option. Wherein did this
man's servitude lie, and why were landlords like the monks of Marmoutier willing to make bargains which were, in effect, costly pur-
chases of a man's liberty?

To understand this, we must ignore the old Latin name which they
used, and see the transaction as a way of establishing a new claim to a
man's loyalty and aid. Land was plentiful: labourers were compara-

tively few. The greatest problem for an estate manager was to ensure full cultivation. Landlords were not above competing for labour. The condition of serfdom, though it did not take away a man's property, prevented him from moving elsewhere. Probably most of those who came into this condition were already working on the land as tenants of the lord to whom they delivered their freedom; henceforth the lord was assured of their continued service—and would pay a price for this assurance. When the employee of a great industrial concern today accepts a substantial sum on condition that he will not move elsewhere, he is doing in a grand way what thousands of men, large and small, were doing in the eleventh century. The modern firm is not interested in securing the services of its tied-man's children: and for good reason —they might be useless. The less selective eleventh-century landlord thought otherwise: the guarantee of service bound also the serf's children. The securing of their labour was a vital part of the bargain.

From this there arose, by way of simple precaution, a custom which came to be regarded as one of the most degrading of all the incidents of serfdom—the payment made by a serf to his lord on the marriage of his daughter; the so-called merchet. In origin, this was the price of the lord's consent to the marriage; the guarantee of his control. This control was not a senseless humiliation. If the serf's daughter married away from the lordship, she and her children were lost to the lord. It was otherwise with the man: the woman came to live with him, the labour of the children was secure. The Marmoutier documents show clearly the difficulties which arose when the daughter of a serf married outside the lordship. A case arose sometime between 1064 and 1100, which shows that the rules about marriage were only slowly worked out under the compulsion of circumstances, and were at first not very rigid. The daughter of a serf of Marmoutier married a serf of the Count of Anjou, had several children and then died. She was an only child and, therefore, heiress to the lands of her parents in the lordship of Marmoutier. When *her* parents eventually died, her children proceeded to divide the inheritance. But the monks of Marmoutier objected: by their mother's marriage, her children were serfs of the Count of Anjou; all kinds of complications would arise if they were allowed to inherit Marmoutier lands. The case went from court to court, and attracted the interest of the Count himself, who declared that he would not allow serfs to be deprived of their inheritance. Finally the monks paid the claimants the truly enormous sum of £ 15, and allowed them to participate in the prayers of the monastery, on condition that they dropped their claim. The monks of Marmoutier wanted their lands cultivated, but not by another man's serfs—the next step would have been to lose the land altogether.

It was not a special degree of misery which drove these men of Marmoutier into serfdom, but the need which was felt on all hands for a more lasting and intimate relationship between landlord and tenant for the cultivation of the soil than that provided by the forms of free society. The new relationship secured advantages to both sides: to the lord, hereditary labour; to the serf a mixture of advantages, from a simple money payment or an additional holding of land to the benefits of religious fraternity. But things did not end here. The filling up of the land, the increasing hold of landlords upon the waste spaces, the elaboration of government, the growing definition and systematization of law, the influences of Roman Law, were the chief factors which during the twelfth and thirteenth centuries affected the position of the serfs. So far as status went, they all worked against the serf. Whether the history of the peasantry in those centuries would have been much different if the idea of serfdom had never been conceived may be doubted. But it is certain that the fact of serfdom was a convenient lever in enforcing the dependence of the peasantry. It was the one all-sufficient argument against any peasants who wanted to subtract their service, or any part of it, from their lords, and against any who resisted the remorseless pressure of landlordly control. We have seen that men in the eleventh century who were given the worst name that could be given to man—*servus*—were yet able to make good bargains with their masters and they could seek to enforce them in courts of law: such bargains would have been unthinkable a hundred or a hundred and fifty years later, and would indeed have been tantamount to recognitions of the man's freedom. By the end of the twelfth century, the processes of government had become more searching, the 'controls' were more elaborate, the status of serfdom was more rigidly defined. No doubt there were compensations—more rapid, more certain justice; rights which, though more restricted, were more assured; a share in a more general prosperity. We can never know whether the gains outweighted the inconveniences, and probably the men themselves would have been unable to tell us.

We are on surer ground when we enquire what they thought about serfdom. There were many ways of looking on it, but broadly we may distinguish a high religious view, and the view of the ordinary man. As to the first, it is relevant to observe the title used by the head of

Christendom in all his acts: *servus servorum Dei*, which could be translated 'serf of the serfs of God'. There was nothing abhorrent in the idea
of servitude—everything depended on its object. All men by sin have
lost the dignity of freedom and have made themselves, in varying degrees, slaves of their passions: the way to freedom lies through a new
subjection, the humiliation of self-negation. The teaching about serfdom in the Schools of the early twelfth century is well represented by
some sentences which come from the influential circle of Anselm of
Laon:

Servitude is ordained by God, either because of the sins of those who
become serfs, or as a trial, in order that those who are thus humbled
may be made better. For servitude is of great help to religion in protect-
ing humility, the guardian of all virtues; and it would seem to be pride
for anyone to wish to change that condition which has been given him
for good reason by the divine ordinance.

This was the teaching of a school which stood for a somewhat heart-
less and uninspired efficiency in scholastic matters, but here is a more
urgent expression of the same point of view: St. Anselm is writing to a
monk who proposed to make a journey to his native land in order to
save his sister from a state of serfdom to which she had been unjustly
depressed:

What concern is it of monks—men who have resolved to flee the
world—what does it matter to them, who serves whom in the world,
or under what name? Is not every man born to labour as a bird to
flight? Does not almost every man serve either under the name of lord
or serf? And is not he who is called a serf in the Lord, the Lord's freeman; and he who is called free, is he not Christ's serf? So if all men
labour and serve, and the serf is a freeman of the Lord, and the freeman is a serf of Christ, what does it matter apart from pride—either
to the world or to God—who is called a serf and who is called free?

It is easy to see that from this point of view secular serfdom had no
terrors. The burdens and restrictions it imposed were of feather weight
compared with those imposed by the radical servitude of unredeemed
nature. At best, this human servitude was a preparatory discipline,
teaching the motions of humility to a will not yet subdued; at worst, it
added only one more lord, and the least tyrannous of them, to the array
of lordly passions under which human nature already groaned. At best,
it taught the first step in religion—humility; at worst, it lessened the
dominion of self-will by subjection to the will of another. Hence it

came about that the ceremonies of initiation into serfdom were often used to symbolize initiation into the liberty of religion. We read of the young St. Odilo, later abbot of Cluny, entering a lonely church and offering himself as a serf to the Virgin, with the token offering of serfdom hung round his neck and with God as his witness. We read also of St. Gerard of Brogne going every second year to Rome 'with ten shillings hanging from his neck to offer himself as a serf to his Lord'. It was an idea which came naturally to the triumphant Crusaders when they entered Jerusalem in 1100, to go to the Holy Sepulchre and offer their *capitale tributum*—their head money—to the Lord. The symbolism of serfdom seemed to these men a fitting expression of the demands made by religion. When theologians extolled the benefits of mundane serfdom as a doorway to religion, and condemned the attempt to throw off this condition as an exhibition of the sin of pride, this was not simply comfortable doctrine for the well-to-do, teaching the poor their place. It sprang from a deep sense of the place of man in the universe, and it was authorized not only by striking acts of religious devotion but by the countless unknown surrenders implicit in the monastic life.

Yet all this did not make for—rather it was incompatible with—any theory such as that of Aristotle that serfdom or slavery was a condition for which some men were marked out by nature. On the contrary, serfdom was regarded as an unnatural state, only justified by the even deeper disharmony in the state of man induced by sin and the conflict with God. This is a theme which recurs again and again in our documents: *lex poli*, so the jingle ran, is not the same as *lex fori*—

> by Heaven's high law all men are free,
> but human law knows slavery.

By what right does human law perpetuate this unnatural condition? If we went a hundred years beyond the limit of this book we should find men devoted to a primitive evangelical purity of life pressing this question with uncomfortable persistence. But in our period there was a sufficient, if not wholly satisfying answer: God wills that the very sins of men shall turn to the relief of human misery; the man who in his pride and arrogance beats down the weak is a sinner indeed, but he establishes a kind of peace. Little good can be expected in the world, but even that little is only to be had by submission to the man who thus strangely becomes God's minister and beareth not the sword in vain. The choice of half a loaf is all that is left to man, and to resist is to throw away even this; the serf still has his life, his family, his livelihood and, by that special mercy which turns all things to good, in his very serfdom, an instrument for the exercise of his religion, the expiation of his sins, and the perfecting of his humility. And then—to emphasize that serfdom like other human institutions existed on sufferance only—there was always manumission. It was the duty of the serf to submit: it was the glory of the lord to free. "Whoever, in the name of the holy and undivided Trinity, moved by charity, permits anyone of his servile dependents to rise from the yoke of servitude to the honour of liberty, may surely trust that in the Last Day, he himself will be endued with everlasting and celestial liberty." There are the words of an eleventh-century act of manumission: they give the only answer to the problem of serfdom which the religious doctrine of the period allowed.

But there was another, less elevated, view of the matter which was shared by the majority of men, free and unfree alike. Even the monk to whom St. Anselm wrote, rejected his advice and made the long journey from England to Italy to try to save his sister from serfdom. To nearly all men serfdom was, without qualification, a degrading thing, and they found trenchant phrases to describe the indignity of the condition. The serf's family was always referred to by lawyers as his brood, his *sequela*, and the poets delighted to exercise their ingenuity in describing the physical deformity of the ideal serf. Hard words break no bones, but they are hard to bear for all that, and they became harder as time went on. Men well knew, however theologians might seem to turn common notions inside out, the difference between the yoke of servitude and the honour of liberty—or, to use the expressive phrase of Giraldus Cambrensis, the *hilaritas libertatis:* "There is nothing", he wrote, "which so stirs the hearts of men and incites them to honourable action like the lightheartedness of liberty; and nothing which so deters and depresses them like the oppression of servitude." If we consider only the practical effects of serfdom and notice how little the lines of economic prosperity follow those of personal status; if we reflect on the many impediments to free action, to which even the mightiest were subjected in such delicate matters as marriage and the bequeathing of property, it may seem surprising that the pride of liberty was so strong, and the contempt for serfdom so general: yet such was the case. However much the hierarchical principle of society forced men into relationships at all levels of society in which rights and restraints were inextricably mixed up, the primitive line which divided liberty from servitude was never forgotten.

Liberty   What men feared and resented in serfdom was not its subordination, but its arbitrariness. The hatred of that which was governed, not by rule, but by will, went very deep in the Middle Ages, and
at no time was this hatred so powerful and practical a force as in the
latter half of our period. The supremacy of Will was itself an evil,
whether the will was one's own or another's: the latter was more uncomfortable; the former more deadly. This instinctive distrust of the
Will comes out in many ways. When Ivo, Bishop of Chartres, wrote to
dissuade a canon, living according to the Rule of St. Augustine, from
becoming a hermit, he raised the objection that the life of the hermit
was a *vita voluntaria*. By this he did not mean that it was a life voluntarily adopted, but that every detail of the life was at the will of the
individual: the life governed by a well-established rule was higher, and
essentially freer. When the thirteenth-century lawyer, Bracton, wanted
a single phrase to sum up the attributes of serfdom, he said that the
serf did not know today what he would have to do tomorrow—he was
at the will of another. As a practical test this definition would have
been quite worthless: most serfs knew very well what they would
have to do tomorrow, probably better than their masters; but the idea
of living according to the will of another struck the imagination—it
expressed better than anything else the degradation of serfdom.

The higher one rose towards liberty, the more the area of action was
covered by law, the less it was subject to will. The knight did not obey
fewer laws than the ordinary freeman, but very many more; the freeman was not less restricted than the serf, but he was restricted in a
different, more rational way. Law was not the enemy of freedom; on
the contrary, the outline of liberty was traced by the bewildering
variety of law which was slowly evolved during our period. The irk-
some rules and tedious gradations of society did not appear, as they
did to a later age, as so many strangle-holds on liberty. High and low
alike sought liberty by insisting on enlarging the number of rules
under which they lived. The most highly privileged communities were
those with most laws. At the bottom of society was the serf, who could
least appeal to law against the arbitrariness of his superiors. At the top
was the nobleman, governed by an immensely complicated system of
rules in his public life, and taught in his private relationships to observe an equally complicated code of behaviour.

It is significant that the men of our period were not greatly interested
in the 'ordinary' freeman. There must have been many men who, to

our eyes which are not adjusted to the fine distinctions of status, appear to have belonged to this miscellaneous group. But to the medieval mind the conception of mere freedom was colourless, almost meaningless, and it was consequently difficult to imagine a freeman without imagining him a member of some privileged group. It should now be possible to see why this was so. Freedom could only be defined by reference to the law, by which those who were free were governed. Freedom was not a status like serfdom; it was a quality which was attached to the status of all who were not serfs. This quality was the quality of rational order. The mere freeman, with no further qualification, was a man who stood on a zero line: it was not easy to decide on which side he stood, and he could easily be pushed across the line into unfreedom. It was only when the quality of freedom was articulated by being attached to the status of knight, burgess or baron that it could be observed, analysed and measured.

It is one of the most striking features of our period that on this subject of freedom common thought and practice joined hands with theological speculation: the conjunction gives solidity to the political experiments of the twelfth and thirteenth centuries. The barons of Magna Carta had little thought for generalities, but a theologian would have found no difficulty in giving their instinctive reactions the authority of a systematic argument. Liberty is a creation of law, and law is reason in action; it is reason which makes men, as we should say, ends in themselves. Tyranny, whether of King John or of the Devil, is a manifestation of the absence of law. The man who lives outside the law, whether under the rule of his own will or that of another, is bound by the iron chains of servitude. The gossiping Franciscan chronicler of the thirteenth century, Salimbene, distinguished five kinds of rule by which a man was disgraced: the rule of women, of serfs, of fools, of boys and of enemies. The common feature of all these forms of tyranny was lack of law; they were destructive of rational order. The inclusion of women in this list deserves notice, because it emphasizes the point that rule over free men should be rational. In practice of course women often exercised rule, and sometimes with conspicuous success. But equally in the theological and chivalric conceptions of the time, women stood for that which was either below or above reason: women, in the person of Eve, was the agent by which sin came into the world, and, in the person of the Virgin, the agent by which Salvation came; in courtly literature, women stood at once for that which was below reason—

caprice—and for a higher principle than reason—love. But liberty, at least in this world's affairs, was a product of the masculine quality of reason, as expressed in law.

It was a characteristic of the higher forms of law, that those who submitted to them must do so by their own choice. There must be a personal act, an oath, a profession, a contract embodied in a public ceremony, renewed by each person in each generation, not descending in the blood like serfdom from some ancestral act. The highest law of all was that in obedience to which a man stripped himself of this world's goods and subjected himself to religious poverty and obedience. But this state had nothing in common—as the writers of the period were almost too anxious to point out—with that ordinary poverty, the common lot of the majority of men, who of necessity were poor. The monk had chosen his poverty and servitude:

O holy band of men living at unity with one another, what can I say that is worthy of you? You hunger and thirst and suffer penury for the name of Jesus. But it is an honourable and sober poverty, not compulsory but freely chosen . . . There is nothing freer, nothing more safe, than holy poverty.

These words, written by a Cistercian monk in the early years of the thirteenth century, occur in a passage which already breathes something of the spirit of Franciscan poverty. But even in this final renunciation there was also the spirit of aristocracy.

Medieval society was prolific in creating forms of association to which entry was obtained by some form of oath. This connexion between freedom and individual acts of acceptance of its responsibilities again emphasizes the rational character of freedom. The serf's unhappy freedom from law was involuntary, but the submission of the knight, the baron, the clerk, the monk, the burgess, to their various codes of law was voluntary. The nobleman was bound by several codes of law —as a Christian, a baron, a knight, a subject of the king; and he could suffer all manner of penalties for a breach of any of these codes of law. Into all these obligations he had entered by an individual contract in the ceremonies of baptism, homage, knighthood and fealty. If he was punished, even by being burnt as a heretic, he could reflect that he was being punished for breach of contract.

NOBILITY  It follows from the foregoing discussion that whereas serfdom was transmitted in the blood, nobility—the highest form of liberty

—was not. Between the eleventh and the thirteenth centuries there is no nobility of blood. This state of affairs was not one which had always existed, nor one which, in large parts of Europe, would continue to exist. At the beginning of the history of the modern European peoples there was a clearly marked aristocracy raised above the level of ordinary freemen by their blood-worth, which was passed on from generation to generation, and which went back perhaps to some mythological beginnings in a descent from the Gods. But by the beginning of the eleventh century this ancient distinction of blood had ceased to have any significance. At the other end of our period, though not universally, we see the dim beginnings of a new nobility of blood claiming legal privileges by virtue of descent. But during our period, nobility had only two roots: property, by which a man entered into a set of relationships determining his place in society; and knighthood, by which he assumed responsibilities and privileges denied to those outside the ranks of the fraternity. The property relationship was born in the act of homage; the knightly relationship in the act of initiation to knighthood. The first gave a man a place in a hierarchy; the second in a brotherhood. The man who had many lords by his homage was on an equality with the king by his knighthood. It is not surprising therefore that the first was the practical working bond between men, while the second had almost from the beginning something of romance and idealism and ineffectiveness.

The act of homage was purely secular and had immediate legal consequences. Being a simple and business-like proceeding it underwent no development, and remained immune from the influences of a changing society. With knighthood, the case is more complicated. It seems to have begun as a social act, perhaps convivial or even boisterous according to one's reading of the minds behind the rough ceremonies. Its first certain appearances are in the middle of the eleventh century and its origins are intimately associated with the rise of the art of fighting on horseback. It is no accident that the time when we first find dukes and counts depicted armed and on horseback on their seals is also the time when we begin to find notices of the knighting of their sons and vassals. Fundamentally knighthood was the rite of entry into the ranks of the mounted warrior. But, while homage gathered no new aura round it as time went on, knighthood responded to every wind that blew: without ever becoming religious it enjoyed the sanction and colour of a religious setting; it obtained a place in the philosophy of political and social life; it inspired a great literature and was swept into a romantic movement wholly alien to its origins. By the second half of the twelfth century, it is possible to talk as if the essence of the ceremony of knighting lay in its religious setting—the taking of the arms from the altar, the implied profession of obedience to the Church, the obligation to protect the poor and punish the wicked. But it is noteworthy that the few existing accounts of knighting suggest something much more secular, and it is hard to say whether, in the hard school of knightly exercises, practice kept pace with theory. Nevertheless, in the thirteenth century, the ceremony of knighting was commonly performed in a church, often on the occasion of a great festival and after a night of vigil: it was firmly fixed in an ecclesiastical—it would perhaps be too much to say, a religious—setting.

The middle years of the twelfth century marked an important stage in this development. It happens that there is a very full description of the ceremony of knighthood in the year 1128, which gives us a clear picture of the procedure at this date at the highest social level. The occasion was the knighting of the young Geoffrey of Anjou by Henry I of England shortly before his marriage with the king's daughter Matilda. In this ceremony, there was no hint of any association with the Church, it was a purely secular affair, and this is the more striking since the occasion was a very great one and the author of our account gives full weight to the religious ceremonies of the marriage which followed. The day of the knighting began with a bath; then the young man was clothed in a linen undergarment, a tunic of cloth of gold, and a purple cloak, silk stockings and shoes ornamented with golden lions. So arrayed, he appeared in public together with the companions who were being knighted with him. Then followed a distribution of horses and arms. Round the neck of Geoffrey was hung a shield with the device of golden lions which also ornamented his shoes, and there was brought for him from the royal treasury an ancient sword, reputed to have been made by the smith Weland. The young men then proceeded to a display of warlike exercises which continued for a week till the wedding took place.

This may be taken as an example of all that was most splendid and 'proper' in the ceremony of knighthood in Northern France and England during the third decade of the twelfth century. But thirty years later, in the book of political wisdom called the *Policraticus* which he completed in 1159, John of Salisbury was able to speak of a new and solemn custom which had grown up, by which the new knight went to church on the day of his knighting, placed his sword on the altar and took it up again as a token (says John) that he offered himself and his sword to the service of God. John of Salisbury's words deserve special attention because he has just been telling us what modern knights do *not* do: they do not for instance take the solemn military oath prescribed by ancient authors; they do not, it seems, take any oath at all. But John sees in their action in coming to the altar, something which for unlettered men has the same force as the written profession of obedience made by bishops and abbots to their superiors.

It would appear therefore that by the middle of the twelfth century it was becoming common for an act of religious dedication to be added to the secular ceremonies. But, though common, it was not necessary. The essential feature was the bestowal of a sword by an established knight on the aspirant to knighthood. When, for instance, in 1173, the grandson of Geoffrey of Anjou was in revolt against his father, Henry II of England, he was knighted as a preparation for battle. The ceremony was performed by William the Marshal, and the author of the Marshal's life disposes of it in very few words: a sword was brought to the young man; he gave it to the Marshal, the best knight in his company; the Marshal girded him, kissed him, "and so he was a knight". The circumstances were unusual for the injured king was hourly expected, but the incident shows what could be done in an emergency.

The addition of the ecclesiastical ceremony to the act of knighthood is somewhat similar to the addition of an ecclesiastical ceremony to the act of marriage, which was increasingly insisted upon by the authorities of the Church during the twelfth century. There were of course great differences: marriage was a sacrament which knighthood, except in the haziest and least technical of senses, was not; and marriage, unlike knighthood, was undeniably governed by the law of the Church. Nevertheless there is a parallel between the attempt to sanctify the institution of knighthood and the ecclesiastical additions to what was essentially a private contract between two persons in marriage. When we recall the horror and aversion with which secular arms were regarded by serious writers in the eleventh century—an aversion which, as we shall see, played an important part in the crisis of the Investiture dispute—this work of sanctifying secular life appears as something of very great moment. It helped to soften the harsh division between the secular and spiritual aspects of society which is implicit in much of the best thought of the period.

The large conclusions which John of Salisbury drew from the addition of a religious sanction to the status of knighthood would perhaps not have been accepted by many laymen.

For what purpose (he asks) is knighthood ordained? To protect the church, to attack infidelity, to reverence the priesthood, to protect the poor, to keep the peace, to shed one's blood and, if necessary, to lay down one's life for one's brethren.

The phrases which, by contrast, might have come more easily from secular lips are such as these: to defend one's rights, to see justice done, to keep one's inferiors and superiors in their place, to be a wise counsellor and a bold fighter, a loyal vassal and a respected lord, and to make the exercise of arms (if one's interests lay in this direction) profitable. There is always a great difference between high theory and low theory. Nevertheless John of Salisbury, high theorist though he was, had conspicuously more room for knighthood in his scheme of things than Gregory VII or St. Bernard in the two previous generations. Gregory VII had sought a sanction for knighthood in the specific service of St. Peter: his *militia sancti Petri* was a desperate remedy, and one with a narrow appeal, justified as it seemed by circumstances of desperate disorder. St. Bernard's ideal of a knighthood dedicated to the cause of re-establishing Christ's kingdom in the Holy Land had a wider appeal, but knighthood was here sanctified by being drawn away from the possibility of doing mischief at home. With John of Salisbury, however, knighthood had its duties and found its fulfilment at home, on a man's native soil. It may seem a far cry from John of Salisbury, demonstrating the necessity for knighthood from Cato and Cicero, illustrating its virtues from the military authors of antiquity, deducing its religious obligations from Roman Law, and finding a modern sanction in the ceremony at the altar, to the country knights—the 'county' folk—of the time of Henry II who sat as jurors, held enquiries into lands and rights, kept records of crime, and were in every way becoming increasingly involved in the work of local government. There is a world of difference here. But though John of Salisbury's learning makes him seem remote from a real life, he knew well how things worked; he had not been the right-hand man of a very active archbishop of Canterbury for nothing. Both the *Policraticus* in its book-learned fashion, and the assizes of the English king—intensely practical, yet in part at least, the work of learned men—bear witness to the important place in peace as well as war which knights were beginning to take in every aspect of government.

While knighthood was thus entering a period of staid and responsible respectability, it was also inspiring a literature which influenced conduct and manners in many important respects. The knights of this new literature had perhaps as much relation to the knights of the time as the private detectives of fiction to the policemen of everyday life. But the portrayal of knightly character in verse and song, in sermons and educational manuals, impressed a unity of social ideals on the Latin world. The themes of Charlemagne and King Arthur, of the Crusade and the formation of the Christian ruler, were all sustained by and developed round the character of the knight. From very humble origins the word 'knight' became charged with an emotional significance, which outlived the social environment of its birth. The literature in which the ideal of knighthood was set forth had probably little influence on the art of government or the practical life of society at large; its impact was on the individual in his social conduct, in the refinement of his emotions and manners. . . .

We have spoken of serfs and knights because these were two distinctive products of the period from the tenth to the twelfth centuries and because it was round these two classes that the social thought of the period crystallized. But it would be wrong to think that most men belonged to these classes, or that they always took the obligations and restrictions imposed on them very seriously. If we were to divide men (leaving aside for the present the members of the ecclesiastical hierarchy and the religious orders) on practical rather than on idealistic lines, we should have to distinguish a whole host of men who either stood outside this classification, or whose condition was only faintly coloured by their being included in the categories of serfs or knights. There would first be the landless men, the most varied and in some ways the freest class of all, stretching from the son of a noble house in search of distinction on the field of battle or in a great man's household, to students, pedlars and labourers. After them would come men, whether serf or free, with only so much land as they and their families could work themselves, and who paid for their land either by rent or labour; then men with more land than they could work, and who either employed the casual labour of others or could demand services as a right from those who in their turn held land from them. There would be men at all stages of prosperity or decay who formed part of the long line of commerce which led from the sheep-runs of England or Spain, or the mines of Germany, or the forests of the Baltic, across half the world; and men who manufactured either for the neighbourhood or for distant markets. There were men who lived exclusively on the services of others either as money-lenders or as employers of labour at the loom

or in the fields, or—grandest of all—those who enjoyed the services
of men as knightly as themselves in war, in administration and in ceremonial duties.

New forms of specialization were constantly breaking up the conventional divisions of society. But it was only slowly that new social
phenomena could be fitted into the framework of thought—the position of the merchant or the hired labourer was still an uneasy one at
the end of our period. Men were not generous or imaginative in the
acceptance of change. Two hundred years earlier knights and serfs
had themselves been the product of an effort at specialization, and
their position in society had been far from clear. Since then a great
deal of law and literature had gathered round them. The age which
saw the creation of military and social organizations like the county
of Anjou also saw the formation of the two classes on which this organization depended: the knights and the serfs. But just as the county
of Anjou was swept into the stream of larger policies in the course of
the twelfth century, so knighthood and serfdom changed their character. They began as local adaptations to circumstance, with no clear
ethical or legal status: both of them practical expedients. In course of
time their practical bearing became obscure—serfdom could disappear
in some areas and be reinforced in others without affecting in any clear
way the position of the peasantry; at the same time knights lost many
of their primitive functions. In the middle of the twelfth century it was
still possible to speak as if only the knight could properly and with
full responsibility and sanction take part in warfare: two generations
later when knights formed only a fraction of a fighting force and when
many skilled men were needed in warfare besides the fighter on horseback, such language would have seemed woefully out of date. Yet both
knighthood and serfdom persisted and continued to reassert their importance in different ways throughout the Middle Ages and beyond.
The local necessities which brought them to birth disappeared but left
them as permanent features of the medieval landscape. Here as elsewhere we have to admire the solidity of the achievement of the tenth
and eleventh centuries, which ensured the survival of the characteristic
institutions of these centuries amidst the widely different prospects
which were gradually opening out.

## Suggestions for Further Reading

DOUGLAS, D. C., *William the Conqueror*. Los Angeles: University of California Press, 1964.

HEER, FREDERICK, *The Medieval World*. London: Weidenfeld & Nicolson, 1962.

KELLY, A., *Eleanor of Aquitaine and the Four Kings*. Cambridge, Mass.: Harvard University Press, 1950.

KNOWLES, DAVID, *The Monastic Orders in England*. Cambridge, England: Cambridge University Press, 1949.

LOPEZ, R. S., *The Birth of Europe*. New York: M. Evans, 1967.

PAINTER, SIDNEY, *French Chivalry*. Baltimore: Johns Hopkins Press, 1940.

PAINTER, SIDNEY, *William Marshal*. Baltimore: Johns Hopkins Press, 1933.

RUNCIMAN, STEVEN, *A History of the Crusades*. 3 vols. Cambridge, England: Cambridge University Press, 1951.

SOUTHERN, R. W., *St. Anselm and His Biographer*. Cambridge, England: Cambridge University Press, 1963.

ULLMANN, WALTER, *The Individual and Society in the Middle Ages*. Baltimore: Johns Hopkins Press, 1966.

# HENRI PIRENNE

# The Impact of Commerce and Urbanization

≈§§≈ To establish the functional parameters of medieval society twentieth-century scholarship had to undertake a searching examination of the course of economic change in western Europe from the fourth to the fifteenth century. The great pioneer in this work, whose views on the pattern of medieval economic change have constituted the standard interpretation that all subsequent research has had to either confirm or amend, was the Belgian scholar Henri Pirenne, who died in 1936 after a very long and distinguished career as professor of medieval history at the University of Ghent.

Pirenne was scarcely influenced by twentieth-century sociology or economic theory. His early work, published between 1890 and the First World War, fell within the tradition of late-nineteenth-century nationalist historiography, and his extremely influential writings of the 1920's and 30's continued to exhibit some of the salient characteristics of historical literature of the 1890's. Like the liberal nationalist historians of the late nineteenth century, Pirenne always thought he was addressing the educated public as a whole and not merely other scholars; this assumption was highly unfashionable among academic historians in the period between the world wars, although fortunately it has enjoyed a strong revival since World War II. Because of Pirenne's consciousness of himself as

FROM Henri Pirenne, *Economic and Social History of Medieval Europe* (New York: Harcourt Brace Jovanovich, Inc., 1937), pp. 1–57.

the instructor of the general public, he took great pains to present his conclusions in a clear and forthright manner in books remarkable for their vivid style and easy comprehension, even when the subjects he was dealing with were in fact highly technical and arcane. Pirenne never hesitated to present his theses in a sweeping and polemical manner, nor did he think it necessary to support his arguments with a heavy barrage of documentation. Having mastered the material of the subject to his own satisfaction, he was content to present his conclusions in as dramatic and direct a way as possible.

Pirenne actually came to economic and social history by way of working on a definitive history of Flanders under the auspices of the Belgian government. He was impressed by the vitality and self-consciousness of the twelfth-century Flemish burgesses, whom he portrayed as achieving a very high degree of communal autonomy, or, as he termed it in one of his books, "Belgian democracy." He saw the process of urbanization from the tenth to the mid-twelfth century—which occurred in all parts of western Europe but most significantly in Flanders, the Rhineland, and northern Italy—as the great turning point in the history of medieval society. Although the bourgeoisie never comprised more than ten percent of the population, he held that the impact of the cities on the economy and then on government, religion, and culture was the decisive force which lifted the medieval world out of its rural primitivism and intellectual sterility.

Therefore to Pirenne a question of the greatest importance for medieval history was the cause of the rise of cities in the tenth and eleventh centuries. Other scholars had already investigated this problem and had suggested various reasons for the beginning of medieval urbanization: the revivification of old Roman cities, the building of fortress towns by kings and lords, and the slow expansion of local market centers. After a thorough examination of the early history of the great medieval Flemish commercial and industrial centers such as Ghent and Ypres, Pirenne rejected all these interpretations. Previous writers had assumed that urbanization preceded the growth of international commerce, but Pirenne contended that the historical process was actually the other way around. First, in the tenth and early eleventh centuries a group of merchants appeared who were engaged in large-scale commerce, principally exchanging the woolen cloth of Flanders for the goods of the Mediterranean world, many of which had been imported from the Orient to Italy. These merchants sought protection from the violence of the feudal world under the walls of an ecclesiastical or governmental center, paying the king, bishop, or lord dearly for this protection. Eventually enough merchants' and craftsmen's houses were built under the walls of the cathedral or fortress that the burgesses (those who lived in the faubourg next to the burg or fortress) could form a community and encircle their own houses with a new wall. When the space within the bourgeois wall filled as the growth of commerce and the general rise in population continued through the eleventh and twelfth centuries, additional faubourgs or suburbs appeared outside the walls of the city and in turn were enclosed with a new wall after fifty or a hundred years. Thus medieval cities grew under the impact of medieval commerce, spreading out in widening concentric circles from the original ecclesiastical or governmental center.

In the last ten years of his life Pirenne turned to the other critical moment in the history of medieval cities, the point at which ancient urban life disappeared in western Europe and the medieval world became a completely rural society until the reemergence of cities, along the lines Pirenne had already traced, in the tenth century. Previous writers had assumed that it was the Germanic invasions of the fifth century that had cut western Europe off from Mediterranean commerce and brought about the deurbanization of France and the Rhineland and the disastrous impoverishment of the Italian cities. But in *Mohammed and Charlemagne*, which was published posthumously, Pirenne contended that the German invasions had had little or no impact on European commercial and urban life. Instead he claimed that it was the expansion of Islam in the late seventh and eighth centuries which finally brought an end to the ancient Mediterranean economy. The Med-

iterranean became "a Moslem lake"; Europe was cut off
from international commerce; a catastrophic deurbanization rapidly occurred; Europe was driven back on its own
resources, and the westerners turned away from the Mediterranean and found new leadership among the feudal
chieftains and monks of northern France and the Rhineland. Thus did the changes in commerce and urban life
create the feudal, rural, early medieval society, just as after
the tenth century they were to shape the much more advanced, city-enriched culture of the high Middle Ages.

The more broad and bold an historical thesis the more
vulnerable to criticism it will be, as no general interpretation is likely to be compatible with all the data that modern
research has turned up. Pirenne was an austere and highly
courageous man; during the occupation of Belgium by the
Germans in the First World War he refused to collaborate
with the conquerors and he was removed from his post
and interned. Similarly, as a scholar Pirenne exhibited an
unshakable self-confidence and boldness and he did not
hesitate to propound an interpretation of the whole structure of economic change in medieval society. In his own
lifetime Pirenne was the dean of academic medievalists and
the voices of criticism were mute; but in the past three
decades his work has been subjected to severe and at times
savage and unfair attack, and many a young medieval
scholar has launched a successful career by claiming to
disprove either one or both of the main themes of the
"Pirenne thesis."

There can be no doubt that recent scholarship, particularly the careful work of Robert Lopez and Robert Latouche, has raised some very grave doubts about the
consistent validity of Pirenne's interpretation. It is now
widely held that Pirenne underestimated the deleterious
impact of the Germanic invasions on the Mediterranean
economy, and it is known that international trade in the
western Mediterranean had in any case been running
downhill since the late second century A.D. Feudal and
manorial society was taking shape long before the expansion of Islam. There is even some doubt as to whether the
Moslem domination of the Mediterranean cut off Italy

from international commerce in as thorough a manner as
Pirenne believed. It also seems to be true that Pirenne's
view of the growth of cities in the tenth and eleventh
centuries was based much too exclusively on the Flemish
experience. In northern Italy there was probably more of
a continuous history of urban life right through the early
medieval period than Pirenne believed. In England and perhaps also in western Germany most of the towns of the
twelfth century had in fact been founded as garrisons and
local markets, rather than as centers of international trade.

Yet all the criticism to which Pirenne's work has been
subjected has not shaken the core of truth in his interpretation of the development of medieval society. Whether or
not the expansion of Islam was the exclusive cause, the
fact remains that in the eighth century European civilization did turn in upon itself, effectively separate itself from
the old Mediterranean world, and under feudal and ecclesiastical leadership find a new focus of power and creativity
in the rural northland. And those medieval cities which
were the most important centers of economy, religion,
culture, and government—not only the Flemish towns but
also London, Paris, Mainz, Cologne, Venice, Florence,
Genoa, Naples, Marseilles, and later Vienna and Barcelona
—were also the centers of international commerce and the
residences of the enterprising and volatile high bourgeoisie
that Pirenne so much admired.

In order to understand the economic revival which took place in
Western Europe from the eleventh century onwards, it is necessary
first of all to glance at the preceding period.

From the point of view which we must here adopt, it is at once
apparent that the barbarian kingdoms, founded in the fifth century
on the soil of Western Europe, still preserved the most striking and
essential characteristic of ancient civilisation, to wit, its Mediterranean
character. Round this great land-locked sea all the civilisations of the
ancient world had been born; by it they had communicated with one
another, and spread far and wide their ideas and their commerce, until
at last it had become in a real sense the centre of the Roman Empire,

towards which converged the activity of all her provinces from Britain to the Euphrates. But the great sea continued to play its traditional rôle after the Germanic invasions. For the barbarians established in Italy, Africa, Spain and Gaul, it remained the highway of communication with the Byzantine Empire and the relations thus maintained enabled it to foster an economic life, which was simply a continuation of that of the ancient world. It will suffice here to recall the activity of Syrian navigation from the fifth to the eighth century between the ports of the West and those of Egypt and Asia Minor, the preservation by the German kings of the Roman gold *solidus*, at once the instrument and the symbol of the economic unity of the Mediterranean basin, and, finally, the general direction of commerce towards the coasts of this sea, which men might still have called, with as much right as the Romans, *Mare nostrum*.

It was only the abrupt entry of Islam on the scene, in the course of the seventh century, and the conquest of the eastern, southern and western shores of the great European lake, which altered the position, with consequences which were to influence the whole course of subsequent history. Henceforth, instead of the age-old link which it had hitherto been between the East and the West, the Mediterranean became a barrier. Though the Byzantine Empire, thanks to its navy, succeeded in repulsing the Moslem offensive from the Aegean Sea, the Adriatic and the southern shores of Italy, the Tyrrhenian Sea fell completely under the domination of the Saracens. They encircled it to the south and the west through Africa and Spain, while the possession of the Balearic Isles, Corsica, Sardinia and Sicily gave them naval bases which completed their mastery over it. From the beginning of the eighth century European commerce in this great maritime quadrilateral was doomed, and the whole economic movement was now directed towards Baghdad. The Christians, says Ibn Kaldun picturesquely, "can no longer float a plank on it". On these coasts, which had once maintained an intercourse based on community of manners, needs and ideas, two civilisations, or rather two foreign and hostile worlds, now faced one another, the worlds of the Crescent and the Cross. The economic equilibrium of antiquity, which had survived the Germanic invasions, collapsed under the invasion of Islam. The Carolingians prevented the Arabs from expanding north of the Pyrenees, but they could not, and, conscious of their impotence, did not even try to recover the sea. The empire of Charlemagne, in striking contrast to Roman and Merovingian Gaul, was essentially a land empire, or (as some would prefer

to express it) a continental empire. And from this fundamental fact
there necessarily sprang a new economic order, which is peculiar to the
early Middle Ages.

Later history, which shows us the Christians borrowing so much
from the higher civilisations of the Moslems, should not be allowed to
foster illusions about their early relations. It is true that in the ninth
century, the Byzantines and their outlying ports on the Italian coast,
Naples, Amalfi, Bari, and above all Venice, traded more or less actively
with the Arabs of Sicily, Africa, Egypt and Asia Minor. But it was
quite otherwise with Western Europe. Here, the antagonism of two
faiths face to face kept them in a state of war with each other. The
Saracen pirates never ceased to infest the littoral of the Gulf of Lyons,
the estuary of Genoa, and the shores of Tuscany and Catalonia. They
pillaged Pisa in 935 and 1004, and destroyed Barcelona in 985. Before
the beginning of the eleventh century, there is not the slightest trace
of any communication between these regions and the Saracen ports of
Spain and Africa. The insecurity was so great along the coast that the
bishopric of Maguelonne had to be transferred to Montpellier. Nor
was the mainland itself safe from attack. We know that in the tenth
century the Moslems established a military outpost in the Alps, at
Garde-Frainet, whence they held to ransom or massacred the pilgrims
and travellers passing from France into Italy. Roussillon in the same
period lived in terror of the raids which they carried beyond the Pyrenees. In 846, the Saracen bands had advanced as far as Rome and laid
siege to the castle of Saint Angelo. In such conditions the proximity of
the Saracens could bring nothing but unalloyed disaster to the Christians of the West. Too weak to think of taking the offensive, they
shrank back upon themselves and abandoned the sea, upon which they
dared no longer venture, to their adversaries. In fact, from the ninth to
the eleventh century the West was bottled up. Though ambassadors,
at long intervals, were still sent to Constantinople, and though pilgrims
in fairly large numbers directed their steps to Jerusalem, they reached
their goal only by a long and difficult journey through Illyrium and
Thrace, or by crossing the Adriatic to the south of Italy, in Greek boats
from Bari. There is thus no justification for citing their voyages, as is
sometimes done, as proof of the persistence of navigation in the
Western Mediterranean after the Islam expansion. It was completely
at an end.

Nor did commercial activity survive it, for the Mediterranean had
been the great artery of commerce. It is easy to show that as long as it

remained active it was this navigation which kept up the trade of the
ports of Italy, Africa, Spain and Gaul and of their hinterland. The
documents, unfortunately all too rare, which we have at our disposal,
show beyond a doubt that in all these countries, down to the Arab
conquest, a class of professional merchants had carried on an export
and import trade, the existence of which is incontestable though its
importance may perhaps be questioned. Through it, the Roman towns
remained the business centres and concentration points of a traffic
which extended from the sea-coast to the north, at least as far as the
Rhine valley, to which were imported papyrus, spices, eastern wines
and oil unloaded on the shores of the Mediterranean.

The closing of the latter through the expansion of Islam in the
seventh century necessarily resulted in the very rapid decline of this
activity. In the course of the eighth century the interruption of commerce brought about the disappearance of the merchants, and urban
life, which had been maintained by them, collapsed at the same time.
The Roman cities certainly continued to exist, because they were the
centres of diocesan administration, and therefore the bishops resided
there and gathered a numerous body of clergy round them, but they
lost both their economic significance and their municipal administration. A general impoverishment was manifest. Gold currency disappeared to give place to the silver coinage which the Carolingians were
forced to substitute for it. The new monetary system, which they
instituted in place of the old Roman gold *solidus*, is clear proof of their
rupture with the ancient economy, or, rather, with the Mediterranean
economy.

It is manifestly erroneous to consider the reign of Charlemagne, as
it almost always is considered, as an era of economic advancement.
This is nothing but a delusion. In reality, compared with the Merovingian, the Carolingian period is an era of decadence or even of
regression from the commercial point of view. Even had he tried,
Charles would have been unable to prevent the inevitable consequences
of the disappearance of maritime traffic and the closing of the sea. It is
true enough that these consequences did not affect the North with the
same intensity as they did the South. During the first half of the ninth
century, the ports of Quentovic (to-day Etaples-sur-la-Canche) and
Duurstede (on the Rhine, above Utrecht) were fairly frequented, and
Frisian boats continued to cross the Scheldt, the Meuse and the Rhine,
and to carry on a coasting trade along the shores of the North Sea.
But we must beware of envisaging these facts as symptoms of renais-

sance. They are nothing more than the prolongation of an activity which dated back to the Roman Empire and which persisted during Merovingian times. It is possible, and even probable, that the habitual presence of the imperial court at Aix-la-Chapelle and the necessity of provisioning its very numerous personnel, contributed not only to the maintenance, but even to the development of trade in the neighbouring territories, and made them the only part of the Empire where some commercial activity is still to be observed. But, however that may be, the Northmen soon put an end to this last survival of the past. Before the end of the ninth century Quentovic and Duurstede were plundered and destroyed by them so thoroughly that they were never to rise again from their ruins.

It might be, and indeed it has sometimes been, thought, that the valley of the Danube took the place of the Mediterranean as the great route of communication between the East and the West. This might indeed have happened, had it not been rendered inaccessible from the very first by the Avars, and, soon afterwards, by the Magyars. The sources show us no more than the traffic of a few boats loaded with salt from the salt-mines of Strasburg. As for the so-called commerce with the pagan Slavs on the banks of the Elbe and the Saale, it was limited to the interloping operations of adventurers, seeking to supply arms to the barbarians, or buying prisoners of war taken by the Carolingian troops among these dangerous neighbours of the Empire, in order to sell them again as slaves. The capitularies show very clearly that there was no normal and regular traffic on these military frontiers, which were in a state of permanent insecurity.

It is quite plain, from such evidence as we possess, that from the end of the eighth century Western Europe had sunk back into a purely agricultural state. Land was the sole source of subsistence and the sole condition of wealth. All classes of the population, from the Emperor, who had no other revenues than those derived from his landed property, down to the humblest serf, lived directly or indirectly on the products of the soil, whether they raised them by their labour, or confined themselves to collecting and consuming them. Movable wealth no longer played any part in economic life. All social existence was founded on property or on the possession of land. Hence it was impossible for the State to keep up a military system and an administration which were not based on it. The army was now recruited only from among the holders of fiefs and the officials from among the great landowners. In these circumstances, it became impossible to safeguard the sovereignty of the head of the State. If it existed in principle, it disappeared in practice. The feudal system simply represents the disintegration of public authority in the hands of its agents, who, by reason of the very fact that each one of them held a portion of the soil, had become independent and considered the authority with which they were invested as a part of their patrimony. In fact, the appearance of feudalism in Western Europe in the course of the ninth century was nothing but the repercussion in the political sphere of the return of society to a purely rural civilisation.

From the economic point of view the most striking and characteristic institution of this civilisation is the great estate. Its origin is, of course, much more ancient and it is easy to establish its affiliation with a very remote past. There were great landowners in Gaul long before Caesar, just as there were in Germany long before the invasions. The Roman Empire allowed the great Gallic estates to stand and they very rapidly adapted themselves to the organisation which prevailed on the estates of the conquerors. The Gallic *villa* of the imperial era, with its reserve set apart for the proprietor and numerous holdings of *coloni*, represents the same type of exploitation as that described by the Italian agronomists in the time of Cato. It went through the period of the Germanic invasions with hardly a change, Merovingian France preserved it and the Church introduced it beyond the Rhine, step by step as the lands there were converted to Christianity.

Thus the organisation of the great estate was not, in any respect, a new fact. But what was new was the way in which it functioned from the moment of the disappearance of commerce and the towns. So long as the former had been capable of transporting its products and the latter of furnishing it with a market, the great estate had commanded and consequently profited by a regular sale outside. It participated in the general economic activity as a producer of foodstuffs and a consumer of manufactured articles. In other words, it carried on a reciprocal exchange with the outside world. But now it ceased to do this, because there were no more merchants and townsmen. To whom could it sell, when there were no longer any buyers, and where was it to dispose of a produce for which there was no demand, because it was no longer needed? Now that everyone lived off his own land, no one bothered to buy food from outside, and for sheer want of demand, the landowner was obliged to consume his own produce. Thus, each estate devoted itself to the kind of economy which has been described rather inexactly as the "closed estate economy", and which was really simply

an economy without markets. It did so not from choice but from
necessity, not because it did not want to sell, but because buyers no
longer came within its range. The lord made arrangements not only to
live on his demesne and the dues of his peasants, but also to produce
at home, since he could not procure them elsewhere, the tools and
garments which he needed for the cultivation of his lands and the
clothing of his servants. Hence the establishment of those workshops
or "gynaeceas", so characteristic of the estate organisation of the early
Middle Ages, which were simply designed to make up for the absence
of commerce and industry.

It is obvious that such a state of things inevitably exposed men to all
the hazards of climate. If the harvest chanced to fail, the supplies laid
up against a scarcity were soon exhausted and it was necessary to tax
all one's wits to get the indispensable grain. Then serfs were sent
round the countryside to get it from some more fortunate neighbour, or
in some region where abundance reigned. In order to provide them with
money the lord caused his plate to be melted down at the nearest mint,
or ran into debt with the abbot of a neighbouring monastery. Thus,
under the influence of atmospheric phenomena, a spasmodic and occasional commerce existed and kept up an intermittent traffic on the
roads and waterways. Similarly, in years of prosperity people sought
to sell the surplus of their vintage or their harvest in the same way.
Finally salt, a condiment necessary to life, was found only in certain
regions, where they had perforce to go and get it. But there is nothing
in all this that can be regarded as commercial activity, in the specific
and professional sense. The merchant was, so to speak, improvised at
the will of circumstances. Sale and purchase were not the normal occupation of anyone; they were expedients to which people had recourse
when obliged by necessity. Commerce had so completely ceased to be
one of the branches of social activity that each estate aimed at supplying all its own needs. This is why we see abbeys situated in regions
without vineyards, such as the Low Countries, leaving no stone un-
turned in their efforts to obtain the gift of estates in the Seine basin,
or in the valleys of the Rhine and the Moselle, so as to be sure each
year of replenishing their wine-cellars.

The large number of markets might seem at first sight to contradict
the commercial paralysis of the age, for from the beginning of the
ninth century they increased rapidly and new ones were continually
being founded. But their number is itself proof of their insignificance.
Only the fair of St. Denys, near Paris (the fair of Lendit), attracted

once a year, among its pilgrims, occasional sellers and buyers from a distance. Apart from it there were only innumerable small weekly markets, where the peasants of the district offered for sale a few eggs, chickens, pounds of wool, or ells of coarse cloth woven at home. The nature of the business transacted appears quite clearly from the fact that people sold *per deneratas*, that is to say, by quantities not exceeding a few pence in value. In short, the utility of these small assemblies was limited to satisfying the household needs of the surrounding population, and also, no doubt, as among the Kabyles to-day, to satisfying that instinct of sociability which is inherent in all men. They constituted the sole distraction offered by a society settled in work on the land. Charlemagne's order to the serfs on his estates not to "run about to markets" shows that they were attracted much more by the desire to enjoy themselves than by considerations of trade.

Thus we seek in vain for professional merchants. None existed, or rather none but the Jews, who alone, from the beginning of the Carolingian era, carried on a regular commerce, so much so that the words *Judaeus* and *mercator* appear almost synonymous. A certain number of them were settled in the south, but the majority came from the Moslem countries of the Mediterranean and reached Western and Northern Europe through Spain. They were the Radanites, perpetual travellers who still kept up a superficial contact with Oriental countries. The commerce in which they engaged was, moreover, exclusively that of spices and precious stuffs, which they laboriously transported by Syria, Egypt and Byzantium to the Carolingian Empire. Through them, a church could procure the incense indispensable to the celebration of the divine offices, and, at long intervals, those rich fabrics of which cathedral treasuries have preserved occasional specimens down to our day. They imported pepper, a condiment which had become so rare and dear that it was sometimes used instead of money, and enamels or ivories of oriental manufacture, which formed the luxuries of the aristocracy. Thus the Jewish merchants addressed themselves to a very limited clientèle. The profits which they realised must have been substantial, but when full allowance is made for this, their economic rôle cannot be considered as anything but that of accessories. Society lost nothing essential by their disappearance.

Thus, from every point of view, Western Europe, from the ninth century onwards, appears in the light of an essentially rural society, in which exchange and the movement of goods had sunk to the lowest possible ebb. The merchant class had disappeared. A man's condition was now determined by his relation to the land, which was owned by a minority of lay and ecclesiastical proprietors, below whom a multitude of tenants were distributed within the framework of the great estates. To possess land was at the same time to possess freedom and power; thus the landowner was also a lord. To be deprived of it, was to be reduced to serfdom; thus the word *vilain* was used both for the peasant living on a domain (*villa*) and for the serf. It is of no importance that here and there among the rural population a few individuals happened to preserve their land and consequently their personal liberty. As a general rule serfdom was the normal condition of the agricultural masses, that is to say, of all the masses. There were, of course, many gradations in this serfdom, for, side by side with men who were still not far removed from the slavery of antiquity, there were to be found descendants of small dispossessed proprietors who had voluntarily commended themselves to the protection of the great. The essential fact was not their legal but their social condition, and socially all who lived on seigneurial soil were now dependents, at once exploited and protected.

In this strictly hierarchical society, the first place, and the most important, belonged to the Church, which possessed at once economic and moral ascendancy. Its innumerable estates were as superior in extent to those of the nobility, as it was itself superior to them in learning. The Church alone, moreover, thanks to the gifts of the faithful and the alms of pilgrims, had at its disposal financial resources which allowed it, in times of scarcity, to lend to necessitous laymen. Furthermore, in a society which had relapsed into general ignorance, it alone still retained those two indispensable instruments of culture, reading and writing, and it was from churchmen that kings and princes had necessarily to recruit their chancellors, their secretaries, their "notaries", in short, the whole lettered personnel without which it was impossible for them to function. From the ninth to the eleventh century the whole business of government was, in fact, in the hands of the church, which was supreme here, as in the arts. The organisation of its estates was a model which the estates of the nobility sought in vain to equal, for only in the Church were there men capable of drawing up *polyptycha*, keeping registers of accounts, reckoning up receipts and expenditure, and, consequently, balancing them. Thus, the Church was not only the great moral authority of the age, but also the great financial power.

Moreover, the Church's conception of the world was admirably adapted to the economic conditions of an age in which land was the sole foundation of the social order. Land had been given by God to men in order to enable them to live here below with a view to their eternal salvation. The object of labour was not to grow wealthy but to maintain oneself in the position in which one was born, until mortal life should pass into life eternal. The monk's renunciation was the ideal on which the whole of society should fix its gaze. To seek riches was to fall into the sin of avarice. Poverty was of divine origin and ordained by Providence, but it behoved the rich to relieve it by charity, of which the monasteries gave them an example. Let the surplus of their harvests, then, be garnered and distributed freely, just as the abbeys themselves advanced freely sums borrowed from them in cases of need.

*"Mutuum date nihil inde sperantes."* Lending at interest, or "usury" (to employ the technical term used for it, which now took on the derogatory meaning which it has retained down to our own day), was an abomination. It had been forbidden from the very beginning to the clergy, and from the ninth century the Church succeeded in prohibiting it also to the laity and in reserving it for the jurisdiction of ecclesiastical courts. Moreover, commerce in general was hardly less disreputable than commerce in money, for it too was dangerous to the soul, which it turned away from the contemplation of its latter end. *"Homo mercator vix aut nunquam potest Deo placere."*

It is easy to see how well these principles harmonised with the facts and how easily the ecclesiastical ideal adapted itself to reality. It provided the justification for a state of things by which the Church itself was the first to benefit. What was more natural than the reprobation of usury, commerce, and profit for profit's sake, in those centuries when each estate was self-supporting and normally constituted a little world of its own? And what could have been more beneficent, when we remember that famine alone compelled men to borrow from their neighbours and hence would at once have opened the door to every abuse of speculation, usury and monopoly, to the irresistible temptation to exploit necessity, if these very abuses had not been condemned by religious morality? Of course, theory and practice are miles apart and the monasteries themselves very often transgressed the Church's order. But, for all that, so deeply did it impress its spirit upon the world, that it took men centuries to grow used to the new practices

demanded by the economic revival of the future and to learn to accept
as legitimate, without too great a mental reservation, commercial
profits, the employment of capital, and loans at interest.

The irruption of Islam into the basin of the Mediterranean in the
seventh century closed that sea to the Christians of the West, but not
to all Christians. The Tyrrhenian Sea, it is true, became a Moslem
lake, but this was not the fate of the waters which bathed Southern
Italy, or of the Adriatic or the Aegean Sea. We have already seen that
in these latitudes the Byzantine fleets succeeded in repulsing the Arab
invasion, and after the check which it experienced at the siege of
Constantinople in 719, the Crescent reappeared no more in the Bosphorus. But the struggle between the two warring faiths continued,
with alternations of success and reverse. Masters of Africa, the Arabs
were bent on seizing Sicily, which they completely dominated after
the capture of Syracuse in 878; but that was the limit of their advance.
The south Italian towns, Naples, Gaeta, Amalfi, and Salerno in the
west, and Bari in the east, continued to recognise the Emperor at
Constantinople, and so also did Venice, which, at the head of the
Adriatic, never had anything seriously to fear from the Saracen
expansion.

The tie which continued to unite these ports to the Byzantine Empire
was, it is true, not very strong, and it grew steadily weaker. The
establishment of the Normans in Italy and Sicily (1029–91) definitely
broke it as regards this region. Venice, over which the Carolingians
had been unable to establish their control in the ninth century, had
been all the more willing to continue under the authority of the Basileus, because he prudently refrained from exerting it, and allowed the
town to be gradually transformed into an independent republic. For
the rest, if the political relations of the Empire with its distant Italian
annexations were not very active, it made amends by carrying on a
very lively trade with them. In this respect, they moved in its orbit
and, so to speak, turned their backs on the West and looked towards
the East. The business of provisioning Constantinople, whose population numbered about a million inhabitants, kept up their exports, and
in return the factories and bazaars of the capital furnished them with
silks and spices which they could not do without.

For urban life, with all the luxury demands which it made, had not
disappeared in the Byzantine Empire as it had done in that of the
Carolingians. To pass from the latter to the former, was to pass into
another world. Here, economic evolution had not been rudely inter-

rupted by the advance of Islam, and an important maritime commerce continued to supply towns peopled with artisans and professional merchants. No more striking contrast could be imagined than that between Western Europe, where land was everything and commerce nothing, and Venice, a landless city, living only by trade.

Constantinople and the Christian ports of the East soon ceased to be the sole objective of the navigation of the Byzantine towns of Italy and Venice. The spirit of enterprise and the search for gain were too powerful and too necessary to allow religious scruples to prevent them for very long from renewing their former business relations with Africa and Syria, although these were now in the power of the infidels. From the end of the ninth century connections were formed which grew steadily more active. The religion of their customers mattered little to the Italians, provided that they paid. The love of gain, which the Church condemned and stigmatised by the name of avarice, was manifest here in its most brutal form. The Venetians exported to the harems of Egypt and Syria young Slavs, whom they carried off or bought on the Dalmatian coast, and this traffic in "slaves" unquestionably contributed quite as largely to their growing prosperity as did the slave trade of the eighteenth century to that of so many French and English shippers. To this was added the transport of timber and iron, with which the countries of Islam were unprovided, although there was no room for doubt that the timber would be used to build vessels and the iron to forge weapons which would be employed against Christians, perhaps even against the mariners of Venice. The merchant, here as always, could see nothing beyond his immediate profit, and bringing off a good business deal. It was in vain that the Pope threatened to excommunicate the sellers of Christian slaves, or that the Emperor prohibited the supply to infidels of articles capable of being employed in warfare. Venice, whither merchants in the ninth century had brought back from Alexandria the relics of St. Mark, went her own way, secure in their protection, and considered the steady progress of her wealth as the just reward of the veneration in which she held them.

That progress was, indeed, uninterrupted. By any and every means, the city of the lagoons devoted itself with astonishing energy and activity to advancing that maritime trade, which was the very condition of its existence. The entire population practised and depended on it, as on the Continent men depended on the land. So serfdom, the inevitable consequence of the rural civilisation of the peasants of this time, was unknown in this city of sailors, artisans and merchants. The hazards of fortune alone established between them social differences independent of legal status. From very early times, commercial profits had created a class of rich traders, whose operations already present an incontestably capitalistic character. The *commenda* appeared in the tenth century, obviously borrowed from the practices of Byzantine customary law.

The use of writing, indispensable to every business movement of any importance, bears indisputable witness to economic progress. A "clerk" formed part of the equipment of every merchant ship sailing abroad and from this we can infer that shipowners themselves had quickly learned to keep accounts and to despatch letters to their correspondents. No reproach, it should be mentioned, was here attached to the business of large-scale commerce. The most important families engaged in it. The doges themselves set the example and were doing so as early as the middle of the ninth century, which seems almost incredible in contemporaries of Lewis the Pious. In 1007, Peter II Orseolo set apart for charitable institutions the profits from a sum of 1,250 livres which he had invested in business. At the end of the eleventh century, the city was full of wealthy patricians, owners of a quantity of shares in ships (*sortes*), whose shops and landing-places (*stationes*) stood close together along the rivo-alto and the isles of the lagoon.

Venice was then already a great maritime power. She had succeeded before 1100 in ridding the Adriatic of the Dalmatian pirates who infested it and in establishing her hegemony firmly on the whole of the east coast of that sea, which she considered as her domain and which remained hers for centuries. In order to preserve control over its entrance to the Mediterranean, she had helped the Byzantine fleet in 1002 to expel the Saracens from Bari. Seventy years later, when the Norman State, set up by Robert Guiscard in southern Italy, threatened her with a maritime competition as dangerous to herself as to the Greek Empire, she allied herself once more with the latter to fight and overcome the peril. After the death of Robert (1076) the dream of Mediterranean expansion conceived by this prince of genius was doomed. The war turned out to the advantage of Venice and with the same stroke she rid herself of the rivalry of Naples, Gaeta, Salerno, and, above all, Amalfi. These cities, which had been absorbed by the Norman State, were dragged down with it, and henceforth abandoned the markets of Constantinople and the East to the Venetians.

For that matter they had already enjoyed an indisputable superiority there for a long time. In 992 the doge, Pietro II Orseolo, had obtained a chrysobull from the Emperors Basil and Constantine freeing the Venetian boats from the customs which they had hitherto had to pay at Abydos. Relations were so active between the port of the lagoons and that of the Bosphorus that a Venetian colony was established in the latter, with judicial privileges ratified by the emperors. In the following years, other establishments were founded at Laodicea, Antioch, Mamistra, Adana, Tarsus, Satalia, Ephesus, Chios, Phocaea, Selembria, Heraclea Rodosto, Andrinople, Salonica, Demetrias, Athens, Thebes, Coron, Modon, and Corfu. At all points of the Empire Venice possessed bases of supplies and penetration, which secured her commercial domination. From the end of the eleventh century she may be said to have held a practical monopoly of transport in all the provinces of Europe and Asia still possessed by the rulers of Constantinople.

Nor did the emperors try to oppose a situation with which it was to their own disadvantage to quarrel. The privilege accorded to the doge in May 1082 by Alexis Comnenus may be regarded as the final consecration of Venetian superiority in the Byzantine empire. Henceforth the Venetians were exempt, throughout the Empire, from very kind of commercial tax, and were thus favoured above the Emperor's own subjects. The stipulation that they should continue to pay duties on foreign merchandise is final proof that thenceforth the whole of the maritime trade of the eastern end of the Mediterranean was in their hands. For, though we are rather badly informed in regard to the progress of their trade with the Moslem lands from the tenth century, everything indicates that it developed in the same way, if not entirely with the same vigour.

The two inland seas, the North Sea and the Baltic, which bathe the coasts of Northern Europe, as the Mediterranean, to which they form a pendant, bathes its southern coasts, presented, from the middle of the ninth century to the end of the eleventh, a spectacle which, profoundly as it differs from that which we have been describing, resembles it nevertheless in one essential character. For here, too, on the coast and, so to speak, on the very edge of Europe, we find a maritime and commercial activity which is in striking contrast with the agricultural economy of the Continent.

We have already seen that the activity of the ports of Quentovic and Duurstede did not survive the Viking invasion of the ninth century. Lacking a fleet, the Carolingian Empire was unable to defend itself against the Northern barbarians as the Byzantine Empire had defended itself against the Moslems. Its weakness had been only too well exploited by the energetic Scandinavians who, for more than half a century, subjected it to annual raids, not only by way of the estuaries of the northern rivers but also by those of the Atlantic. But the Northmen must not be represented as mere pillagers. Masters of the sea, they could and did combine their aggressions. Their object was not and could not be conquest; though they won a few settlements on the Continent and in the British Isles, that was the most they could do. But the incursions which they pushed so deeply into the mainland were essentially great razzias. Their organisation was obviously carefully planned; they all set off from a fortified camp as centre, where booty collected from neighbouring regions was piled up while awaiting transport to Denmark or Norway. The Vikings, in fact, were pirates, and piracy is the first stage of commerce. So true is this that from the end of the ninth century, when their raids ceased, they simply became merchants.

To understand Scandinavian expansion, however, it must also be remembered that it was not directed exclusively towards the West. While the Danes and the Norwegians threw themselves on the Carolingian Empire, England, Scotland and Ireland, their neighbours, the Swedes, turned to Russia. From our point of view it is immaterial whether they had been asked for assistance by the Slav princes in the valley of the Dnieper in their struggle with the Patzinaks, or whether, in search of gain, they made a spontaneous thrust towards the Byzantine shores of the Black Sea, by the great natural route which from remotest times had been followed by Greek merchants from the Chersonese and the Sea of Azov seeking Baltic amber. It is enough to state that from the middle of the ninth century they established entrenched camps along the Dnieper and its tributaries, similar to those that their Danish and Norwegian brothers were establishing at the same date in the basins of the Scheldt, the Meuse and the Seine. Constructed at so great a distance from their mother country, these *enceintes* or, to use the Slavonic word, *gorods*, became permanent fortresses, from which the invaders dominated and exploited the not very warlike people who surrounded them. It was there that they amassed the tribute imposed on the vanquished and the slaves taken from among them, as well as the honey and furs which they obtained from the virgin forests. But before long, the position which they occupied inevitably led them to engage in trade.

Southern Russia, where they had installed themselves, lay, in fact, between two areas of superior civilisation. To the east, beyond the Caspian Sea, stretched the caliphate of Baghdad, to the south, the Black Sea bathed the shores of the Byzantine Empire and led to Constantinople. The Scandinavians in the basin of the Dnieper at once felt this double attraction. The Arab, Jewish and Byzantine merchants, who were already frequenting this region before their arrival, showed them a road which they were more than ready to follow. The country conquered by them put at their disposal products particularly suited for trade with rich empires leading a life of refinement: honey, furs and above all slaves, the demand for whom from Moslem harems, as well as from the great estates, promised the same high profits which tempted the Venetians.

Constantine Porphyrogenitus, in the tenth century, has left us a picture of the Scandinavians, or rather the Russians (to give them the name by which the Slavs knew them), assembling their boats each year at Kiev, after the melting of the ice. The flotilla slowly descended the Dnieper, whose innumerable rapids presented obstacles which had to be got round by towing the barks along the bank. Having reached the sea, it sailed along the coast to Constantinople, the goal of the long and perilous voyage. There the Russians possessed a special quarter, and their trade with the great city was regulated by treaties, of which the oldest dated back to the ninth century. The influence which she soon came to exercise over them is well known. It was from her that they received Christianity (957–1015); it was from her that they borrowed their art, their writing, the use of money and a good part of their organisation. There can be no more striking witness to the importance of the trade they kept up with the Bosphorus. At the same time they were making their way, through the valley of the Volga, to the Caspian Sea and trafficking with the Jewish and Arab merchants who frequented its ports.

But their activity was not confined to this. They exported merchandise of all sorts to the north, spices, wines, silks, goldsmiths' work, etc., which they obtained in exchange for their honey, furs and slaves. The astonishing number of Arab and Byzantine coins discovered in Russia mark, as with the silver point of a compass, the trade routes which crossed it, converging either from the course of the Volga, or from that of the Dnieper to the Dvina and the lakes which are attached to the Gulf of Bothnia. There, the commerce from the Caspian and Black Seas joined the Baltic and continued through it. Across the im-

mense stretches of continental Russia Scandinavian navigation was
thus linked with the oriental world. The island of Gothland, in which
there have been dug up even more hoards of Islamic and Greek coins
than have been found in Russia, appears to have been the great entre-
pôt of this traffic and its point of contact with Northern Europe. It is
tempting to believe that the booty gathered by the Northmen in England and France was there exchanged for the precious goods brought
from Russia.

In any case, it is impossible to doubt the part played by Scandinavia
as a middleman, when we consider the astonishing progress of its
navigation in the tenth and eleventh centuries, that is to say, during
the period which succeeded the invasion of the Danes and Norwegians
in the West. It is quite clear that they ceased to be pirates and became
merchants after the example of their Swedish brothers; barbarian
merchants, perhaps, who were always ready to become pirates again
on the slightest occasion, but merchants all the same, and what is more,
merchants navigating the high seas. Their deckless ships now carried
the articles of trade which came to Gothland far and wide. Trading
posts were founded on the Swedish coast and on the shores, still
Slavonic at this period, of the extensive littoral which lay between the
Elbe and the Vistula; in the south of Denmark, excavations made quite
recently at Haithabu (north of Kiel) have revealed the existence of an
emporium, whose ruins bear witness to its importance during the
course of the eleventh century. This commercial activity naturally
extended to the harbours of the North Sea, well known to the northern
navigators who had devastated its hinterland for so long. Hamburg on
the Elbe and Tiel on the Waal became, in the tenth century, ports
actively frequented by the Northmen's ships. England received a still
greater number of them and the trade carried on by the Danes conferred on them a superiority which the Anglo-Saxons could not resist
and which reached its height when Canute the Great (1017–35) united
England, Denmark and Norway in an ephemeral empire. The trade
which was thus carried on from the mouths of the Thames and the
Rhine to that of the Dvina and the Gulf of Bothnia is attested by the
discovery of English, Flemish and German coins in the basins of the
Baltic and North Sea. The Scandinavian sagas, in spite of the late date
at which they were written down, still preserve the memory of the
risks run by the intrepid seamen, who ventured to far-away Iceland
and Greenland. Daring young men went to join their fellow-country-
men in Southern Russia; Anglo-Saxons and Scandinavians are found

at Constantinople in the bodyguard of the emperors. In short, the Nordic people gave proof at this time of an energy and a spirit of enterprise which reminds us of the Greeks in the Homeric era. Their art was characterised by a barbarous originality, which nevertheless betrays the influence of that East with which their commerce brought them into communication. But the energy which they displayed could have no future. Too few numerically to retain the mastery over the immense expanses where their ships had sailed, they had to yield place to more powerful rivals, when the extension of commerce to the Continent brought about a revival of navigation to compete with their own.

Continental Europe was bound soon to feel the force of the two great commercial movements which appeared on its borders, the one in the Western Mediterranean and the Adriatic, the other in the Baltic and the North Sea. Responding as it does to the craving for adventure and the love of gain which are inherent in human nature, commerce is essentially contagious. Moreover, it is by nature so all-pervasive that it necessarily imposes itself on the very people whom it exploits. Indeed it depends on them by reason of the relationship of exchange which it sets up and the needs which it creates, while it is impossible to conceive of commerce without agriculture, since it is sterile itself and needs agriculture to supply food for those whom it employs and enriches.

This ineluctable necessity was imposed on Venice from its very foundation on the sandy islets of a lagoon, on which nothing would grow. In order to procure a livelihood its first inhabitants had been forced to exchange salt and fish with their continental neighbours for the corn, wine and meat which they could not have obtained otherwise. But this primitive exchange inevitably developed, as commerce made the town richer and more populous, and at the same time increased its demands and sharpened its enterprise. At the end of the ninth century, it was already commandeering the territory of Verona and above all the valley of the Po, which provided an easy avenue for penetration into Italy. A century later its relations had extended to a number of points on the coast and mainland: Pavia, Treviso, Vicenza, Ravenna, Cesena, Ancona, and many others.

It is clear that the Venetians, taking the practice of trade with them, acclimatised it, so to speak, wherever they went. Their merchants gradually found imitators. It is impossible, in the absence of evidence, to trace the growth of the seeds sown by commerce in the midst of the agricultural population. That growth was no doubt opposed by the Church, which was hostile to commerce, and nowhere were bishoprics more numerous and more powerful than south of the Alps. A curious episode in the life of St. Gerald of Aurillac (d. 909) bears striking witness to the incompatibility of the moral standards of the Church with the spirit of gain, that is to say, the business spirit. As this pious lord was returning from a pilgrimage to Rome, he met in Pavia some Venetian merchants, who asked him to buy oriental stuffs and spices. Now, he had himself purchased in Rome a magnificent pallium which he took the opportunity of showing to them, mentioning how much he had paid for it. But when they congratulated him on his good bargain, since according to them the pallium would have cost considerably more in Constantinople, Gerald, reproaching himself for having defrauded the vendor, hastened to forward him the difference, considering that he could not take advantage of it without falling into the sin of avarice.

This anecdote admirably illustrates the moral conflict which the revival of commerce was to provoke everywhere, and which indeed never ceased during the whole of the Middle Ages. From the beginning to the end the Church continued to regard commercial profits as a danger to salvation. Its ascetic ideal, which was perfectly suited to an agricultural civilisation, made it always suspicious of social changes, which it could not prevent and to which necessity even compelled it to submit, but to which it was never openly reconciled. Its prohibition of interest was to weigh heavily on the economic life of later centuries. It prevented the merchants from growing rich with a free conscience and from reconciling the practice of business with the prescripts of religion. For proof of this we need only read the many wills of bankers and speculators, directing that the poor whom they had defrauded should be repaid and bequeathing to the clergy a part of the property which at the bottom of their hearts they felt to be ill-gotten. If they could not refrain from sin, at least their faith remained unshaken and they counted on it to obtain absolution for them on the day of judgment.

It must, however, be recognised that this ardent faith contributed largely all the same to economic expansion in the West. It played a great part when the Pisans and Genoese took the offensive against Islam at the beginning of the eleventh century. Unlike the Venetians, in whom the spirit of gain ruled supreme, these cities were impelled by hatred of the infidel and by enterprise alike to wrest the mastery of the Tyrrhenian Sea from the Saracens. An unending struggle was waged between the two religions face to face there. In the beginning it had constantly turned to the advantage of the Mohammedans; in 935, and again in 1004, they had pillaged Pisa, doubtless with the intention of suppressing the first feeble efforts at maritime expansion there. But the Pisans were determined to expand, and the following year they defeated a Saracen fleet in the Straits of Messina. The enemy had their revenge by invading and destroying their bold competitors' port, but the Pisans, exhorted by the popes and lured by their adversary's wealth, resolved to continue a war which was at once religious and commercial. With the Genoese, they attacked Sardinia and succeeded in establishing themselves there in 1015. In 1034, emboldened by success, they ventured as far as the coast of Africa and for a time made themselves masters of Bona. A little later, their merchants began to frequent Sicily and it was to protect them that in 1052 a Pisan fleet forced the entrance of the port of Palermo and destroyed its arsenal.

From that time fortune turned in favour of the Christians. An expedition, to which the presence of the Bishop of Modena added all the prestige of the Church, was directed against Mehdia in 1087. The sailors saw in the sky the archangel Michael and St. Peter leading them into battle. They took the town, massacred "the priests of Mohammed," pillaged the mosque and imposed an advantageous commercial treaty on the vanquished. The Cathedral of Pisa, built after this triumph, symbolises to perfection both the faith of the Pisans and the wealth which their victories were beginning to bring them. Pillars, precious marbles, gold and silver ornaments, curtains of purple and gold carried away from Palermo and Mehdia adorned it. It is as though they wished to symbolise by its splendour the revenge of the Christians upon the Saracens, whose wealth was a thing of scandal and of envy.

Islam fell back before the Christian counter-attack and lost its hold over the Tyrrhenian Sea, which had been a Moslem lake. The launching of the first crusade in 1096 was to mark its definite overthrow. In 1097, the Genoese sent a fleet with reinforcements and supplies to the Crusaders besieging Antioch, and the following year obtained from Bohemond of Tarento a *fondaco* with commercial privileges, which was the first of a long series to be obtained in due course by the maritime towns on the coast of the Holy Land. After the capture of Jerusalem the relations of Genoa with the Eastern Mediterranean increased rapidly. In 1104, she possessed a colony at St. John of Acre to which King Baldwin ceded a third of the town, a street by the sea and the rent of six hundred gold bezants out of the customs. Venice set up counting-houses at Tyre, Sidon, St. John of Acre and Kaffa. Pisa devoted herself with growing energy to provisioning the states founded in Syria by the crusaders. Moreover, the commercial revival which had begun on the coast of Italy soon reached that of Provence. In 1136, Marseilles already occupied an important place, her citizens having founded a settlement at St. John of Acre. From the other side of the Gulf of Lyons, Barcelona was already ushering in her future prosperity, and, just as in former times the Moslems had engaged in the Christian slave trade, so Moorish slaves captured in Spain furnished her with one article of her traffic.

Thus the whole Mediterranean was opened, or rather re-opened, to western navigation. As in the time of Rome, communications were established from one end to the other of this essentially European sea. The exploitation of its waters by Islam was at an end. The Christians had recaptured the islands whose possession guaranteed its mastery, Sardinia in 1022, Corsica in 1091, Sicily in 1058–90. It matters little that the Turks soon destroyed the ephemeral principalities founded by the Crusaders, that the country of Edessa was reconquered by the Crescent in 1144 and Damascus in 1154, that Saladin took Aleppo in 1183, then, in 1187, Acre, Nazareth, Caesarea, Sidon, Beyrout, Ascalon, and finally Jerusalem, and that in spite of all their efforts the Christians never recovered until our own day the domination of Syria which they had won in the first crusade. However important it may be in general history, and however heavily it has weighed since on the destinies of the world, the Turkish thrust did not shake the position that the Italian towns had gained in the Levant. The new offensive of Islam extended only to the mainland. The Turks had no fleet and did not attempt to create one. Far from harming them, Italian trade on the coasts of Asia Minor was to their advantage, for by it the spices brought by the caravans of China and India to Syria continued to be carried to the West by Italian ships. Nothing could have been more profitable than the persistence of a navigation which served to maintain the economic activity of the Turkish and Mongolian lands.

Undoubtedly the Italian fleets continued to lend an increasingly active co-operation to the crusades down to the day when the defeat of St. Louis at Tunis (1270) brought them to an end and marked a definite check both in the political and in the religious sphere. It would not be untrue to say that without the support of Venice, Pisa and Genoa, it would have been impossible to persist so long in these fruitless enterprises. Only the first crusade was carried out by the land route, the transport by sea of masses of men going to Jerusalem being at that time still unfeasible. The Italian ships contributed nothing beyond supplies for the armies. But almost immediately the demands of the Crusaders upon their navigation galvanised it into incredible life and vigour. The profits realised by army contractors have been immense in all ages, and it cannot be doubted that the Venetians, Pisans, Genoese and Provençals, finding themselves suddenly rich, hastened to put new ships on their stocks. The establishment of the crusading states in Syria ensured the regular use of these means of transport, without which the Franks would have been unable to maintain themselves in the East. Thus they were prodigal of privileges to the towns whose services were indispensable to them, and from the end of the eleventh century helped them to set up their *fondaci* and *échelles* and all along the coasts of Palestine and Asia Minor, and of the Aegean islands. Before long, indeed, they began to make use of them for military operations. During the second crusade the Italian boats carried the troops of Louis VII and Conrad III along the coast of Anatolia, to the Holy Land. The third crusade furnishes a characteristic proof of the growth of Italian and Provençal tonnage, which was considerable enough to transport the troops of Richard Coeur de Lion and Philip Augustus. From then onwards, all subsequent expeditions were carried out exclusively by the sea route. It is well known how the Venetians exploited the situation by diverting to Constantinople the fleet equipped for the fourth crusade, whose commanders, unable to pay the agreed price for the passage, were compelled to abandon the direction of the whole enterprise to them and how they finally used the fleet for the siege and capture of Constantinople. The ephemeral Latin empire then set up on the shores of the Bosphorus was largely a creation of Venetian policy, and when it disappeared (1261), Venice had to resign herself to allowing the Genoese, who, in order to outwit her, had worked for the restoration of Michael Palaeologus, to dispute with her the economic supremacy of the Levant.

Thus the one lasting and essential result of the crusades was to give the Italian towns, and in a less degree, those of Provence and Catalonia, the mastery of the Mediterranean. Though they did not succeed in wresting the holy places from Islam, and though no more than a few places on the coast of Asia Minor and in the islands remained of their early conquests, at least they enabled Western Europe not only to monopolise the whole trade from the Bosphorus and Syria to the Straits of Gibraltar, but to develop there an economic and strictly capitalistic activity which was gradually to communicate itself to all the lands north of the Alps.

Islam did not react against this triumphant advance until the fifteenth century and the helpless Byzantine Empire was forced to submit to it. From the beginning of the twelfth century its supremacy in the eastern Mediterranean was at an end. It rapidly fell under the influence of the maritime towns, which now monopolised its import and export trade. Sometimes in an endeavour to shake off their yoke, the emperor tried to play off the Pisans and Genoese against the Venetians, or allowed the populace to massacre the detestable foreigners indiscriminately, as, for example, in 1182. But he could not do without them, and willy-nilly had to abandon Byzantine commerce to them, even more completely than Spain in the seventeenth century was to abandon hers to the Dutch, the English and the French.

The revival of maritime commerce was accompanied by its rapid penetration inland. Not only was agriculture stimulated by the demand for its produce and transformed by the exchange economy of which it now became a part, but a new export industry was born. In both directions the lead was taken by the Lombard plain, admirably situated as it was between the powerful commercial centres of Venice, Pisa and Genoa. Country and towns shared equally in production, the former with its grain and wines, the latter with their linen and woollen stuffs. As early as the twelfth century Lucca was manufacturing silk fabrics, the raw material for which came to her by sea. In Tuscany, Sienna and Florence communicated with Pisa by the valley of the Arno and shared in her prosperity. Behind Genoa the movement spread to the coast of the Gulf of Lyons and reached the basin of the Rhône. The ports of Marseilles, Montpellier and Narbonne traded all over Provence as did Barcelona over Catalonia. So vigorous was the trade of the maritime countries that in the eleventh century it began to spread northwards through the Alpine passes, which the Saracens of Garde-Frainet had blocked so dangerously in the tenth century. From Venice it reached Germany by the Brenner, the Saône and Rhine valleys by the Septimer and St. Bernard, and the Rhône valley by Mont Cenis. The St. Gothard was long impassable, but eventually a suspension bridge was slung from rock to rock across the gorge and it too became a route of transit. In the second half of the eleventh century we hear of Italians in France. It is more than probable that they were already frequenting the fairs of Champagne at this period and met there the flow of commerce from the coast of Flanders.

Indeed, the economic revival which was in process of achievement in the Mediterranean, was matched on the shores of the North Sea by a revival which, if it differed from it in extent and character, proceeded from the same causes and produced the same result. As we have seen above, the Northmen had established, in the estuary formed by the arms of the Rhine, the Meuse and the Scheldt, a mart which soon attracted trade from far and wide along these rivers. In the eleventh century Tiel already appears as a commercial centre frequented by many merchants and in communication by way of the Rhine valley with Cologne and Mainz, which now show signs of considerable activity. No other proof is needed than the six hundred *mercatores opulentissimi* mentioned in 1074 in the first of those towns by Lampert of Hersfeld, although we may doubt the figure quoted and it is impossible to know what was the chronicler's standard of wealth. At the same period, a trade developed in the Meuse valley, extending as far as Verdun by way of Maastricht, Liége, Huy and Dinant. The Scheldt enabled Cambrai, Valenciennes, Tournai, Ghent and Antwerp to communicate with the sea and the large rivers which emptied their waters among the Zealand Islands. The harbour of Bruges at the end of the Gulf of Zwyn, now silted up, was so convenient that from the end of the eleventh century ships began to put in there in preference to other ports, and the future glory of the city was thus ensured.

It is certain that at the end of the tenth century Scandinavian trade kept Flanders in close relations with the North Sea and Baltic countries. Coins struck by Counts Arnold II and Baldwin IV (965–1035) have been discovered in Denmark, Prussia and even Russia. Her trade was naturally still more active with England. The tariff of London tolls, between 991 and 1002, mentions the Flemings as being among the foreigners who traded in the city. The Channel was less frequented than the North Sea, but there was a regular trade between the Norman and English coasts, by way of Rouen and the estuary of the Seine, and thence along the river to Paris and to the confines of Champagne and Burgundy. The Loire and the Garonne, by reason of their distance, did not experience until later the effects of the commercial revival in the northern seas.

Flanders soon came to occupy a privileged position, which it was to keep until the end of the Middle Ages. Here we meet with a new factor, industry, which was nowhere else in operation at so early a date and with such remarkable results. Already in the Celtic era, the

Morini and Menapii in the valleys of the Lys and the Scheldt had been manufacturing the wool from the large flocks of sheep which they kept in that country of lush meadows. Their primitive cloth manufacture was perfected during the long Roman occupation, when their conquerors introduced them to the technical methods of the Mediterranean. So rapid was its progress that in the second century Flanders was exporting cloth as far as Italy. The Franks, who invaded the region in the fifth century, continued the tradition of their predecessors. Until the coming of the Northmen in the ninth century, Frisian boatmen regularly carried cloths woven in Flanders along the rivers of the Low Countries; under the name of *pallia fresonica,* their beautiful colours made them so popular that Charlemagne could find nothing better to send as a gift to the Caliph Haroun-al-Raschid. The destruction of commerce by the Scandinavian invasions naturally interrupted this export. But when, in the course of the tenth century, the pillagers became traders whose boats reappeared on the Meuse and the Scheldt in quest of merchandise, the cloth manufacture found a market once again. The fineness of the cloths soon caused a demand for them along all the coasts frequented by the Northern seamen and, to meet that demand, their manufacture increased to proportions hitherto unattained. It was already so considerable that at the end of the tenth century native wool was insufficient for its needs, and wool had to be imported from England. The superior quality of English wool naturally improved that of the cloth, the sale of which increased as its fame grew. In the course of the twelfth century the whole of Flanders became a country of weavers and fullers. Cloth-making, which up till then had been carried on in the country, was concentrated in the merchant towns, which were founded on all sides and supplied an ever-growing commerce. It was cloth which created the nascent wealth of Ghent, Bruges, Ypres, Lille, Douai and Arras. Already an essential article of maritime trade, it now brought into existence an extremely important trade by the land routes. From the beginning of the twelfth century Flemish cloth was being taken by sea to the fair of Novgorod, while the Italians were coming to Flanders to buy it in exchange for the spices, silks, and goldsmiths' work which they imported from south of the Alps. But the Flemings themselves frequented the famous fairs of Champagne, where, midway between the North Sea and the Alps, they met buyers from Lombardy and Tuscany. These carried Flemish cloth in enormous quantities to the port of Genoa, whence under the name of *panni francesi* they were taken by sea as far as the ports of the Levant.

Of course, Flanders was not the only place where cloth was manufactured. Weaving is by nature a domestic occupation, which is known to have existed from prehistoric times and is met with wherever there is wool, i.e., in all countries. It was only necessary to stimulate its production and perfect its technique for it to become a real industry. This was not neglected. In the thirteenth century, Genoese notarial instruments mention the names of a number of towns which were sending cloth to that port: Amiens, Beauvais, Cambrai, Liége, Montreuil, Provins, Tournai, Châlons, etc. Nevertheless, Flanders and soon afterwards its neighbour, Brabant, occupied an unrivalled place among their competitors. The proximity of England enabled them to obtain excellent wool on the best terms and in much larger quantities than the latter. In the thirteenth century the overwhelming superiority of the Flemish industry is reflected in the admiration which it inspired in foreigners. Throughout the history of medieval Europe no other region presented this character of an industrial country which distinguished the basin of the Scheldt. It offers, in this respect, a contrast to the rest of Europe which brings to mind England in the eighteenth and nineteenth centuries. Nowhere else was it possible to equal the finish, the flexibility, the softness and the colours of these fabrics. Flemish and Brabantine cloth was, indeed, a cloth *de luxe*, and it was this which made its success and assured its world-wide expansion. In an age when the means of transport were not sufficiently developed to be adaptable to the circulation of cheap and heavy goods, the first place in international commerce belonged to merchandise of great value and medium weight. In short, the success of Flemish cloths is to be explained, like that of spices, by their high price and the ease with which they could be exported.

In striking contrast to the Italian towns, Flanders and Brabant, as they became more industrialised, became also less interested in the maritime commerce for which their geographical situation seemed to have destined them. They abandoned it to the foreigners whom their industry attracted in ever-increasing numbers to the port of Bruges, Scandinavians in the eleventh century, and, later, Hansards. In this respect it is tempting to compare them with modern Belgium, in so far as it is permissible to compare the Middle Ages with our own times, taking into account their relative economic development. In the same territory once occupied by them, does not the Belgium of to-day present the same paradoxical spectacle of extraordinary industrial productivity combined with a relatively insignificant marine?

As long as Mediterranean commerce continued to draw Western Europe into its orbit, urban life went on in Gaul as well as in Italy, Spain and Africa. But when the Islamic invasion had bottled up the ports of the Tyrrhenian Sea after bringing the coasts of Africa and Spain under its control, municipal activity rapidly died out. Save in southern Italy and in Venice, where it was maintained thanks to Byzantine trade, it disappeared everywhere. The towns continued in existence, but they lost their population of artisans and merchants and with it all that had survived of the municipal organisations of the Roman Empire.

The "cities", in each of which there resided a bishop, now became no more than centres of the ecclesiastical administration of their dioceses. Thus they preserved considerable importance, no doubt, from the religious point of view, but from the economic point of view none. At most, a small local market, supplied by the peasants round about, provided for the daily needs of the numerous clergy of the cathedral and of the churches or monasteries grouped around it and those of the serfs employed in their service. At the big annual festivals the diocesan population and pilgrims flocking into the city kept up a certain activity, but in none of this are any signs of a revival visible. In reality these episcopal cities were merely living on the country. The bishops and abbots within their walls lived on the rents and dues which they obtained from their estates, and their existence thus rested essentially on agriculture. The cities were the centres not only of religious but also of manorial administration.

In time of war their old walls furnished a refuge to the surrounding population. But during the period of insecurity which set in with the dissolution of the Carolingian Empire, the need for protection became the first necessity of a people threatened in the South by the Saracen incursions and in the North and West by those of the Normans, to which were added, at the beginning of the tenth century, the terrible cavalry raids of the Hungarians. These invasions led on all sides to the construction of new places of refuge. In this period Western Europe became covered with fortified castles, erected by the feudal princes to serve as a shelter for their men. These castles, or, to use the term by which they were customarily designated, these *bourgs* or *burgs*, were usually composed of a rampart of earth or stones, surrounded by a moat and pierced with gates. The *vilains* from round about were requisitioned to construct and maintain them. A garrison of knights resided inside; a donjon served as the lord's dwelling-place; a church of canons looked after the needs of religion; and barns and granaries were set up to receive the grain, smoked meats and dues of all kinds levied on the manorial peasants, which served to feed the garrison and the people who, in times of peril, came huddling into the fortress with their cattle. Thus the lay burg, like the ecclesiastical city, lived on the land. Neither had any real economic life of its own. They were perfectly compatible with an agricultural civilisation for, far from opposing it, they may be said to have served in its defence.

But the revival of commerce soon completely altered their character. The first symptoms of its action are observable in the course of the second half of the tenth century. The wandering life of the merchants, the risks of every sort to which they were exposed, in an age when pillage formed one of the means of existence of the smaller nobility, caused them from the very beginning to seek the protection of the walled towns and burgs, which stood at intervals along the rivers or natural routes by which they travelled. During the summer these served as halting-places, during the bad season as wintering-places. The most favourably situated, whether at the foot of an estuary or in a creek, at the confluence of two rivers, or at a spot where the river ceased to be navigable and cargoes had to be unloaded before they could proceed farther, thus became places of passage and of sojourn for merchants and merchandise.

Soon the space that cities and burgs had to offer these newcomers, who became more and more numerous and embarrassing in proportion as trade increased, was no longer sufficient. They were driven to settle outside the walls and to build beside the old burg a new burg, or, to use the term which exactly describes it, a *faubourg* (*foris-burgus*), i.e., an outside burg. Thus, close to ecclesiastical towns or feudal fortresses there sprang up mercantile agglomerations, whose denizens devoted themselves to a kind of life which was in complete contrast to that led by the people of the inside town. The word *portus*, often applied in documents of the tenth and eleventh centuries to these settlements, exactly describes their nature. It did not, in fact, signify a port in the modern sense, but a place through which merchandise was carried, and thus a particularly active place of transit. It was from it that in England and in Flanders the inhabitants of the *port* themselves received the name of *poorters* or *portmen*, which was long synonymous with *bour-*

*geois* or *burgess* and indeed described them rather better than the latter, for the primitive bourgeoisie was exclusively composed of men living by trade. The reason why they came, before the end of the eleventh century, to be known by the word *bourgeois*, which was really much better suited to the inhabitants of the old burgs, at the foot of which they settled, is to be found in the fact that very early the mercantile group too surrounded itself by a wall or palisade for the sake of security, and thus became a burg in its turn. This extension of meaning is all the more easily comprehensible, since the new burg very soon overshadowed the old. In the most active centres of commercial life, such as Bruges, it was already at the beginning of the twelfth century surrounding the fortress, which had been its nucleus, on all sides. The accessory had become the essential, the new-comers had triumphed over the old inhabitants. In this sense it is strictly true to say that the medieval town, and consequently the modern town, had its birth in the faubourg of the city, or of the burg which determined its site.

The collection of merchants in favourable spots soon caused artisans also to collect there. Industrial concentration is as old as commercial concentration. We can observe it with particular plainness in Flanders. Cloth-making, which had at first been carried on in the country, emigrated of itself to places which offered a sale for its products. There weavers found wool imported by the merchants, fullers' and dyers' soap and dye-stuffs. A real industrial revolution, of which we do not, unfortunately, know the details, accompanied this transformation of a rural industry into an urban one. Weaving, which had up to then been an occupation carried on by women, passed into the hands of men, and at the same time the old small *pallia* were replaced by pieces of cloth of great length, which were better suited for export and have remained the stock size used in the cloth manufacture up to the present day. There is good reason also for supposing that a change took place at this time in the looms used by the weavers, if only to allow a warp measuring for twenty to sixty ells to be fitted to the beam.

In the metallurgical industry of the Meuse valley an evolution analogous to that which took place in the Flemish cloth industry may also be observed. Copper-working, which perhaps dates back to the bronze-working which was actively developed there at the time of the Roman occupation, received a powerful impetus when the revival of navigation on the river gave it the chance to produce for export. At the same time, it became concentrated at Namur, Huy, and above all at Dinant, towns whose *marchands batteurs* went to the mines of Saxony for their copper in the eleventh century. Similarly, the excellent stone in which the region of Tournai abounded was worked in that town, and the manufacture of baptismal fonts became so active that we meet with them as far away as Southampton and Winchester. In Italy, the story is the same. Silk-weaving, introduced by sea from the East, became concentrated at Lucca, while Milan and the Lombard towns, soon imitated by Tuscany, devoted themselves to the manufacture of fustians.

The essential difference between the merchants and artisans of the nascent towns and the agricultural society in the midst of which they appeared, was that their kind of life was no longer determined by their relations with the land. In this respect they formed, in every sense of the word, a class of *déracinés*. Commerce and industry, which up till then had been merely the adventitious or intermittent occupations of manorial agents, whose existence was assured by the great landowners who employed them, now became independent professions. Those who practised them were incontestably "new men". Attempts have often been made to derive them from the servile personnel attached to the domestic workshops of the manor, or the serfs who were charged with feeding the household in times of scarcity and in time of plenty disposed of their surplus production outside. But such an evolution is neither supported by the sources nor probable. There is no doubt that territorial lords here and there preserved economic prerogatives in the nascent towns for a fairly long time, such prerogatives, for instance, as the obligation of the burgesses to use the lord's oven and mill, the monopoly of sale enjoyed by his wine for several days after the vintage, or even certain dues levied from the craft gilds. But the local survival of these rights is no proof of the manorial origin of urban economy. On the contrary, what we note everywhere is that from the moment that it appears, it appears in a condition of freedom.

But the question immediately occurs, how are we to explain the formation of a class of free merchants and artisans in the midst of an exclusively rural society, where serfdom was the normal condition of the people? Scarcity of information prevents us from replying with that precision which the importance of the problem demands, but it is at least possible to indicate the chief factors. First, it is incontestable that commerce and industry were originally recruited from among landless men, who lived, so to speak, on the margin of a society where land alone was the basis of existence. Now these men were very numerous. Apart altogether from those, who in times of famine or war left their native soil to seek a livelihood elsewhere and returned no more, we have to remember all the individuals whom the manorial organisation itself was unable to support. The peasants' holdings were of such a size as to secure the regular payment of the dues assessed upon them. Thus the younger sons of a man overburdened with children were often forced to leave their father in order to enable him to make his payments to the lord. Thenceforth they swelled the crowd of vagabonds who roamed through the country, going from abbey to abbey taking their share of alms reserved for the poor, hiring themselves out to the peasants at harvest time or at the vintage, and enlisting as mercenaries in the feudal troops in times of war.

These men were quick to profit by the new means of livelihood offered them by the arrival of ships and merchants along the coasts and in the river estuaries. Many of the more adventurous certainly hired themselves to the Venetian and Scandinavian boats as sailors; others joined the merchant caravans which took their way more and more frequently to the "ports". With luck, the best among them could not fail to seize the many opportunities of making a fortune, which commercial life offered to the vagabonds and adventurers who threw themselves into it with energy and intelligence. Strong probability would suffice to support such a reconstruction of the facts, even if we did not possess, in the story of St. Godric of Finchale, a valuable example of the way in which the *nouveaux riches* were then formed. Godric was born toward the end of the eleventh century in Lincolnshire of poor peasant stock and, forced, no doubt, to leave his parents' holding, he must have had to use all his wits to get a living. Like many other unfortunates in every age he became a beachcomber, on the lookout for wreckage thrown up by the waves. Shipwrecks were numerous and one fine day a lucky chance furnished him with a windfall which enabled him to get together a pedlar's pack. He had amassed a little store of money, when he met with and joined a band of merchants. Their business prospered and he soon made enough profit to enable him to form a partnership with others, in common with whom he loaded a ship and engaged in coastal trade along the shores of England, Scotland, Flanders and Denmark. The partnership prospered. Its operations consisted in taking abroad goods which were known to be scarce there and bringing back a return cargo, which was then exported to places where the demand was greatest and where, in consequence, the largest profits could be realised.

The story of Godric was certainly that of many others. In an age when local famines were continual, one had only to buy a very small quantity of grain cheaply in regions where it was abundant, to realise fabulous profits, which could then be increased by the same methods. Thus speculation, which is the starting-point in this kind of business, largely contributed to the foundation of the first commercial fortunes. The savings of a little pedlar, a sailor, a boatman, or a docker, furnished him with quite enough capital, if only he knew how to use it. It might also happen that a landowner would invest a part of his income in maritime commerce. It is almost certain that the nobles on the Ligurian coast advanced the necessary funds to build the Genoese ships and shared in the profits from the sale of cargoes in the Mediterranean ports. The same thing must have happened in other Italian cities; at least we are tempted to assume so when we observe that in Italy a large proportion of the nobility always lived in the cities, in contrast to their brothers north of the Alps. It is only natural to suppose that a certain number of them were in some way interested in the economic revival which was developing around them. In these cases landed capital unquestionably contributed to the formation of liquid capital. However, their share was secondary, and though they profited by the recovery of trade, it was certainly not they who revived it.

The first impetus started from outside, in the South with Venetian and in the North with Scandinavian navigation. Western Europe, crystallised in its agricultural civilisation, could not of itself have become so rapidly acquainted with a new sort of life, in the absence of external stimulus and example. The attitude of the Church, the most powerful landowner of the time, towards commerce, an attitude not merely passive but actively hostile, is quite enough proof of that. If the first beginnings of commercial capitalism partly evade our notice, it is much easier to follow its evolution during the course of the twelfth century. In the vigour and relative rapidity of its development it may, without exaggeration, be compared with the industrial revolution of the nineteenth century. The new kind of life which offered itself to the roving masses of landless men had an irresistible attraction for them, by reason of the promise of gain which it offered. The result was a real emigration from the country to the nascent towns. Soon, it was not only vagabonds of the type of Godric who bent their steps thither. The temptation was too great not to cause a number of serfs to run away from the manors where they were born and settle in the towns, either as artisans or as employees of the rich merchants whose reputation spread throughout the land. The lords pursued them and brought them back to their holdings, when they succeeded in laying hands on them. But many eluded their search, and as the city population increased, it became dangerous to try to seize the fugitives under its protection.

By concentrating in the towns industry was able to supply their export trade more and more largely. Thus the number of merchants steadily increased and with it the importance and the profits of their business. At that time of commercial growth, it was not difficult for young men to find employment as assistants to some rich master, to share in his business and in the end to make their own fortunes. The *Gesta* of the bishops of Cambrai relate in detail the story of a certain Werimbold, who, in the time of Bishop Burchard (1114–30), entered the service of a wealthy merchant, married his daughter and developed his business to such a degree that he himself became rich. He purchased a great deal of land in the town, built a magnificent house, bought off the toll collected at one of the gates, constructed a bridge at his own expense and in the end left the greater part of his property to the Church.

The foundation of large fortunes was certainly at this period a common phenomenon in all centres where an export trade was developing. Just as landowners had in the past showered gifts of land on the monasteries, so now merchants used their fortunes to found parish churches, hospitals, almshouses, in short, to spend themselves in religious or charitable works for the benefit of their fellow-citizens and the good of their own souls. Indeed, religion may well have spurred many of them on to win a fortune, which they intended to dedicate to the service of God. It should not be forgotten that Peter Waldo, the founder in 1173 of the Poor Men of Lyons, which shortly gave rise to the sect of the Waldenses, was a merchant and that, almost at the same date, St. Francis was born at Assisi in the house of another merchant. Other *nouveaux riches*, more bitten with worldly ambition, sought to raise themselves in the social hierarchy by giving their daughters in marriage to knights; and their fortune must have been very large to have stifled the aristocratic reluctance of the latter.

These great merchants, or rather *nouveaux riches*, were naturally the leaders of the bourgeoisie, since the bourgeoisie itself was a creation of the commercial revival and in the beginning the words *mercator* and *burgensis* were synonymous. But while it developed as a social class this bourgeoisie was also forming itself into a legal class of a highly original nature, which we must now consider.

The needs and tendencies of the bourgeoisie were so incompatible with the traditional organisation of Western Europe that they immediately aroused violent opposition. They ran counter to all the interests and ideas of a society dominated materially by the owners of large landed property and spiritually by the Church, whose aversion to trade was unconquerable. It would be unfair to attribute to "feudal tyranny" or "sacerdotal arrogance" an opposition which explains itself, although the attribution has often been made. As always, those who were the beneficiaries of the established order defended it obstinately, not only because it guaranteed their interests, but because it seemed to them indispensable to the preservation of society. Moreover, the bourgeois themselves were far from taking up a revolutionary attitude towards this society. They took for granted the authority of the territorial princes, the privileges of the nobility and, above all, those of the Church. They even professed an ascetic morality, which was plainly contradicted by their mode of life. They merely desired a place in the sun, and their claims were confined to their most indispensable needs.

Of the latter, the most indispensable was personal liberty. Without liberty, that is to say, without the power to come and go, to do business, to sell goods, a power not enjoyed by serfdom, trade would be impossible. Thus they claimed it, simply for the advantages which it conferred, and nothing was further from the mind of the bourgeoisie than any idea of freedom as a natural right; in their eyes it was merely a useful one. Besides, many of them possessed it *de facto*; they were immigrants, who had come from too far off for their lord to be traced and who, since their serfdom could not be presumed, necessarily passed for free, although born of unfree parents. But the fact had to be transformed into a right. It was essential that the villeins, who came to settle in the towns to seek a new livelihood, should feel safe and should not have to fear being taken back by force to the manors from which they had escaped. They must be delivered from labour services and from all the hated dues by which the servile population was burdened, such as the obligation to marry only a woman of their own class and to leave to the lord part of their inheritance. Willy-nilly, in the course of the twelfth century these claims, backed up as they often were by dangerous revolts, had to be granted. The most obstinate conservatives, such as Guibert de Nogent, in 1115, were reduced to a wordy revenge, speaking of those "detestable communes" which the serfs had set up to escape from their lord's authority and to do away with his most lawful rights. Freedom became the legal status of the bourgeoisie, so much so that it was no longer a personal privilege only, but a territorial one, inherent in urban soil just as serfdom was in manorial soil. In order to obtain it, it was enough to have resided for a year and a day within the walls of the town. "City air makes a man free" (*Stadtluft macht frei*), says the German proverb.

But if liberty was the first need of the burgess, there were many others besides. Traditional law with its narrow, formal procedure, its ordeals, its judicial duels, its judges recruited from among the rural population, and knowing no other custom than that which had been gradually elaborated to regulate the relations of men living by the cultivation or the ownership of the land, was inadequate for a population whose existence was based on commerce and industry. A more expeditious law was necessary, means of proof more rapid and more independent of chance, and judges who were themselves acquainted with the professional occupations of those who came under their jurisdiction, and could cut short their arguments by a knowledge of the case at issue. Very early, and at latest at the beginning of the eleventh century, the pressure of circumstances led to the creation of a *jus mercatorum*, i.e., an embryonic commercial code. It was a collection of usages born of business experience, a sort of international custom, which the merchants used among themselves in their transactions. Devoid of all legal validity, it was impossible to invoke it in the existing law courts, so the merchants agreed to choose among themselves arbitrators who had the necessary competence to understand their disputes and to settle them promptly. It is here undoubtedly that we must seek the origin of those law courts, which in England received the picturesque name of courts of *piepowder* (*pied poudré*), because the feet of the merchants who resorted to them were still dusty from the roads. Soon this *ad hoc* jurisdiction became permanent and was recognised by public authority. At Ypres, in 1116, the Count of Flanders abolished the judicial duel, and it is certain that about the same date he instituted in most of his towns local courts of *échevins*, chosen from among the burgesses and alone competent to judge them. Sooner or later the same thing happened in all countries. In Italy, France, Germany and England the towns obtained judicial autonomy, which made them islands of independent jurisdiction, lying outside the territorial custom.

This jurisdictional autonomy was accompanied by administrative autonomy. The formation of urban agglomerations entailed a number of arrangements for convenience of defence, which they had to provide for themselves in the absence of the traditional authorities, who had neither the means nor the wish to help them. It is a strong testimony to the energy and the initiative of the bourgeoisie that it succeeded by its own efforts in setting on foot the municipal organisation, of which the first outlines appear in the eleventh century, and which was already in possession of all its essential organs in the twelfth. The work thus accomplished is all the more admirable because it was an original creation. There was nothing in the existing order of things to serve it as a model, since the needs it was designed to meet were new.

The most pressing was the need for defence. The merchants and their merchandise were, indeed, such a tempting prey that it was essential to protect them from pillagers by a strong wall. The construction of ramparts was thus the first public work undertaken by the towns and one which, down to the end of the Middle Ages, was their heaviest financial burden. Indeed, it may be truly said to have been the starting-point of their financial organisation, whence, for example, the name of *firmitas*, by which the communal tax was always known at Liége, and the appropriation in a number of cities *ad opus castri* (i.e., for the improvement of the fortifications) of a part of the fines imposed by the borough court. The fact that to-day municipal coats of arms are surrounded by a walled crown shows the importance accorded to the ramparts. There were no unfortified towns in the Middle Ages.

Money had to be raised to provide for the expenses occasioned by the permanent need for fortifications, and it could be raised most easily from the burgesses themselves. All were interested in the common defence and all were obliged to meet the cost. The quota payable by each was calculated on the basis of his fortune. This was a great innovation. For the arbitrary seigneurial tallage, collected in the sole interest of the lord, it substituted a payment proportionate to the means of the taxpayer and set apart for an object of general utility. Thus taxation recovered its public character, which had disappeared during the feudal era. To assess and collect this tax, as well as to provide for the ordinary necessities whose numbers grew with the constant increase of the town population, the establishment of quays and markets, the building of bridges and parish churches, the regulation of crafts and the supervision of food supplies, it soon became necessary to elect or allow the setting up of a council of magistrates, consuls in Italy and Provence, *jurés* in France and aldermen in England. In the eleventh century they appeared in the Lombard cities, where the consuls of Lucca are mentioned as early as 1080. In the following century, they became everywhere an institution ratified by public authority and inherent in every municipal constitution. In many towns as in those of the Low Countries, the *échevins* were at once the judges and administrators of the townsfolk.

The lay princes soon discovered how advantageous the growth of the cities was to themselves. For in proportion as their trade grew on road and river and their increasing business transactions required a corresponding increase of currency, the revenues from every kind of toll and from the mints likewise flowed in increasing quantities into the lord's treasury. Thus it is not surprising that the lords assumed on the whole a benevolent attitude towards the townsfolk. Moreover, living as a rule in their country castles, they did not come in contact with the town population and thus many causes of conflict were avoided. It was quite otherwise with the ecclesiastical princes. Almost to a man they offered a resistance to the municipal movement, which at times developed into an open struggle. The fact that the bishops were obliged to reside in their cities, the centres of diocesan administration, necessarily impelled them to preserve their authority and to oppose the ambitions of the bourgeoisie all the more resolutely because they were roused and directed by the merchants, ever suspect in the eyes of the Church. In the second half of the eleventh century the quarrel of the Empire and the Papacy gave the city populations of Lombardy a chance to rise against their simoniacal prelates. Thence the movement spread through the Rhine valley to Cologne. In 1077, the town of Cambrai rose in revolt against Bishop Gerard II and formed the oldest of the "communes" that we meet with north of the Alps. In the diocese of Liége the same thing happened. In 1066 Bishop Théoduin was forced to grant the burgesses of Huy a charter of liberties which is several years earlier than those whose text has been preserved in the rest of the Empire. In France, municipal insurrections are mentioned at Beauvaise about 1099, at Noyon in 1108–9, and at Laon in 1115.

Thus, by fair means or foul, the towns gained peaceably or by force, some at the beginning, others in the course of the twelfth century, municipal constitutions suitable to the life of their inhabitants.

Originating in the "new burgs", in the *portus*, where the merchants and artisans were grouped, they were soon developed to include the population of the "old burgs" and the "cities", whose ancient walls, surrounded on all sides by the new quarters, were falling into ruin like the old law itself. Henceforth, all who resided within the city wall, with the sole exception of the clergy, shared the privileges of the burgesses.

The essential characteristic of the bourgeoisie was, indeed, the fact that it formed a privileged class in the midst of the rest of the population. From this point of view the medieval town offers a striking contrast both to the ancient town and to the town of to-day, which are differentiated only by the density of their population and their complex administration; apart from this, neither in public nor in private law do their inhabitants occupy a peculiar position in the State. The medieval burgess, on the contrary, was a different kind of person from all who lived outside the town walls. Once outside the gates and the moat we are in another world, or more exactly, in the domain of another law. The acquisition of citizenship brought with it results analogous to those which followed when a man was dubbed knight or a clerk tonsured, in the sense that they conferred a peculiar legal status. Like the clerk or the noble, the burgess escaped from the common law; like them, he belonged to a particular estate (*status*), which was later to be known as the "third estate".

The territory of the town was as privileged as its inhabitants. It was a sanctuary, an "immunity", which protected the man who took refuge there from exterior authority, as if he had sought sanctuary in a church. In short, the bourgeoisie was in every sense an exceptional class. Each town formed, so to speak, a little state to itself, jealous of its prerogatives and hostile to all its neighbours. Very rarely was a common danger or a common end able to impose on its municipal particularism the need for alliances or leagues such, for example, as the German Hanse. In general, urban politics were determined by the same sacred egoism which was later to inspire State politics. For the burgesses the country population existed only to be exploited. Far from allowing it to enjoy their franchises, they always obstinately refused it all share in them. Nothing could be further removed from the spirit of modern democracy than the exclusiveness with which the medieval towns continued to defend their privileges, even, and indeed above all, in those periods when they were governed by the crafts.

## Suggestions for Further Reading

*Cambridge Economic History*, Vols. I and II, 2d ed. Cambridge, England: Cambridge University Press, 1967.

LATOUCHE, ROBERT, *Birth of the Western Economy*. London: Methuen & Co., Ltd., 1961.

LOPEZ, R. S., AND I. RAYMOND, *Mediterranean Trade in the Medieval World*. New York: Columbia University Press, 1955.

MUNDY, J. H., AND P. RIESENBERG, *The Medieval Town*. New York: Van Nostrand Reinhold, 1958.

MUMFORD, L., *The City in History*. New York: Harcourt Brace Jovanovich, Inc., 1961.

PIRENNE, HENRI, *Medieval Cities*. Princeton, N. J.: Princeton University Press, 1946.

PIRENNE, HENRI, *Mohammed and Charlemagne*. New York: Meridian Books, 1957.

RORIG, FRITZ, *The Medieval Town*. Berkeley: University of California Press, 1967.

THRUPP, SYLVIA, *The Merchant Class of Medieval London*. Ann Arbor: University of Michigan Press, 1962.

WHITE, LYNN, *Medieval Technology and Social Change*. Oxford: Clarendon Press, 1962.

# DENO J. GEANAKOPLOS

# The Heritage of Byzantium

⋙ For several decades the only research institute of medieval history in the United States, that at Dumbarton Oaks in Washington, D. C., was devoted not to western medieval history but to Byzantium. (Recently a distinguished institute for canon law studies has been created and is now located at Berkeley.) Because of the financial support and academic persuasion provided by Dumbarton Oaks, American medieval scholarship has achieved great distinction in Byzantine studies, particularly in the art and culture of Byzantium. Indeed, American medievalists have been far more original and convincing in interpreting medieval Greek culture than they have been in handling the Latin West. The other great center of Byzantine scholarship has been in France, although, not surprisingly, Bulgarian, Russian, and native Greek scholars have made some important contributions. French Byzantine scholarship has a long history, going back to the patronage of the Sun King, Louis XIV, himself.

Cultural historians and sociologists may well ask whether American fascination with medieval Byzantium derives from something more profound than the idiosyncrasies of the millionaire who endowed Dumbarton Oaks. It may be asked: Does the United States of the twentieth century, like the France of Louis XIV, fall under the model of an *ancien régime*, so that scholars inevitably

FROM Deno J. Geanakoplos, *Byzantine East and Latin West* (New York: Harper & Row, Publishers, 1966), pp. 11–54.

have a great sensitivity to, and admiration for, Byzantium, that arch-example of *ancien régime?*

An *ancien régime* is a culture and society that cannot change itself in fundamentals so that the more it changes in personnel and appearances, the more it does the same things, and the more passionate the controversies, the more the social, cultural structure of one era resembles that of the previous era. France from 1650 to 1789—some would say right down to the present—is an *ancien régime.* So, perhaps, is the United States since the time of Theodore Roosevelt and Woodrow Wilson. So certainly was Byzantium from the time of Justinian I until the fall of Constantinople to the Turks in 1453. The one possible turning point, the iconoclastic controversy of the eighth century which had the potential of transforming the political and social structure and the value system of the Eastern Roman Empire, in the end was aborted and Byzantium went on its customary way, endlessly refining the governmental, economic, and cultural heritage derived from the late Roman Empire.

Yet *anciens régimes* have their value in that only in such systems can the resources of society be applied to nonsocial or antisocial purposes: the medieval Greeks poured vast wealth and human talent into monumental art and architecture, as did France of the eighteenth century; while the American *ancien régime* commits its treasure and brain power into sending people to the moon even though the misery of the blacks and the poor goes on unabated decade after decade. And, one supposes, future historians will admire our monumental space achievements and forget about the social cost in human suffering that results from this dysfunctional allocation of resources—just as American and French Byzantinists celebrate the art of medieval Constantinople while forgetting about the common man who had to pay dearly for these memorials to Emperor and God.

Medieval western Europe, at least before 1200 or so, was no *ancien régime,* but rather a violent, disordered, unstable, creative, ever-changing frontier society; and like all such frontier societies, it borrowed heavily from more sophisticated civilizations. Medieval Europe naturally tapped the culture and technology of the *ancien régime* in Constantinople, although the ways in which it applied and used these borrowings was nearly always novel and distinctive. To take an example, the western medievals borrowed Byzantine ideas and ceremonies of sacred kingship, but their purpose was to increase social order by giving legitimacy to warrior chieftains. Of course, it can be argued that the Byzantine impact on the West was singularly unfortunate in that it kept driving the westerners back toward traditional centuries-old Mediterranean institutions and values, inhibiting the triumph of a distinctively new culture.

Deno J. Geanakoplos, a Yale professor, is among the most learned and clear-headed of American Byzantinists. In this study he convincingly demonstrates the great debt (for better or worse—Geanakoplos assumes for the better) of the West to the medieval Greek heritage.

❧

It is frequently asserted that from a cultural point of view the chief function of Byzantium was to serve for over one thousand years as the bulwark of Christendom against invading infidel hordes and in this capacity to preserve for the world the literary and philosophic heritage of ancient Greece. There is no doubt of course of the signal service rendered by Byzantium as a preserver of Greek learning. After all, the Greek language and literature had virtually disappeared from the German-dominated West of the so-called Dark Ages. But Byzantium was certainly more than a mere passive repository of ancient civilization. On the contrary, as her culture developed, it reflected a remarkable amalgamation not only of the philosophy and literature of Greece, but of the religious ideals of Christianity—which in the East underwent a development significantly different from that of the Latin West—and thirdly, of a certain transcendent, mystical quality that may at least partly be attributed to the diverse influences of Syria, Egypt, the Jews, even Persia. These three elements, then, Greco-Roman classicism (including the governmental tradition of Rome), the Byzantine brand of Christianity, and what we may call the oriental component, were blended by the Byzantines into a unique and viable synthesis that made Constantinople, at least until 1204, the cultural capital of all Christendom. It was this many-faceted cultural amalgam, as we shall attempt to show, that enabled Byzantium to play a far from insignificant part in the formation of western civilization.

Now to analyze the Byzantine cultural influence on the West is a complex problem spanning more than a millennium of history and involving, in one way or another, most of the countries of Europe. One could perhaps make facile generalizations about the natural tendency of the less developed western civilization to draw upon or be influenced by the more complex, sophisticated Byzantine. But one must not forget that as the medieval period progressed, Byzantium and the West were becoming increasingly estranged—indeed by perhaps the ninth century they had become almost two different worlds—and that many westerners, especially those who did not come into direct contact with the East, were not receptive to Byzantine influences. To demonstrate a *definite* cultural impact of the Christian East on the West can accordingly sometimes be a rather difficult, even elusive matter, particularly in regard to those fields which are less tangible in nature or in which the evidence remaining is inadequate. In order therefore to deal with the problem on as firm ground as possible and at the same time to provide a kind of historical frame of reference, we shall consider first the points of actual physical contact between Byzantium and the Latin West during the medieval period—that is, the specific channels through which cultural transmission could and seems to have taken place. Then, having established such a pattern of contacts, we shall . . . examine . . . selected cultural fields in which it can be asserted that the Byzantines affected western civilization—philosophy, science, law, political theory and diplomacy, music, art, and such lesser known but important aspects as religious piety, commercial practice, and more refinement in the manner of living.

Originally constituting two halves of the ancient Roman Empire, the eastern (Byzantine) and the western (Latin) areas in the early centuries of the Christian era had possessed certain cultural elements in common, Christianity and the Greco-Roman tradition. In the East, however, the Greek element continued from the Hellenistic period onward to predominate, while in the West the Latin language and culture obtained. Moreover, while the East technically preserved an unbroken continuity of the Roman Empire—as late as 1453 the Byzantines continued to call themselves Roman not Greeks—the western areas early fell to the German invaders and, with the passing of time, the German element largely displaced in the West the more refined Greco-Roman. This emergence of a strong Germanic strain in the western cultural synthesis is to be contrasted to the Byzantine synthesis, with its inclusion of an Oriental component, absent in turn from the West.

In the sixth century, under the Emperor Justinian, Byzantium recaptured much of Italy and established the so-called exarchate of Ravenna, a fact which once again brought an important area of the West into direct dependence upon Byzantium. The exarchate—and this included the city of Rome—remained in Byzantine hands until 751 when Ravenna was finally captured by the Lombards. Before its collapse, however, Ravenna had become a center for the radiation of Byzantine cultural influence, especially in connection with Byzantine art and the dissemination of Byzantine, that is Roman law.

More significant for our study are the areas of Sicily and southern Italy, which were Byzantine provinces until the ninth and eleventh centuries respectively. What served to maintain—some scholars would prefer to say 're-establish'—the Hellenization of these areas, especially in southern Italy after the period of antiquity, was the successive waves of Greek exiles who emigrated there from the East. Thus in the seventh century refugees from Syria, Palestine, and Egypt fled to southern Italy (especially Calabria) before the attacks of the Arabs. And in the eighth and ninth centuries, according to certain scholars, as many as 50,000 eastern monks and, to a lesser extent, ecclesiastics arrived in Calabria in order to escape the persecutions of the Byzantine Iconoclast Emperors [Iconoclasm opposed the veneration of religious images (icons)]. Whether the Greek language spoken by the population of southern Italy was derived from the ancient Greek of Magna Graecia or was rather the product of subsequent Byzantine influence we may pass over here. The significant point is that by the eleventh century parts of southern Italy, primarily Calabria, had become almost completely Byzantinized in both culture and religion and that as late as the fifteenth century it would constitute the leading outpost of Byzantine influence in the West.

Even the Arab conquest of Sicily in the ninth century did not put an end to Greek influence on the island. For the Arabs were fascinated by ancient Greek and, to a much lesser degree, Byzantine science and philosophy. Indeed, when subsequently in the late eleventh century, the Norman invaders took the island from the Arabs, Greco-Byzantine culture continued to be a vital element in the island-civilization. Under

the Norman King Roger II and his successors, for example, three
official languages were employed in the documents of the Sicilian
chancery, Latin, Greek, and Arabic. Moreover, the Normans appointed as ministers of state such learned Greeks as Eugene the Emir
and the more famous Henry Aristippus, who, at a time when western
Europe knew only a fragment of one of Plato's dialogues, the *Timaeus*,
translated into Latin two more Platonic works. Though relations between Byzantium and Norman Sicily were generally hostile, we know
that gifts were not infrequently exchanged by their rulers, sometimes
including valuable Greek manuscripts of philosophic or scientific content such as the famous *Almagest* of Ptolemy.

Among the first Italians to have had active commercial contacts
with Constantinople—and the Italians were to have the closest relations
economically with the East—were the citizens of Amalfi, in southern
Italy. The cultural results of those connections of Amalfi are hard to
assess, though we know, for example, that in the eleventh century the
wealthy Amalfitan family of the Pantaleone, with residence in Constantinople, had transported to Amalfi, for installation in that city's cathedral, magnificent bronze doors which had been cast in Byzantium. The
rising Italian maritime cities of Genoa and Pisa followed the Amalfitan
example and by the twelfth century had established, in the heart of
Constantinople, substantial quarters for the residence of their own merchants. Each community had a Latin church for the use of its people
and though the sources, which primarily concern activities of merchants, do not afford many specific examples of cultural exchange
with the Greeks, we may cite the names of such Pisan men of letters
as Burgundio of Pisa, Leo Tuscus and his brother Hugo Eterianus.
These were interested not only in Greek philosophy, but what is more
striking in this period of Latin suspicion of the Greek church, in Byzantine ecclesiastical writings.

Of the many Italian commercial colonies in the East the most important was certainly that of Venice. From at least as early as the
ninth century Veneto-Byzantine relations had been close, the Doge
acquiring the title of *Protosevastos* and a high enough place in the
imperial Byzantine hierarchy of titles. In exchange for Venetian naval
aid against Byzantium's enemies, the Greek Basileus had authorized
the establishment of a Venetian colony in the heart of Constantinople,
along the Golden Horn, the citizens of which were soon able to enjoy
complete freedom from payment of taxes and even exemption from im-

perial Byzantine law—what we would call extraterritoriality. In the twelfth century this Venetian colony numbered perhaps 20,000 persons out of a total population in Constantinople of 800,000 to a million people. The contrast with Venice itself with an estimated 64,000 in 1170, and with Paris, then the West's largest city with a population of less than 100,000, is remarkable.

To be sure, the Venetian colonists, having the mentality of merchants, were rarely interested in anything but commercial profit. Thus of course they learned to speak enough Greek for their commercial transactions. But this was the colloquial vulgar Greek (the lingua franca of the East) and it was not sufficient as a rule to permit the reading of classical works or the exchange of ideas on a higher intellectual level. (The literary Greek of Byzantine intellectual circles was different from the spoken, every-day Greek.) Exceptions do exist such as the case of the famous James of Venice, who a recent scholar believes was a Greek living in Venice. James translated Aristotle's *Ethics* into Latin and acted as interpreter at ecclesiastical disputations held before the imperial Greek court on questions of difference between the Greek and Latin churches. Such occasions must surely have afforded some opportunity for cultural exchange.

What brought the people of the West and the Byzantines into direct contact on a far greater scale, however, was the vast movement of the Crusades, which began at the end of the eleventh century. Entire western armies now passed through Constantinople on the way to the Holy Land, and pilgrims flocked eastward via Constantinople, all being exposed to the richer and more cosmopolitan manner of living of the medieval Greeks. Inevitably, jealousies and antagonisms between the two peoples now began to develop and with the passing of time to increase. The shattering climax came in 1204 with the notorious Fourth Crusade, when the western armies, led by the Venetians, diverted their crusade from Jerusalem to Constantinople and actually captured the Byzantine capital. After a barbaric sack of three days, a tremendous amount of booty—sacred relics associated with the life of Christ and the saints, precious manuscripts, silver and gold religious treasures, and countless objects of art—was seized in this richest of Christian cities and carried back to adorn the churches and palaces of the West. The enumeration of this booty and the recounting of its seizure fill several volumes in the works of a noted French scholar of the history of the Christian East during the Crusades.

As a result of the Fourth Crusade a Latin Empire was established on the ruins of the Byzantine state. Attempts were made by the western conquerors, and especially the pope, to Latinize the Greek people by forcible conversion to the Roman faith. But this unwise policy, as might be expected, provoked the violent opposition of the mass of the Greek population. The Latin Empire existed until 1261, when Constantinople was recaptured by the Greeks. Then the hitherto predominant Venetian influence in Byzantium diminished, to be displaced by that of the Byzantine allies, the Genoese. The Venetians, however, managed to retain control of certain of their Greek colonies in the East—several points in the Peloponnesus, the Aegean isles, and especially the great island of Crete. With the Ottoman Turkish advance on the Byzantine territory of Asia Minor in the fourteenth and fifteenth centuries, the Greek animosity toward the Latins began of necessity to be mollified. And in fact some of the Byzantines, especially of the court circles, came to view the West not only as the sole source of possible aid against the Turk but, still later, even as a place of refuge from Turkish domination.

Before and for at least a century after 1453 [when Constantinople fell to the Turks], then, large numbers of Greeks—a veritable diaspora of intellectuals, merchants, mercenaries, and others—poured into the West, many of whom sought asylum in Venice. By the end of the fifteenth century there was a very substantial Greek colony established in that city. This was in fact the greatest colony of Greeks to be established in the West after 1453. The Greeks of this community were granted the right to build a church and they also possessed a large dockyard, or *scala*, on an important Venetian canal for the loading and shipment of goods abroad. We shall see that, from the cultural viewpoint, these Greek émigrés to the West were to play a significant role in the development of humanistic learning in the Renaissance.

There is time only for brief mention of several other Italian centers affected by or radiating Byzantine influence during the medieval period. Further reference should certainly be made to the papal capital Rome, which, after the fall of Ravenna and throughout the entire Middle Ages, had intimate contact with Byzantines or Byzantine ideas. A large community of Greek monks seems always to have lived in Rome, and up to the third century Greek was even the language of the Roman liturgy. Moreover, during the later seventh and early eighth centuries many of the popes themselves—eleven of thirteen to be precise—were

Greek or Syrian in origin and shared the cultural proclivities of the East.

Other western areas further removed from the East were also at one time or another in direct contact with Byzantium. In the early ninth century, the German court of Charlemagne at Aachen [Aix-la-Chapelle] was exposed to considerable Byzantine influence, as we know from the architectural evidence of its palace chapel as well as from certain Byzantine art works and textiles that remain. In the tenth century more intensive Byzantine influence was felt at the German court as a result of the marriage of the future Holy Roman Emperor Otto II to the Byzantine princess Theophano. So imbued did their young son, the half-Greek Otto III, become with Byzantine political ideals that he adopted Byzantine titles for his court and envisioned the reunion of both East and West in one Empire in the manner of Justinian.

Similarly, we hear that there were at various times communities of Greek merchants or monks in early medieval France—such as at Narbonne. And in the later medieval period, French crusaders were to bring back from the East Byzantine art objects, new ideas, and different building techniques, the adoption of which helped gradually to make for a more refined mode of life. Because of the distance involved the Byzantine influence on England was perhaps the least penetrating of all. But sporadic traces of such influences do remain such as, for example, in the late Anglo-Saxon and possibly Norman use of the imperial Byzantine title Basileus, to apply to their kings; and in the Northumbrian sculptured stones of the seventh century, so extraordinarily Byzantine in feeling and execution. Inspiration for the latter probably came from the East, however, rather through the mediation of the English connection with Rome.

There is one-western area, Spain, where the influence of Greek and to a lesser degree of Byzantine philosophy and science were of capital importance for their effect on western culture as a whole. These influences, however, came through the mediation not of the Byzantines but of another people, the Arabs. In the early years of the Islamic expansion, the Arabs had come into contact with heretic Nestorian and Monophysite refugees from the Byzantine East and from these they acquired an interest in ancient Greek philosophy and science, especially the Aristotelian. These Greek works the Arabs carried with them into Spain, and it was from this region that in the twelfth and thirteenth centuries the bulk of Aristotle and other Greek scientific treatises were brought back to the Christian West, with the results we shall note shortly.

These, then, are the principal foci, direct and indirect, for the reception and diffusion of Byzantine culture in the western world. Now that we have pointed out the chief lines of possible transmission and provided in the process a historical background, let us concentrate on certain selected areas of culture in order to show in each case what the Byzantine contribution seems to have been.

## PHILOSOPHY AND SCIENCE

First let us consider the important realm of philosophic and scientific ideas. According to the famous French scholar Etienne Gilson, western medieval and Renaissance intellectual thought underwent two fundamental crises in the course of their development, both under the impact of the re-introduction of Greek philosophy. First in the twelfth and thirteenth centuries with the reception of Aristotle from Arabic Spain, and, second, in the fifteenth century when an interest in Plato was diffused in the West following the coming to Florence of a Byzantine delegation to negotiate religious union with Rome. Now it cannot of course be said that a knowledge of the Greek language *per se* was indispensable for advance in culture. After all, classical Latin was also a flexible and highly expressive language. But the point is that reception of the ancient Greek philosophic works brought along with them that greatest gift of ancient Greece to the world—the emphasis on natural reason. In the period of the so-called Dark Ages such an attitude contrasted starkly with the unquestioning, superstitious *Weltanschauung* of the West regarding nature and the world. Hence it is clear how traumatic it must have been for the more thoughtful western man suddenly to come upon works of Aristotle with his convincing explanation of the cosmos based solely on reason and entirely without reference to the supernatural elements of Christianity.

But as we have elsewhere observed, the Aristotelian philosophy and science that entered the West in the twelfth century did not come directly from Byzantium but via the Arabs of Spain. The point is that this Aristotelian thought was colored by Muslim theological interpretation which, aside from being non-Christian (as on the question of the eternity of matter), sometimes had even confused Aristotelianism with aspects of Neo-Platonism. It was not until after the Latin conquest of Constantinople in 1204 that most of the original Greek texts, of Aristotle and other scientific writers, in more or less unadulterated form, were made available to western scholars. It is a striking commentary on the distrust felt by the West for the Greek 'schismatics', as the Byzantines were referred to, that for a considerable period the westerners actually preferred the second- or even third-hand Arabic version of Aristotle to the purer version the Byzantines could provide.

The introduction of the 'Muslim' Aristotle from Spain provoked such a sensation in western intellectual circles that the pope, sensing danger for the church, had to forbid the reading of portions of that author at the University of Paris, then the chief center of theological study in the West. But as usually happens with this type of censorship, the prohibition proved impossible to implement. Latin scholars, dazzled by the wealth of new material in Aristotle and other Greek authors, simply refused to obey. And ultimately the great Dominican Thomas Aquinas was appointed to minimize the danger by attempting to reconcile Aristotle's cosmology with that of Catholic Christianity— with the results that are well known.

It is worth noting that fully five hundred years before St. Thomas, a conciliation of Christian faith—but this time of Orthodoxy—with Aristotelian reason had already been attempted in the Byzantine East by the theologian John of Damascus [d. 750]. A copy of John's famous *Fountain of Wisdom*, which is still perhaps the basic work for the theology of the Orthodox Church, was apparently known to and utilized by Aquinas in the composition of his own great *Summa Theologica*. It was also Aquinas who suggested a vast undertaking to William of Moerbeke, the Latin Archbishop of Corinth—a revised, literal translation made directly from the Greek of almost all of Aristotle's works, including the famous political treatise, the *Politics*.

For the most part, medieval western translations of Greek writings were limited to logical treatises, the sciences, and, to a much lesser extent, to theology. Significantly, they failed to include classic Greek poetry, history, and much of philosophy—that is, the more humanistic writings. And the latter works did not in general come to the West until the period of the Renaissance. We have no time here to discuss specific works of this nature. But we should note that the original texts—say of the Greek tragedies—had in many cases been established in Constantinople by Byzantine scholars at the time of Photius [c. 820– 892?] and Arethas and especially in the thirteenth and fourteenth centuries and then brought westward mainly by Greek refugees or exiled scholars who settled in Venice and other Italian centers. One has only to examine a list of the personnel of the famous Academy of Aldus Manutius in Venice, which, at the end of the fifteenth and early sixteenth centuries, printed many first editions of these influential Greek texts and which counted among its editors many Greeks, including the famous Cretan Marcus Musurus and the Constantinopolitan humanist-diplomat Janus Lascaris.

Of parallel significance to Aristotelianism for the development of western thought and learning, as we have noted, was the introduction in the fifteenth century of Platonic philosophy. This, however, is exclusively to be associated with Byzantium and was not the result of mediation through the Arabs. To be sure certain Neo-Platonic works had earlier been known to the West. Already in the ninth century, during the so-called Carolingian Renaissance, the Irish scholar John Scotus Erigena had secured from the library of Charles the Bald, the King of the Franks (to whose predecessor Louis the Pious it had been sent by the Byzantine Emperor), a copy of the work of the Byzantine Neo-Platonist Maximos the Confessor. Erigena also had at his disposal in the writing of his famous *On the Division of Nature*, the work of the most highly influential mystic of the entire medieval world, the early Byzantine Dionysius the Areopagite, which Erigena translated into Latin. Dante in his *Paradiso* drew on material from Dionysius' *Celestial Hierarchy* and even the fourteenth century German mystic, Meister Eckhart, owed something to the profound mysticism of Dionysius.

In the Byzantine East, where pure Platonism was usually suspect to the church, the last significant revival of genuinely Platonic thought took place in the fourteenth and fifteenth centuries at Constantinople and especially at Mistra, near ancient Sparta. There the philosopher and social reformer Gemistos Pletho had founded a virtual cult of Platonic studies. In the West, on the other hand, Plato had been practically unknown since antiquity (despite the good intentions of Boethius in the sixth century and the pervasive Neo-Platonic thought reflected in Augustine). And it was not until the coming to Italy of Pletho and other Greeks to attend the famous Council of Florence in 1438–39 that the original Platonic texts once again were brought into direct contact with the mainstream of the western tradition. To save Constantinople, now completely surrounded by the Turks, the Greek Emperor, in a last desperate measure, had assembled a large number of his prelates and officials (many of whom were also scholars) and gone to Florence in the hope of securing military aid through religious union with the West. The papal price for western help against the Turks of course was the submission of the Greek church to Rome. The proceedings of this Council, the greatest medieval confrontation between East and West, lasted one and a half years, during which period opportunity was afforded for the westerners to acquire from the Greeks a knowledge and an appreciation of Platonic philosophy. Cosimo de' Medici, the ruler of Florence, was in fact so impressed by Pletho that he soon founded his Platonic Academy, whence, ultimately, interest in Plato became diffused throughout the entire West.

On the purely religious side the Florentine Marsilio Ficino achieved a synthesis of Platonic and Christian thought, which had an important impact on the religious outlook of many western humanists. According to some modern scholars the reception of Plato's philosophy did more to widen the intellectual horizon of the West during the Renaissance than any other single factor. Certain other authorities, however, take a narrower view. They believe that the most significant contribution of Platonic philosophy consisted rather in an emphasis on a mathematical type of thinking derived from certain Pythagorean materials incorporated in Plato. It was this mathematical emphasis, in contrast to the medieval western Aristotelian stress on logic that, according to this theory, paved the way for the advent of modern western science, especially acceptance of the Copernican theory.

If the Italian Ficino was responsible for producing the first complete Latin translation of the Platonic dialogues, it was, as is not always realized, a Byzantine or rather a post-Byzantine—Marcus Musurus, the Cretan editor of the Venetian Aldine Press—who made the first printed edition of the original Greek text. To this work Musurus prefixed his famous 'Hymn to Plato', a composition which, at least from the philological point of view, some scholars rank as the finest piece of Greek poetry written since antiquity.

Mention must be made, if only briefly, of the most celebrated ancient Greek scientific work that passed to the West—the *Mathematike Syntaxis* of Ptolemy (known better under its Arabic title of *Almagest*), a mathematical explanation for the universe which was to dominate the astronomical thinking of the West up to the time of Copernicus. It is known that in the twelfth century the Byzantine Emperor Manuel I Comnenus sent a copy of this work as a diplomatic gift to the Norman king of Sicily, Roger II. And it was from this manuscript that the first Latin version was made. William of Moerbeke, mentioned above, also translated a great part of the corpus of Archimedes. And at the very end of the Byzantine period, the fifteenth century philosopher Gemistos Pletho's introduction of the *Geography* of Strabo to the West influenced Renaissance conceptions of the configuration of the earth and, thus, indirectly, was a contributory factor leading to Columbus' discovery of America.

The Byzantine scientific tradition was essentially unoriginal, being based on ancient Greek, Hellenistic, and Roman achievements. But despite this broad heritage in natural science, the Byzantines, much like their ancient Greek forebears, were unable to develop a technical equipment, technology that is, and thus were usually unable to apply their sometimes not inconsiderable theoretical knowledge to practical use. Nevertheless, we may point out a few instances in which the Byzantines seemed to have anticipated certain modern technological developments. Kallinikos' invention of the famous Greek fire and the Byzantine technique of shooting this fire from copper tubes, constituted, according to several modern authorities, 'the prototype of modern gunpowder . . . , starting the military technicians not merely of Byzantium but of Islam, China, and the West on the trail of ever more combustible mixtures'. Though the watermill for producing power dates from the ancient world, it is quite possible that the overshot water-wheel (in which water runs over the top of, not underneath, the wheel) was an improvement of the early Byzantine period. In the sixth century Anthemius of Tralles (architect of St. Sophia) not only wrote on parabolic mirrors, but, as a joke, harnessed steam pressure to simulate a small earthquake. In the same century John Philoponus rejected the Aristotelian notion of the impossibility of producing a vacuum and even anticipated Galileo's experiment that two weights dropped from the same height reach the ground at approximately the same time. Finally, the famous mechanical *automata* of the Byzantine court (the rising throne, lions roaring, and birds singing), used to impress foreign visitors such as the tenth century Bishop Liudprand, may indirectly have influenced the development of the western mechanical clocks of the fourteenth century.

## LITERATURE

Apart from a certain influence on western historical writing as revealed through such works as the papal librarian Anastasius' ninth century translation of the Byzantine chronicler Theophanes, the Byzantine influence on western medieval literature was small. Creativity in Byzantine literature was relatively rare, except in the sometimes remarkable poetry found in the Byzantine hymnology and the unique eleventh century epic poem, 'Digenes Akritas'. Byzantium never produced a Dante, though probably the most learned scholar of the entire medieval world was the ninth century Patriarch Photius. This deficiency in literary creativeness is usually attributed (perhaps with a certain exaggeration) to the slavish Byzantine imitation of the ancient literary models. The cultured Byzantine felt that ancient Greek literature had reached such a state of perfection that in many respects it was impossible to surpass, a fact which led not only to the close Byzantine imitation of ancient rhetorical style but, more important, to the use by most writers of an artificial form of ancient Greek rather than the living vernacular spoken by the Byzantines themselves. It was this anomalous situation, somewhat analogous to that of an American attempting to write in Chaucerian English, that served in large part to stultify creativity in Byzantine literature.

Since Byzantium was the medieval repository for the ancient Greek literary treasures, it was from there or Byzantine southern Italy that they passed to the West. The medieval Greeks preserved the works of Homer, Aeschylus, Sophocles, Euripides, Aristophanes, and other poets and dramatists when they were unknown to or had been lost to the western world. And it is this work of preservation that some critics have termed Byzantium's most significant cultural contribution to the modern world.

While the classic dramatists were read in the East, they were never apparently performed on the stage, probably because of ecclesiastical objection to their pagan character and occasional immoral themes. As for Homer, he was read by all eastern school boys. But his work did not become familiar to western scholars until the fourteenth century when, at Petrarch's and Boccaccio's commission, Pilatus, a Greek of southern Italy, translated the Iliad and Odyssey into Latin prose. The version was not very successful (he did not know Latin too well), nor was Pilatus very effective in teaching Greek to Petrarch and Boccaccio. (It may not have been entirely his fault since dictionaries and other such aids were then unavailable, nor did the two Italian humanists really like Pilatus.) Nevertheless, Pilatus provided Boccaccio with material for his *Genealogy of the Gods*, the first exposition since antiquity of the Greek myths in their original pagan setting. It was at Boccaccio's initiative, moreover, that Pilatus, in 1361, was appointed

at Florence to the first chair of the Greek language to be established
in western Europe. A subsequent and more important holder of this
post (1396) was the distinguished Byzantine nobleman Manuel
Chrysoloras, during whose tenure so many leading Italian statesmen
and humanists came to study with him that the formal study of classical Greek letters may be said to have begun in the Renaissance.

Researchers differ sharply over the problem of the origin of the so-
called Franco-Greek romances, epic poems of the fourteenth and fifteenth centuries about love and adventure which were popular in both
the Greek East and the West. Some scholars believe that their genesis
is to be traced to the medieval Byzantine East, others to the courtly love
poems of France. Still others consider their prototype to be the novel
of Greek antiquity. Certainly, in the late medieval period, Byzantine
poets translated into their own language French and Italian narratives
of love and combat and also, perhaps to an even greater extent, created
their own works of this genre, examples being 'Floire and Blanchfleur',
Lybistros and Rhodamne' and 'Belthandros and Chrysantza'. Moreover, it is well-known that a number of twelfth century French romances of adventure had their setting in southern Italy, Constantinople, or Rome, and that the names of some of the characters in these
works are distortions from the Greek. Thus, whatever the origin of
the form of the so-called Franco-Greek romance, it may at least be
affirmed that a mutual interaction of Byzantine and western elements
in the development of this type of literature is clearly indicated.


## MEDICINE

In the early medieval period the only medical knowledge available
to western Europe consisted of scattered fragments, in Latin translation, of the ancient Greeks Hippocrates, Galen, Soranus and Dio-
scorides. The revival of western medicine began in the late tenth or
early eleventh century at the medical school of Salerno in southern
Italy, where the traditions of Latin, Greco-Byzantine, Arabic, and Jewish medicine met and were blended. Half-legendary tradition has it that
the founders of the Salerno school were Salernus who taught in Latin,
a certain Pontos who taught in Greek, Adela who instructed in Arabic,
and Helinus who taught in Hebrew. Of the several elements represented here it is generally believed that the Byzantine, aside from the
ancient Greek proper, was rather negligible. But further research
on the neglected field of Byzantine medicine may reveal that this view

may have to be qualified. It is already known for example that a late twelfth century Latin physician at the same medical school, Roger of Salerno, was influenced by the treatises of the Byzantine doctors Aetius and Alexander of Tralles of the sixth century, and Paul of Aegina of the seventh.

Arabic medicine was based largely on the ancient Greek, though in several areas, such as the science of vision, symptomatology and pharmacology the Arabs were able to make a few original contributions. In Byzantium the tradition of the ancients of course also obtained, and though the Byzantines seem to have made few if any important advances (our knowledge of Byzantine medicine is, however, still extremely scanty), they achieved in certain respects a rather high state of practical application. Thus, we know that in the twelfth century the capital city Constantinople had two well organized hospitals staffed by medical specialists (including women doctors), with special wards for various types of diseases and systematic methods of treatment. This situation of course was not typical of the entire Empire, nor of all classes. Yet it is to be contrasted sharply with conditions in the West where, in the early period in general, apart from Salerno, gross superstition was rife.

Arabic, and to a lesser extent, Byzantine medical practice was accordingly far advanced over the contemporary western. Eastern physicians had learned to recognize the decay of tissues and in the case of dentistry to treat and fill decayed teeth and do extractions. With the transmission to western Europe in the twelfth and thirteenth centuries of much ancient medical learning from the Arabs of Spain, Sicily, and North Africa, and to some extent also from the medieval Greeks, the body of western medical knowledge began to increase. It was the ancient medical and anatomical texts of Hippocrates and Galen, gradually in more complete form, both in Arabic and Greek versions, that in the fourteenth century were used in the rising medical schools of the West —at Bologna, Padua, Paris and Montpellier. Thus the most influential anatomical textbook in the fourteenth century in the West—indeed it was to remain the most popular until Vesalius in the sixteenth century—was the *Anatomia* of Mondino di Luzzi, a work based largely on Galen, the Byzantine Theophilus, and Arabic authorities.

Much used in the examination of the pulse and the urine, the commonest method of diagnosis in the medieval period, was the treatise of the above-mentioned Theophilus of seventh century Byzantium. But the principal medical work of the Byzantine era was that of the seventh century Paul of Aegina. Emphasizing the practical aspects of medicine, its surgical section was celebrated for its excellence and had considerable influence on the medical science of the West as well as of the Arabs. Another Byzantine treatise, that of the thirteenth century Nicholas Myrepsos, remained the principal pharmaceutical code of the Parisian medical faculty until 1651, while the Byzantine tract of Demetrios Pepagomenos (thirteenth century) on gout was translated and published in Latin by the great post-Byzantine humanist Marcus Musurus, in Venice in 1517.

## INDUSTRY

Before the Latin conquest of Constantinople in 1204 the Byzantines were noted for their industrial techniques—techniques carried over in some cases from the ancient Greco-Roman world, but in others involving processes perfected in Byzantium. Silk manufacture, especially the making of magnificent gold-embroidered brocades and the designing of patterns on rich materials, though partly inspired from the ancient Near East, became a specialty of the medieval Greeks. Remarkable for their longevity are some of the Byzantine textiles still remaining, such as those found in the tomb of Charlemagne dating from the ninth century. The products of Byzantine silk manufacture were so prized by the West that when, early in the twelfth century, the Norman King Roger II attacked Byzantine Greece, he took special care to transport to Palermo the most skilled Theban and Peloponnesian silk workers. The historian of science George Sarton believes that this marked the beginnings of silk production in the West. But it is perhaps more likely that the production of the finer western silk may be dated from this time.

We have already referred to the Byzantine reputation for the casting of bronze doors—examples of which are still to be found in the cathedral of Pisa, the church of St. Paul-outside-the-walls in Rome, at the great monastery of Monte-Cassino, the cathedral of Amalfi and elsewhere. Byzantium until 1204 was also Europe's chief center for the making of glass. After that date the industry began to revive in the West, especially in Venice. There can be little doubt but that the many centuries of Venetian trade with the East and particularly her conquest of the Greek capital in 1204 had a good deal to do with her newly found technological supremacy for which she soon became famous. Interestingly enough, one of the best accounts we have of medieval glass-making, a treatise of the German priest Theophilus, dating from the early twelfth century, prominently mentions the Byzantine methods of manufacturing certain types of glassware such as plate glass and drinking vessels decorated with gold leaf.

## ADMINISTRATION, POLITICAL THEORY, LAW AND DIPLOMACY

In contrast to the medieval West, where a relatively loose, atomized feudal system obtained, Byzantium, for most of the period, had a highly centralized state organization with a well-developed civil service —a type of government in which virtually all activities were at the command of the emperor. These two elements, the autocracy and the civil service dependent upon it, were basic factors in providing Byzantium with the strength to withstand almost continual foreign invasions and domestic crises.

The autocratic tradition of Byzantium served as an inspiration for the development of a number of medieval western governments. Thus, for example, part of the basis for the Norman ideas of kingship in Sicily, as well as some of the Norman court ceremonial (including the king's own costume), seem to have been borrowed directly from Byzantine usage and from the absolutist concept of the Basileus as vicegerent of God, the ruler of both state and church in the world. (The portrait of Roger II in the Martorana of Palermo is a good example.) This Byzantine concept was opposed to both the earlier western theory of pope and emperor as wielders of the two swords, and the later papal claims to universal spiritual and temporal sovereignty. We know that Roger II of Sicily, when seeking to bolster his claim to control of the Sicilian church *vis-à-vis* the papacy, instructed a Greek monk of his kingdom, Nilos Doxopatres, to draw up a treatise expounding the old Byzantine theory of the pentarchy, that is of the equality of all five patriarchs, including the pope, in the governance of the Christian church (though the pope was conceded a primacy of honor). It is probable that the autocratic Byzantine type of government also inspired some of the German Hohenstaufen ideas of royal power and, according to Diehl, helped to shape the subsequent European concept of the divine right of kings.

If the autocracy played a basic role in maintaining the strength of the Byzantine state, it was law which bound together Byzantine society. And it is the Roman law, codified by the Byzantine Emperor

Justinian and transmitted via Italy to the West which is perhaps Byzantium's chief practical legacy to the modern world. For while the West was steeped in Germanic, barbaric law with its primitive ordeals and trials by battle, the Greek East was enjoying the benefits of Roman law, which had been leavened by the ideals of Stoicism and other philosophies on the basis of the long experience of the East. It was these concepts of Romano-Byzantine jurisprudence even more than the practical legal enactments themselves that have had the greatest effect on modern western law.

Contrary to common belief, the evolution of Byzantine law did not cease with the reign of Justinian. Because of the great social changes which came about in the Empire the code had to be modified and even expanded by the Macedonian dynasty in the tenth century, at which time all laws were systematically reshaped in Greek. It was the Macedonian code, even more than that of Justinian, which occupied the central position in Byzantine jurisprudence of the tenth century and afterwards.

Previously, in the eighth and ninth centuries, three other codes had been drawn up by the Isaurian dynasty, the rural code or farmers' law, the military code for soldiers, and an 'admiralty law' based on the old Rhodian sea law. Of the three the latter had a considerable impact on the West. Originally developed in antiquity by the mariners and merchants of the Greek island of Rhodes, the Rhodian sea law had been adopted by the Hellenistic cities and then by Rome as a model of maritime law. In the Byzantine East where it became the official or semi-official sailor's code and 'admiralty law', it offered practical, time-tested regulations for the handling of collision cases between ships and for such 'proto-capitalist' problems as the relation of the owner of a ship to the cargo owner in the event the cargo was lost. As time went on, provisions of the code seem to have been transmitted, by custom, to the early Italian maritime cities, which, as we have seen, were in close relation with Constantinople. One of the Italian sea codes, possibly the first, that of Amalfi (enacted ca. 1000 A.D.) seems to have been based upon it. As Byzantine trade declined, however, from the twelfth century onward and Italy secured the primacy in sea power, the Rhodian sea law *per se* fell more and more into disuse. But some of its more important concepts continued to survive and inspired the development of certain of the commercial and maritime practices of Genoa, Pisa, Venice, and even of the famous 'Consolato del Mare', the early Catalan legal code (written down ca. 1300) of more distant Barcelona.

Regarding navigation it appears that as the great western commercial cities of the Mediterranean began to develop their trade, they borrowed a number of nautical and commercial terms from the Greek East. For example the Byzantine (but originally Latin) term *scala* (landing place for merchandise) was used in the Italian documents from the eleventh century onward. The word *gripos* (a Byzantine type of net or fishing boat) also came into common usage in parts of the Mediterranean, especially Italy, as did the Byzantine *palamarion* (a rope or cable), the latter found in Genoese, Venetian, as well as Catalan documents of the thirteenth century and later. Perhaps an even more interesting derivation is that of the old Viking term *dreki*, referring to the larger type of Viking ship, the prow of which was decorated with the head of a dragon or other animal, and which one scholar believes may have been borrowed ultimately from the Byzantine term *drakon* (dragon). (How this term actually came to the North is another question.) It should be pointed out, however, that a recent survey of nautical and maritime terms in use in the Mediterranean would seem to indicate that, especially from the thirteenth century onward, more terms of this type were borrowed by the Byzantines from western usage than vice versa. Examples are the Venetian *cassela*, chest; *marangon*, ship's carpenter; *galion*, warship (which is first mentioned in a Pisan twelfth century document); and the blended Venetian term *arma*, meaning rigging of a ship, which fused with the older Latinism *arma*.

An obvious but important area of cultural transmission, hitherto hardly investigated, is the possible influence of Byzantine statecraft, more precisely diplomatic practice, on the medieval West. Though Byzantine diplomatic methods were originally derived, at least in part, from Rome and the Hellenistic east, Byzantium developed these to a degree of finesse otherwise unknown in the medieval period. Some Byzantine treatises dealing in whole or in part with diplomatic policy and statecraft were composed (Emperor Constantine VII's *On the Administration of the Empire* is perhaps most significant for example), which provided detailed instructions based on theory and experience as to the most expedient ways to handle difficult political situations. Venice, whose relations with Byzantium were always closer than those of other western powers, seems to have profited most from the Byzantine example. Indeed, a comparison of Venetian and Byzantine diplomatic practice in the late medieval and Renaissance period—for instance, the transmission by ambassadors of periodic reports to the home government (*relazioni*) or the organization of an intelligence service—would probably reveal no small degree of direct or indirect Byzantine influence. It may be recalled that Venice, from the eleventh and twelfth centuries, had a large colony in the very heart of Constantinople and that early a substantial number of Greeks had settled in Venice.

In view of what has been discussed in this section, we may make an important but little realized assumption: that Byzantium, with its perfected administrative system, offered to the feudal western world, especially in the great city of Constantinople, something lost to the West since antiquity—a living example of a remarkably developed and organized society under the rule of public authority.


## GUILDS

Up to perhaps the twelfth century Constantinople was Europe's chief center of commercial activity. And, as such, its gold coin, termed bezant by the West, was for long accepted as the standard of exchange throughout Europe. Given these economic connections between East and West—interrupted to be sure but never wholly destroyed by the Arabic invasions—it is of no little interest that the western guild system closely resembles, in certain respects, the system which for long obtained at Byzantium.

As we know from the tenth century Byzantine Book of the Prefect, all Greek traders and merchants of the capital (and probably of the other cities as well) were organized into corporations or guilds which were under the direct control of the eparch or prefect of Constantinople. Cattle traders, butchers, fish-mongers, bakers, spice and silk merchants, the latter of both raw and finished silk, shipwrights, even notaries, money changers and goldsmiths—all had to belong to the guild organization. As in the later western system regulations were carefully prescribed: no man could belong to two guilds, the hours of wages and labor were carefully regulated, attempts to forestall or corner the market were forbidden, along with disclosure of the secrets of manufacture.

An important distinction is the fact that, unlike the West where the authority of the state had virtually disappeared, the Byzantine system was not primarily intended to serve the interest of the producers and merchants, but mainly to further governmental control of economic life in the interest of the state. What the actual degree of Byzantine influence may have been on the western guilds has not yet been determined. And of course one cannot overlook the fact that guilds, although with a different purpose, existed already in the late Roman world, the Byzantine being an extension of the Roman. More important perhaps is the fact that similar circumstances might well have evoked similar kinds of responses even in areas distant from one another. Yet until a careful and detailed comparison of the medieval guilds of East and West is made, it is hard to believe that the long familiarity of the Italian maritime republics with Byzantine economic life—many Italian cities possessed commercial colonies in Constantinople itself—had nothing to do with the development of western guild organization and practice.

## GRACIOUS LIVING

One result of East-West contact that may not immediately come to mind is the impact of the more refined Byzantine way of life on the lower western standard of living. Byzantine cloths, especially silks and silk brocades, as well as Byzantine utensils and other objects were eagerly sought in the West, and their adoption helped to lead to what we might call a more gracious mode of living. The simpler wooden and occasional stone fortresses and residences of the western nobles were gradually replaced during the crusading period by a type of castle with round towers, a construction which permitted a better defense and deployment of forces and which possibly had been inspired by Byzantine usage. The Normans of Sicily undoubtedly learned something of what they know about masonry construction from the Byzantines. Eleanor of Aquitaine, Queen of France in the twelfth century, who is often credited with introducing more refinement into the lives of the western nobility, especially the women, acquired some of her tastes in the Arabic and Byzantine East while accompanying the French armies of the Second Crusade. Previous to this, in the tenth century when, as we have noted, the Byzantine princess Theophano married the German Emperor Otto II, and brought to what she called 'barbarian Germany' a large Greek entourage, she scandalized the German inhabitants by taking baths (then considered unhealthy by the westerners) and by wearing rich silken garments. One outspoken German nun said she had a dream in which Theophano appeared in hell for these transgressions! And only a few years later Theophano's cousin, Maria Argyra, shocked the good Peter Damiani, an ascetic Italian monk, by introducing the use of forks to the city of Venice.

The many products of exquisite Byzantine craftsmanship brought westward over the centuries—icons, ivory and jewel carvings, illuminated manuscripts, gold and silver chalices, bronze doors, intricate glassware and other luxury goods—would seem to point to a considerable amount of Byzantine influence. But it is not always easy to determine how much of western Europe was actually affected, and to what degree. Another way to show influence of this kind on a more or less permanent basis would be by citing examples of western words—language is after all the most important bearer of ideas—the origin of which has been shown by philologists to be Byzantine. The wide range of terms adduced below will serve to suggest some of the variety of fields in which the East may have influenced the West.

For example, we have from Venice the term gondola (a Venetian boat) which comes from the Byzantine word *kontoura*, a small boat, and which derived originally from the Greek *kontouros*, meaning 'short-tailed'. From the area of Ravenna comes the Italian *anguria*, cucumber, which derives from the Byzantine *angurion*. In the field of administration, the English word cadaster (register of real estate) is from the Byzantine *katastihon*. In music the French and English *timbre* is from the Byzantine *tympanon* (tambourine), itself from the ancient Greek *tympanon*, a kettle-drum. The Spanish *botica* (pharmacy) comes from the Byzantine *apotheke* meaning storehouse. And, in connection with fabrics, the old French word *samit* (English samite, referring to a heavy silk fabric) comes from the Byzantine *examitos*, 'six threaded'. With respect to furniture the French and English word *tapis* (carpet), Catalonian, *tapit*, is from the Byzantine *tapeti*. In medicine, the Spanish *quemar*, meaning 'to burn', comes from the Byzantine or late Greek *kaema*, meaning a cauterization (a derivative of the ancient Greek *kaio*, to burn). One could go on with many more examples of this kind. But we may observe here only that in the age-old and intricate Mediterranean game of cultural give-and-take, Byzantine material was not always taken over directly by the receiving western culture but was sometimes mediated through a third one, for example the Arabic, just as Byzantium itself on occasion served as a mediator between other cultures.

## RELIGIOUS PIETY: MUSIC AND THE LITURGY

In recent years, with the growth of interest in the Greek church, it has become increasingly realized that that element of Byzantine civilization which was able to weld together the diverse aspects of her culture and provide its greatest distinctiveness was the Orthodox religion. The peculiar ethos of Byzantine piety was expressed most clearly in the eastern liturgy, a vivid ceremonial in which the worshipper, through personal identification with the drama transpiring in the church, was able, even more than in western liturgy, to experience a kind of mystical foretaste of the blessed life of the hereafter. The importance of the liturgy was so central to Byzantine culture in general that we shall devote some space to a discussion of it.

One, if not the chief example, of the artistic creations of Byzantine religious piety is the hymn—those of Romanos the Melodist, for example, or of John of Damascus or the Patriarch Sergius, one of whom wrote the celebrated Akathistos Hymnos. These Byzantine hymns were a combination of metrical poetic text and music, together designed to underline and emphasize the devotional, other worldly character of the liturgy. Since we are as yet not certain exactly how the music of these hymns sounded (much more work remains to be done in this area) we can perhaps best compare their poetry to such thirteenth century western hymn texts as the Dies Irae or to Jacopone da Todi's Stabat Mater—masterpieces which are at least equalled in expressiveness by the Byzantine hymns. (Many scholars acknowledge, incidentally, that the western mass as a whole was probably not nearly so moving as the Byzantine, and it was not until as late as the end of the fifteenth or beginning of the sixteenth century, with the composition of the highly polyphonic liturgical music of the great Palestrina that it may be considered to surpass the Byzantine liturgy.)

For a long time musicologists have been intrigued by certain similarities to be found in Greek and Latin church music, and particularly by the affinity between Byzantine chant and the western Gregorian, as well as by the fact that certain passages of the Catholic liturgy contain isolated Greek words or phrases. One obvious explanation for such similarities is of course the common Syrian-Hebrew background of both the Christian East and West. But significant too are the subsequent influences that flowed westward from Byzantium. We have already mentioned . . . the existence of Byzantine colonies in many areas of western Europe, especially with respect to the sixth and seventh century Greco-Syrian merchants in southern Gaul. More important, culturally, were the Byzantine monks who brought their ritual with them and who continued, in such places as the Greek monastery of Grottaferrata near Rome, to write original Greek hymns until past the eleventh century. We know that the famous fourth century Gallic monk St. Martin of Tours was in contact with and deeply influenced by the great champion of Nicene orthodoxy, St. Athanasius, and the monastic tradition of the East. In Rome itself, as we have seen, during the first three centuries Greek was the language of the Roman mass and it does not seem at once to have been supplanted by Latin. Still today in the Good Friday service of the Roman Church, according to the noted scholar E. Wellesz, one may hear sung the alternating chant, first of the Greek words 'Hagios athanatos eleison hemas', then of the Latin equivalent, 'Sanctus immortalis, miserere nobis'. Wellesz cites also the interpolation of the Greek trisagion ('Holy, holy, holy') in the western service, which we know came to the West shortly before 529 by way of Burgundy, the rulers of which were then in close rapport with the Byzantine court.

Another consideration of importance is the fact, previously mentioned, that virtually all the popes of the late seventh and eighth centuries were Greeks or Syrians. Thus the western melody of 'Ave [Maria] gratia plena' ('Hail Mary full of grace') has been shown to be connected directly with the Greek Pope Sergius of the seventh century and was originally sung to the Greek text 'chaire keharitomene'. Still another but curious example is the Latin hymn, 'Ave sponsa incorrupta' of Chester (England) which includes a terribly garbled Greek line 'Karikaristo menitra toche partine', the original words of which had come from the Byzantine troparion, 'chaire keharitomene theotoke parthene'. Not all accretions of Greek phrases in Latin service books are of course to be attributed to remnants of a common ecclesiastical heritage. In certain cases, they might rather be ascribed to the influence of Charlemagne and his learned circle (who, according to one scholar, might even have received Byzantine influences in church music via the Muslims of southern Spain, with whom Charlemagne's court had frequent contacts.) Charlemagne, we are told, after hearing members of a Greek embassy to his court chanting their religious hymns, became so attracted that he ordered the Byzantine hymns to be translated into Latin.

Claims for extensive western borrowings from Byzantine religious music are still a matter of some dispute. It is not yet entirely clear, for example, what influence the Byzantine musical system of *echoi* (a grouping of tones in a kind of scale and constituting a melody type) may have had on the western modal system. On the other hand, there is a reasonable degree of agreement that Pope Gregory the Great, whether or not he should be credited with the reform of the western ecclesiastical chant, was deeply influenced by the eastern hymnody. And this despite the fact that as long-time papal apocrisiarius (ambassador) in Constantinople he had refused to learn Greek on the grounds that the Byzantine clergy were too worldly! But it seems significant that he set about reorganizing his Schola Cantorum, a training school for instruction in the chant, immediately after his return from Byzantium, where we know that he was a frequent observer of the practice of the Byzantine chant at the cathedral of St. Sophia.

Another vestige of Byzantine music that still remains today had to do with the acclamations, or *polychronia*, which were addressed to a newly enthroned emperor. It is worthy of note that at the coronation of Charlemagne in St. Peter's on Christmas day of the year 800, the populace assembled in the Basilica broke forth, at the appropriate moment, into a form of Byzantine *polychronion*—a practice which is today still preserved in the Orthodox salutation to a newly appointed bishop. Though we evidently cannot credit the medieval Greeks with the invention of the organ, Constantinople was the early medieval center for organ building: we know that in 757 Pepin, King of the Franks, requested and received an organ from the Byzantine Emperor.

Much more evidence of western indebtedness to eastern religious music—and quite possibly a few of the reverse as well—will probably be found by researchers. One hindrance to such a study has been the undue emphasis placed on the schism between the two churches—a fact which has led some too readily to believe that little cultural interaction was possible, at least after 1054, the date commonly taken as marking the complete rupture between the Greek and Latin churches. But this interpretation is probably much exaggerated, because for centuries the two great bodies of Christians had looked upon one another as part of one undivided Christian church. Indeed, the schism did not become truly definitive, it would seem, until as late as 1204, when the Latins captured Constantinople and forced the Greek population to accept Roman Catholicism. On the lower levels in fact the ordinary man of East and West was hardly ever aware of any religious rupture until long after 1054 and probably not until well into the twelfth century.

Another subject of significance, the study of which is only now developing, is the influence of Byzantine piety, especially of the Greek 'Basilian' monks, on western monastic life. When during the ninth, tenth and early eleventh centuries many Byzantine monks fled the

Arabic invasions of Sicily and southern Italy to move further north, they brought with them the traditional ideals and practices of Byzantine monasticism, especially of the ascetic type. Because of the piety of these monks they were, in this period, almost always well received, and we find examples of Byzantine-Latin symbiosis in certain western monasteries such as at Monte Cassino, where in the late tenth century the famous Greek monk St. Nilus lived with Latin monks and wrote hymns to St. Benedict. (At this time Monte Cassino even had a Greek abbot.) In Rome, at Sts. Boniface and Alexius, Basilian and Benedictine monks lived together, each under its own rule, all under a Greek abbot. The Byzantine traits that most attracted and influenced the West were the high degree of Byzantine spirituality, and the monks' sanctity of life (including their manner of prayer), in a period of general western corruption and ecclesiastical degradation. The severe Basilian ideal of manual labor—at this time western monks usually employed serfs to do their work—and the patristic erudition of some of the Greek monks also seem to have inspired their western counterparts. It is interesting that the monastic houses of the West most connected with the Cluniac reform movement—St. Vannes at Verdun, Cluny under Hugh, and others, had the closest relations with the Greek monks. It is therefore very possible that Byzantine influence may have played a certain role in the western reform movement of the period. This, incidentally, is a consideration which has hitherto been generally overlooked.

Finally, in connection with the development of popular piety in particular, one might profitably investigate the influence of Byzantine ideas on western attitudes regarding veneration of the Virgin— Mariology, that is. After all, when Mariology in the West was still in a rather undeveloped phase, the cult of the Virgin, who was looked upon as the protectress of Constantinople, was second to none in the East. In the late eleventh century a new and influential form of popular literature emerged in the West, the so-called Stories of *Miracles of the Virgin.* These, more imaginative than previous legends of this type, were concerned with the miraculous intervention of the Virgin in the lives of her devotees and, now like the more extravagant stories of the East, came to emphasize her compassion for individuals, not so much her interest in churches or religious corporations as such. Some of the stories of course were taken over from ancient Latin tradition, but it seems certain that a not inconsiderable number now came from the Byzantine East. Thus the famous reformer Peter Damiani, one of the earliest collectors of such stories, tells us that one of his chief sources of information was the Cardinal-priest Stephen, a Burgundian who had served as papal legate to Constantinople in the mid-eleventh century.

No less important than the newly developing emphasis on veneration of the Virgin was the influence of the many sacred relics of the early Christian church which had begun to flow westwards, already before the twelfth century and especially after the mass despoiling of the Greek churches by the Latins in 1204. This wealth of relics in certain ways helped to bring about an alteration even in the appearance of western churches, and thus, together with the increased emphasis on Mariology, made a deep impression on the developing western forms of public and private devotion in this period.

## ART

Unlike the Byzantine service to literature which in many respects may appear to have been mainly a holding operation from antiquity, the Byzantine contribution to art was essentially original and attained a degree of expressiveness that has rarely been equalled. Byzantine art, in particular its painting, has been much in vogue recently, especially because of its relatively abstract character as well as richness of color. We shall have to limit our remarks here to the more important aspects of Byzantine art, concentrating especially on Italy where its influence was greatest.

It is no exaggeration to say that Italy, from the sixth to the thirteenth century, was an artistic province of Byzantium. In its many monuments of painting and mosaics can be seen the distinctive traits of Byzantine art—its power, mysticism, color and line—qualities which sought to represent to the viewer something more than the appearance of nature, rather to evoke emotions expressing the reality of the other world.

We may begin with the Byzantine mosaics at Ravenna, especially the portraits of the Emperor Justinian, his consort Theodora, and the imperial court. The refulgent cubes (tessera) of colored glass and stone, set at various angles, reflect the light in such a way as to suggest the celestical richness of the court of God's vicar on earth. In these mosaics and also the wall paintings of the Ravenna churches, in some of those of Rome throughout the various medieval centuries (of the artist Cavallini for instance), and in the Norman cathedral of Monreale in Sicily with the imposing figure of the Byzantine Pantocrator in the apse, the tradition of the East is clearly apparent. Further north, in

Venice, which was almost a Byzantine city as Diehl puts it (or 'another Byzantium' as Bessarion declared in the fifteenth century), the mosaics of St. Mark's cathedral—the building itself almost an exact replica of the church of the Holy Apostles in Constantinople—also belong to the artistic sphere of Byzantium. Modeled evidently after St. Mark's is the dome structure of the church of Saint-Front in Perigeux, France, while still further to the north, in Charlemagne's capital of Aachen, Germany, Charlemagne's palace chapel was modeled after San Vitale in Ravenna, itself an imitation of the church of Saints Sergius and Bacchus in Constantinople. Also to be found at Aachen are bronze doors and other specimens of Byzantine or Byzantine-inspired workmanship.

While looking with admiration at the great monuments of Byzantine art, the medieval westerner prized even more the smaller but precious works of the Byzantine craftsmen. Some ivory carvings sent as gifts to western princes or prelates still remain, and the French monastery of St. Denis possessed textiles ornamented with figures of eastern type. Along with their creations the Byzantine craftsmen themselves not infrequently moved to the West and they, probably even more than the products of their art, seem to have been responsible for suggesting new ideas and methods to local western artists. Thus in the seventh century when the Greek monk and later Archbishop of Canterbury Theodore of Tarsus came to Britain, his entourage may have included easterners expert in the technique of sculpture. Similarly, the painted figures of the Evangelists in the Lindisfarne gospels were modeled basically on Byzantine or Italo-Byzantine originals and we know of the Byzantine style in Northumbria and Mercia, and in the tenth and eleventh centuries in Wessex. At Monte Cassino in southern Italy, in the eleventh century, under the aegis of the Abbot Desiderius, Byzantine art objects—bronze doors among them—were purchased in Constantinople and sent to adorn the great abbey. And later, during the twelfth century, the interior of the great French monastery church of Cluny was decorated by frescoes in so Byzantine a style that they may even have been done by a native Greek.

We must touch, lastly, on the difficult problem of Byzantine influence on the art of the Italian Renaissance. A few scholars believe that even the beginnings of realism in western painting, usually connected with the name of the Italian Giotto (as the Italian sources put it Giotto freed himself from 'la maniera greca', meaning the Byzantine style), should rather be attributed to the inspiration of Byzantine art. Whether this be true or whether it was, as seems more likely, the result of a parallel though independent development of Italian and Byzantine art reverting back in each case to ancient Hellenistic models, there is no doubt that in the late thirteenth and fourteenth centuries a good deal of Byzantine painting was becoming more interested in showing emotion, more personal and individualized—in short more realistic and humanized. We may cite as evidence of these qualities the Byzantine masterpieces at the monastery of the Chora (Kariye Camii) in Constantinople, in the churches of Milesevo, Sopocani, and Gracanica in Yugoslavia, to a lesser extent in the churches of Mistra (near Sparta), and the very recently uncovered paintings at St. Nicholas Orfanos and in other churches of Thessalonika. Certain similar characteristics are to be found in Italy in the works of the Florentine artist Cimabue, the Sienese Duccio, and in certain other Italian Trecento painters.

In the view of the critics Charles Diehl and especially the more recent authority André Grabar, it was Italian painting, through the Byzantine influence exerted on Duccio and Giotto, that derived the greater benefit from the renewed contact of the Byzantines with paintings in the Hellenistic spirit. For despite their superb creations the Byzantine artists inspired by the realistic aesthetic of the Hellenistic models remained in the minority. And during the course of the fourteenth century, when their Italian contemporaries were advancing to the freer art forms which were to become characteristic of the Italian Renaissance, Byzantine painting in general reverted to the more conventional Byzantine forms. Nevertheless, despite this reversion to the older, more traditional methods (a phenomenon perhaps attributable, according to Grabar, to Byzantine mistrust of anything connected with the Latins), some paintings were produced during this period which equal or surpass in brilliance and decorativeness the best works of the earlier Byzantine epochs. What is particularly striking is that scenes in these fourteenth century paintings display almost a new type of experimental boldness which, in the elongated, attenuated figures and the extraordinary coloring used, seems in certain respects to anticipate the style of El Greco.

These two developments in Byzantine painting, then, both a part of the remarkable Palaeologan Renaissance of the thirteenth to the fifteenth centuries (remarkable because a Renaissance in both art and letters could occur while the Empire itself was collapsing on every side), have been termed by art historians the Macedonian and Cretan schools of painting. Macedonian refers in general to the shorter-lived,

more realistic art of the end of the thirteenth and first decades of the
fourteenth century radiating primarily from the center Thessalonika.
The so-called Cretan refers to the reversion to (or in some cases continuation of) the more traditional modes of painting, found especially
at Mt. Athos or on Crete itself, and extending through the sixteenth
century and even later. Because of a growing awareness today of the
complexity of Byzantine painting in this period, however, such a distinction between the two schools seems too rigid and is indeed often
difficult to make clear in the paintings that have survived. It may therefore be better, as some scholars are now doing, to scrap the use of
these particular terms which were originally coined a half century ago
by the French art historian Millet.

Sometimes overlooked even by art historians is the presence of
Greek painters in Italy after the fall of Constantinople in 1453—men
who continued to produce works in the more or less traditional Byzantine manner until as late as the seventeenth century. Their paintings,
often referred to as belonging to the Cretan school, are admittedly not
of primary importance. But they are frequently of quality, especially
those produced by the group of painters living in the Greek community
of Venice. . . .

It is the opinion of modern Greek art historians as well as certain
western critics that the celebrated El Greco, born Domenikos Theo-
tokopoulos on the Venetian-held island of Crete some four or five
decades after the fall of Constantinople, may be termed, from certain
viewpoints, one of the last of the 'Byzantine' painters. El Greco studied
for four years in Venice and later adopted as his permanent residence
the Castilian city of Toledo. But despite the undeniable influence of
these two centers on the formation of his technic and style, he never
seems to have forgotten his Byzantine heritage. Indeed a remarkable
document very recently discovered seems to indicate that he lived in
Crete until the age of 25, not merely until 18 as was previously
believed. The point is that this greatest of all Greek painters may have
been more deeply influenced in his early years by the Cretan-Byzantine
style of his native island than most western scholars have been willing
to admit. In that period painters were apprenticed rather early, so that
by the age of 25 'Maestro' El Greco should already have had some ten
years experience in the Byzantine style.

Italy, then, the prime area of Byzantine artistic influence, owed
much to Byzantium: not only the models from which many Italian
artists worked, not only the bronze doors, gorgeous fabrics, enamels

and richly illuminated manuscripts which were brought to the West, but, of more underlying importance, the symbolic pattern of church decoration and even the iconographical schemes for some of the more important religious motifs. Thus, it may be said that all through the medieval period, from the sixth century probably even to the beginning of the Renaissance in the fourteenth, Byzantine art profoundly influenced that of Italy and, through Italy, many areas of western Europe.

## CONCLUSION

What may we say in conclusion about the impact of Byzantine culture on the West? How is its influence to be assessed? It must be pointed out, first, that such important facets of Western culture as parliaments, Gothic architecture, and Scholasticism, above all the *basic* institutions of feudalism, manorialism, and chivalry were essentially Germano-Latin in origin, there being little or no Byzantine influence whatever. Indeed in connection with feudalism, chivalry, and Scholasticism certain influences seem rather to have flowed from West to East. But though not a few examples may be cited of medieval Greek acculturation to individual western practices, especially among the Byzantine upper classes, the Byzantine influence on the West seems to have been far stronger than the reverse. This was partly because at least up to the twelfth or early thirteenth century western civilization in almost all aspects was markedly inferior to the eastern (in classical Greek learning of course few westerners could equal the Greeks until the High Renaissance), and also because owing to its developing antipathy to the West, the East in general—the lower classes, monks and lesser clergy in particular—strongly resisted the adoption of Latin customs.

Though it must be clear from our investigation that there was a more or less continuing influence of Byzantium on western culture from the fourth all the way to at least the end of the fifteenth century, it is no less manifest that the degree of influence varied greatly from field to field, depending not only on the pattern of contacts but on the attitudes and receptivity of the various western areas. Italy for example was more deeply influenced than more distant, rather conservative France and immeasurably more than England. Nor is it easy to ascertain how deeply the Byzantine influences we have discussed penetrated the various classes of the western social structure, though it would seem that because of greater contacts with the East and a generally more flexible attitude the upper classes and merchants were most affected.

It should not be overlooked also that our judgements as to the degree of influence must of necessity be tempered by the scarcity of the evidence remaining as well as by the status of scholarly research at the moment. It is easier to show, on the basis of the extant artistic monuments, what the eastern influence may have been in art than, say, in the development of the guild system, where we are reduced to hypothesis or deduction. Similarly we should consider, I think (as is usually not done), the evidence of such phenomena as vocabulary borrowings—borrowings which in most cases would not have taken place unless there were at least some degree of cultural transfer involved. On the other hand, the mere presence in the West of a great many Byzantine luxury items should not mislead us into assigning the same importance to these as cultural agents as we would attach to the adoption of Byzantine ideas, institutions, or techniques—considerations which in the long run were to prove of more permanent value.

With these qualifications and bearing in mind that western culture was at bottom Germano-Latin, we may then affirm our findings that Byzantium, through its amalgamation of classicism and the more original 'Byzantine' elements of its culture, above all its unique brand of Christianity which permeated every facet of medieval Greek life, was able, directly or indirectly, to influence a great many aspects of western cultural development: in certain types of art and architecture, in the sphere of industrial techniques, in law and statecraft, in navigational terms and regulations, the recovery of classical Greek literature and possibly the composition of the romance, in the development of a more refined mode of living and in some forms of religious piety and music as well as in religious thought. In these aspects of *most* of the cultural areas meaningful to medieval man there seems to have been some tangible specific evidence of Byzantine influence in one area or another of western European society. Once more, however, it should be emphasized that these influences ranged from the very minor in some spheres to the very substantial in others.

No doubt the Byzantine contributions were more passive and less creative in certain fields, for instance in literature, philosophy, and science, which had in the main been taken over from the ancient Greeks and which, especially in the case of Aristotle, were first transmitted to the West via the Arabs. Yet even in their vaunted preservation of the ancient literary masterpieces the Byzantines were able to make a few contributions of their own. For example they developed certain philological methods of scholarship—methods which if sometimes faulty, nonetheless had more impact than is usually realized on the development of Renaissance textual criticism and which therefore could not help but influence the meaning and interpretation of the ancient texts transmitted (the ancient tragedies for instance). Even in the domain of science, despite their almost worshipful devotion to ecclesiastical tradition as well as to the authority of the ancient Greek writers, a few Byzantines seem to have broken out of these restraints and at least to have anticipated certain later western scientific developments. Moreover, as we have observed, in several other areas there can be no doubt that the Byzantines were able to make truly *original* contributions, specifically in art and architecture, in forms of religious piety and ecclesiastical literature, and, perhaps not least, in providing to the West something often overlooked by historians—a living example of a state with a highly centralized administration and tradition of statecraft under the rule of public law. In view of these considerations it is obvious that Byzantine civilization was far from being the mere 'fossilization of antiquity' that western historians were wont to term it not many years ago.

In sum, then, it was the rich content, the diverse elements *both ancient and medieval*, of Byzantium's unique cultural synthesis, that enabled it to attract the interest of the westerners and, little by little and despite the frequent reluctance or outright hostility of the Latins, to provide them with inspiration and guidance. And so in 1453 when Constantinople finally succumbed to the Turks, not only had Byzantium handed over its previous legacy of ancient Greek culture to the West—now prepared in part by the East itself to receive it—but, no less important, the West had assimilated a good deal of the products of Byzantium's own creativity. As a consequence of what might be called this long-term process of cultural infiltration, Byzantium played a much more pervasive role than is generally realized in molding the civilization of the medieval and hence, indirectly, of the modern, western world.

## Suggestions for Further Reading

BAYNES, N. H., and H. MOSS, eds., *Byzantium.* London: Oxford University Press, 1948.
DEMUS, OTTO, *Byzantine Art and the West.* New York: New York University Press, 1969.

DIEHL, CHARLES, *Byzantium: Greatness and Decline.* New Brunswick, N.J.: Rutgers University Press, 1957.

GRABAR, A. *Byzantine Painting.* Geneva: Skira, 1953.

HUSSEY, J. M., *The Byzantine World.* London: Hutchinson, 1957; New York: Harper and Row, 1961.

HUSSEY, J. M., *Church and Learning in the Byzantine Empire.* New York: Oxford University Press, 1937.

LINDSAY, J., *Byzantium into Europe.* New York: Humanities Press, 1951.

MOSS, H., *The Birth of the Middle Ages.* London: Oxford University Press, 1961.

OSTROGORSKY, G., *History of the Byzantine State.* Oxford: Basil Blackwell, 1956.

RUNCIMAN, STEVEN, *Byzantine Civilization.* London: Macmillan, 1933.

RUNCIMAN, STEVEN, *The Last Byzantine Renaissance.* New York: Cambridge University Press, 1970.

VASILIEV, A., *History of the Byzantine Empire,* 2d ed. Madison, Wisconsin: University of Wisconsin Press, 1964.

VRYONIS, S., *Byzantium and Europe.* New York: Harcourt Brace Jovanovich, Inc., 1967.

# FRIEDRICH HEER

# *Church and State*

◄§§► The struggle between the German Emperor Henry
IV and Pope Gregory VII in the 1070's and 80's has long
been regarded as one of the most dramatic and significant
confrontations in the medieval world. Some German historians of medieval political and social ideas, in particular
Fritz Kern and Gerd Tellenbach, have in fact regarded the
conflict over the ideology of the Gregorian reform as the
central, determining event in the whole pattern of medieval
history. For them, this conflict represented a contest to the
death between opposed views of world order. In the end
neither royal nor papal ideology prevailed, but the ideas
and feelings engendered by the conflict shaped the subsequent course of medieval civilization.

How was it that the Church became the central institution in European life? For the answer to this difficult question we must go back to the barbarian Germanic invasions
of western Europe in the fifth century. The initial cata-
clysmic result was political and social disorganization and
a tremendous decline in culture and literacy from about
450 to 750 A.D. Roman ideals and institutions of government, administration, and law were either abandoned or

FROM Friedrich Heer, *The Intellectual History of Europe,*
translated by Jonathan Steinberg (New York: World Publishing Co., 1966), pp. 70–78; and Friedrich Heer, *The Medieval
World,* translated by Janet Sondheimer (London: Weidenfeld
& Nicolson and New York: Praeger Publishers, 1962), pp. 270–
281.

vulgarized almost out of existence. The Latin Church remained the only meliorative institution in society, the possessor of all literacy, and the font of all ethics and ideals of progress and public order. Between 750 and 950 the Benedictine monks and the papacy succeeded in convincing certain intelligent and ambitious Germanic kings, like the Frankish king Charlemagne and the Anglo-Saxon ruler Alfred, to accept the Church's ideals and to try to turn the tide of barbarism and anarchy. The classical literary and ethical heritage was substantially recovered, the papacy began to exercise some effective leadership over the whole Latin Church, and theocratic kings like Charlemagne, with the invaluable assistance of clerical chief ministers, tried to establish peace and a degree of centralized control. The Carolingian rulers of the ninth century engaged in a bold attempt to achieve the political unity of Europe. This great experiment failed and the empire disintegrated about 900 because the forces of localism, reflected in feudal and manorial institutions, were too strong; because the Carolingian dynasty failed to produce a great personality after Charlemagne; and because the Scandinavian and Hungarian invasions of the late ninth and early tenth centuries produced new confusion and disorder. But the dominant forms of government, economy, social organization, ecclesiastical leadership, and art and literature characteristic of the Carolingian empire survived its breakup and were perpetuated and intensified in the Romanesque world of the late tenth and early eleventh centuries.

The German emperors of the Ottonian-Salian line during the late tenth and eleventh centuries perpetuated and accentuated the Carolingian ideology of Christian monarchy. It was the vehement espousal of this ideology by Henry III—the father and immediate predecessor on the throne of Henry IV—which combined with a strong personality, gave him the inspiration to become the greatest king of the mid-eleventh century. The all-knowing and omnipotent God, Henry III believed, had designated the emperor to be his vice-regent on earth and to image the heavenly peace and order. What of the pope? Did not he claim the same prerogatives? Occupants of the See of

Peter had made such claims repeatedly in centuries past and
had secured wide consent to their claim to be the vicar of
Christ on earth. Nor would Henry III or any other leader
of European society in the mid-eleventh century gainsay
such claims. But since the early tenth century the papal
throne had been the prize fought over by factions of
gangster Roman nobility, with the result that the pope's
effective leadership in the Church was nonexistent in the
year 1050, and the bishop of Rome's vicarage of Christ
had become a mere shibboleth having little or no meaning
in practice. The great bishops and abbots of Germany—
and also of England and France—thus ignored the pope
and turned for leadership to the theocratic kings of northern Europe. As the greatest of these by far, the Emperor
Henry III could regard himself as God's chief representative on earth. The bishop of Rome, it was conceded by
Henry and his ecclesiastical supporters, had special authority in the realm of theology, but it was the emperor
who was the leader of the Christian people and the effective
authority in setting right the order of the Church. Therefore Henry appointed at will the great ecclesiastics of his
empire, investing them with the symbols of their office, and
held it both his right and duty to correct the scandalous
situation in Rome. So Henry summoned and presided at
a Church synod at which the Italian pope was deposed
as morally unworthy, and instead the emperor designated
worthy German churchmen as bishops of Rome. In 1048
Henry appointed one of his own kinsmen as pope, and this
learned and devout German ecclesiastic, who took the title
of Leo IX, began a far-reaching reform of papal government. All this, Henry believed—and the churchmen who
gathered at his court confirmed his opinion—was only in
fulfillment of the power, the glory, and the responsibility
bestowed upon him as the Lord's anointed.

An eleventh-century theocratic king, like Henry III—
and an important duke or count as well—was constantly
surrounded by churchmen who were his advisers, friends,
and civil servants. All the literate work of eleventh-century
government was in the hands of the king's clerical secretaries, who were frequently rewarded for their services

by eventual appointment to bishoprics and abbacies. The more outstanding of the great bishops and abbots spent several months a year at the royal court advising the king on matters of state as well as on the Church. In the eleventh century there was no line of demarcation between the world and the Church. The anointed king was a consecrated churchman; the leading churchmen were indispensable royal officials and the king's chief ministers.

These political and social institutions and values formed the background to the crucial investiture controversy. And out of the investiture controversy came the doctrines and attitudes that shaped the relations between church and state in the high Middle Ages. This theme, so central to medieval civilization, has been treated by many scholars, but perhaps never as succinctly and incisively, with such a subtle weaving of the intellectual and social aspects of the problem, as in the following study by Friedrich Heer, Professor of the History of Ideas at the University of Vienna. Heer draws upon the great traditions of German intellectual history, but advances upon earlier scholars who wrote in the 1920's and 30's by placing ecclesiastical and cultural forms in a sociological perspective. This is cultural history of the highest quality.

◦§◦

The most momentous of all the actions and movements of modern European history was the Gregorian Reform. From this reform sprang the curial Papacy and the national states, the reforming nobility, the crusading movement, humane urban civilization, scholasticism, modern European mysticism and the spiritualism, philosophical rationalism and philosophical materialism of the last few centuries. Europe's theology and philosophy of history and all the reformations and revolutions of the thirteenth to the nineteenth centuries were profoundly dependent upon the Gregorian movement.

The mixture of classical, folk-archaic and Christian elements in western Europe between the fifth and tenth centuries could only be integrated by a mighty purge. The symbiotic growth of various complex institutions had to be crushed, if Europe was to resist the mighty pressures exerted by it. The pre-Gregorian West was helpless against the seductive power of the East. While the West was struggling with the internal problems left by the collapse of Carolingian hegemony and slowly rebuilding under the Ottonine emperors, important events were taking place in the East. In 860 the Russians first successfully attacked Byzantium. In 988 Prince Vladimir married the Byzantine Princess Anna and was baptized. Russia began to imitate Byzantium and to become its heir. Under Yaroslav the Wise (1016–54), the critical years of German domination over the Papacy, Byzantine Russia achieved an early pinnacle of culture and power. The German King Conrad II [ruled 1024–1039] and his ally, Knut the Great [of Denmark and England], were lured into an alliance with Yaroslav against Poland, which was to be the Original Sin of Germany's political history. It undermined the power of Poland, western Europe's sea wall against Russia, Byzantium and Turkey.

At the same time Byzantium itself began to develop fresh and significant energies in political, intellectual and religious life. In 1045 a college of philosophy and law was founded at Constantinople. The monastic, highly intellectualized mysticism of Simeon (1025–92) suggests that the Byzantine spiritual revival was more than mere political ambition or ideological preparation for a fresh campaign in the sphere of foreign policy. By its history and traditions Byzantium was the master of cultural and matrimonial politics. It subverted the surrounding world by the travels of its monks and humanists and the marriages of its women. Byzantium was a nightmare which haunted the minds of the early Gregorian reformers.

A third threat to the West was Islam. During the eighth, ninth and tenth centuries, Spain developed a cultural power and splendour against which the West simply could not compete. Especially during the reign of Abdarrachaman III, theology, philosophy and mystical science flourished. In the following century, Avicenna, who died in 1037, and Gebirol-Avicebron continued to enrich the speculative life of Spain. By the eleventh century, its magnetic power must have been tremendously strong. The suppression of the 'Visigothic' Mozarabic liturgy in 1071 and 1090 was undoubtedly a desperate counter-attack by the Church. The omniscient, blurred and misty erudition of an Alcuin, the superficial humanism of a Lupus of Ferrières, the cosmic speculations of an Eriugena were incapable of resisting the East or Islam. The totalitarian monism of imperial state theology and of pantheistic intellectualism were too seductive.

Obviously, certain spiritual lines would have to be drawn. If an outward stand was to be made, inner freedom was necessary. Hence, there had to be a line between the spiritual and the secular. The clerical

Church must be freed from blood (the archaic society) and from soil (imperial domination of the Church). Otto III, as the Apostle-Emperor, had taken the title and hierarchical position of St Paul, who according to a widespread tradition stood higher than St Peter. *Servus Jesu Christi*, the servant of Christ, was St Paul's name for himself, and it was 'as a second St Paul' that the Emperor accepted the call to cleanse the Augean stable at Rome. In a Bull of 980, the Emperor was called the guardian of the Holy Spirit. He led and protected the Church and Christendom. He appointed popes and bishops and advanced the reformation of the monasteries. As a reincarnation of Charlemagne, Otto the Great and Otto III, the Emperor Henry III [1039–1056] exercised the same office. His proclamations, the manifestoes of his principles and policies, adopted the sacred, political formulas of Otto I's chancellery. The high point of imperial domination over the Church came at Sutri in 1046 when the Emperor, as Vicar of God and Head of the Church, deposed three popes and appointed a new one of his own. At first he was unopposed, because he was the leader of that movement of monastic reform which was fighting, in the name of the Holy Spirit, against the 'old world of sin'. As Protector of Cluny, and in alliance with the Peace of God movement in Aquitaine, Henry gave his Empire peace as a union of the law and grace. He granted freedom to the reformed monasteries by releasing them from their servitude to the bishops and nobility of the old world and taking them under the protection of his Empire and (his) Church. It was a lofty and perilous undertaking to protect the Holy Spirit and to carry out the condemnation of the old world, one which was entirely beyond the power of young Henry IV [1056–1106], who was both badly educated and advised. He was a son of the old world who simply did not understand one word of the new language. It was no wonder that he succumbed to [Pope] Gregory VII, the 'new father'.

The man who began the papal revolution was Humbert, Cardinal of Silva Candida, a son of that Burgundian land which, during the next thousand years, was to be the home of so many conservative and revolutionary spiritualists: Bernard of Clairvaux, the mystics of the fourteenth and fifteenth centuries, Poiret, Rousseau and Albert Schweitzer. Humbert exposed the Carolingian and Ottonian imperial Church as a lie. The German emperors, he argued, had violated the Church of God with their simoniac clergy, their liturgy and their bishops. Freedom for the Holy Spirit and the Church implied the liberation of the clergy from their unworthy servitude to secular lords, from whom they purchased spiritual offices (simony). The Church, now established as a Church of the clergy, was to be freed from the secular empire. The election of bishops and popes was reserved strictly to the clergy which, for the first time, constituted a clerical class in contrast to everything secular.

Every successful revolution creates a new language. New words and slogans bring into focus problems which men have ignored or regarded as unimportant. A good example of this process is what Humbert and his reforming movement did to simony. They took the professional ecclesiastical reformer's technical term for the sale of spiritual offices and made it the battle cry of a revolution which tore the whole of the Carolingian world to pieces. Simony became the name for the adulterous cohabitation of empire and Church under the German emperors, simoniac the word for most of the imperial bishops and higher clergy of the old world. Their consecrations were invalid, the sacraments they administered were without effect. Peter Damian, the great leader of the conservative revolution, the partner, friend and opponent of Humbert and Gregory VII, maintained the unconditional objectivity and validity of sacraments and consecrations administered in the correct form—as did the whole of the middle ages with him. Humbert denied it. For him the sacraments and consecrations of simonists were empty signs. In other words, he declared the grace-bearing activity of 98 percent of existing bishops and priests invalid. What Humbert wanted was a purely spiritual Church, freed by the Holy Spirit from bondage to the world, the world which had eaten its way deep into the very heart of the Church. His devastating criticism of the secularized Church and his denial of the objectivity of the sacraments were to inspire every left-wing reformer, heretic and spiritualist from the twelfth century on.

If Humbert was to establish his own orthodoxy, and impose the standard of his own true spirituality upon the Church, he had to be extremely careful with his own more radical followers. The reform movement could easily get out of hand, once it had really begun to split all the entities hitherto regarded as indivisible. What would be left after nature and supernature, God and the world, spirit and matter had been completely severed? Hence his battle with Berengar of Tours, whom he forced to recant despite the sympathy and protection of Damian and Gregory VII. Berengar, like Humbert himself, was a spiritual descendant of Augustine, the radical spiritualist Augustine, and like Humbert (at least in his doctrine of the unity of the Church) a follower of Eriugena. Again like Humbert, he battled against the popular conception of the unity of God and the world, of spirit and nature. The difference was that Humbert was concerned with the purity of the spiritual Church and Berengar was concerned with the purity of concepts. Berengar viewed with horror the vulgar notion of communion current amongst the uneducated clergy and uninstructed laity. People believed that they were really and literally devouring the flesh and blood of Christ. Berengar denied the belief vigorously and asserted that the material substance of wine and bread were absolutely distinct from the spiritual meaning of the sacrament. The one was mere matter and the other pure spirit. In effect he denied the union of God and the world as expressed in the mystery of the Sacrament. Since he denied that the wine and bread were changed into the blood and flesh of Christ, they became mere signs, a remembrance of Christ who instituted the Sacrament of the altar as his memorial.

The intimate connection between Berengar's intellectual spiritualism and the political spiritualism of Humbert is obvious. The difference between them was, however, vital. If Humbert's Church of the spirit, his Roman Church, did not truly dispense salvation, it could not survive. Berengar's thought threatened the Roman Church with destruction by attacking its most valuable attribute. The hands of its priests had to give God literally to each of its believers in the administration of the Sacrament of the altar. The capacity to offer the Sacrifice of Christ was the exclusive guarantee of the power of saving grace, without which the Church of Rome had no claim against the three ancient realms of salvation: Byzantium, the powerful German emperors, and the salvation system of archaic society. Humbert drew up a formula of belief which he forced Berengar to swear: after the consecration, the bread and wine are the true body and blood of the Lord. This final, decisive, victory of 1079 was the end of decades of struggle.

In 1054, in Hagia Sophia, Humbert had excommunicated Cearularius, the Patriarch of Constantinople. This was *the* schism, *the* break between East and West! Violent, fanatical, partisan and unfair, like all great fighters, Humbert championed the superior purity and spirituality of unleavened bread against the Greeks who clung to the leavened bread of the ancients. The split between East and West led to the transformation of Western Eucharistic doctrine from a spiritual to a Christological concept and thus to a new kind of Eucharistic devotion outside the Mass. It is important to remember how precariously the Western Eucharistic doctrine stood. The ancient kingdoms and all the archaic sacraments binding God and the world had been destroyed by the new spiritualism. The new sacraments of the Roman clerical church were not yet firmly rooted in popular consciousness. It is understandable that Humbert regarded the Byzantine doctrine of the Eucharist as *preuma* or 'pure spirit' with bitter hostility. He charged that Byzantium had been spiritually conquered by Islam. This was how Humbert saw its spiritualist monotheism, its identification of God and the emperor and its indifference to the passion of the Son of God. For all its obvious injustice, the rebuke contained a kernel of profound truth. East Rome's political monotheism was spiritually very near to Islam. Moreover, Byzantine influences had permeated the West through work of the Spanish *émigrés* in the Carolingian empire. Significantly, Christopher Dawson has called the Ottonian, Salic empire of the tenth and early eleventh centuries 'a kind of Germanic Tsardom', and Rosenstock-Huessy argues that the danger of Western Christendom's becoming a caliphate during this eleventh century was very real.

Humbert realized this. As soon as he returned from Constantinople, he began his struggle with the Carolingian empire by attacking it on the fundamental level of premise and axiom. This was the reason that this first revolution in the West was so effective and so much the model for all succeeding revolutions. Only at the end were its opponents able to set up tenuous ideologies against it. The papal revolutionaries established their own new principles and basic axioms. In his polemical works, Humbert rarely attacked the individual emperors, even the Carolingians. It was the Ottonian *system* of domination over the Church that was the essential evil. Its source was the Carolingian liturgy and sanctified social order. In 1059, at the reform Council of Sutri, Humbert officially exposed the Carolingian Church as the primary instigator of ecclesiastical sin. The councils of the Carolingian Church in 794 and 797 gave the monks licence for that lavish eating and drinking which was their ruin. The sacred culture of feasting and carousing . . . was denounced as a foul practice. With the agreement of all the Roman-Gregorian reformers, Humbert then began his onslaught on the Carolingian liturgy. Humbert and the new Romans wanted to revive golden Rome, the golden St Peter's of the fourth to eighth centuries, and to make it what Leo the Great, the victor over the Huns, had meant when he called the Roman Church 'a holy stock, an elect people, a priestly and royal citizenship (*civitas*), raised by the

See of Peter to be the head of the world'. This golden Rome, pure and holy, had been shamefully degraded, because the barbarians and the German emperors had ruined the liturgy.

Instinctively Humbert and Gregory VII recognized that it was here that the 'wicked middle age' had made its most important inroad into the heart of the Church. The Roman liturgy of the fourth to sixth centuries was an expression of the victory won by the *Kyrios Christus* over the *Kyrios Nero*. The *domus aurea*, the earthly Emperor-God's golden house, had been conquered by the Word spoken by the God-Emperor Christ. Arrayed in the might of the Roman emperor's sacred colours, Christ, the high priest, had assumed the emperor's place. But, in the eyes of the reformers, this Roman liturgy had been degraded by the barbarian emperors and made into *their* liturgy—a pretentious glorification of their own holy majesty. In their exaltation of themselves, they dared to use the royal psalms of the Old Testament. This accusation had a certain basis in fact. Charlemagne had entrusted the revision of the *Sacramentarium Gregorianum* [Gregorian chant, the traditional liturgy] to Alcuin, and further reforms were introduced into his edition of it by Paulus Diaconus, and later on by Helisachar, the chancellor of Louis the Pious. The German emperors—the Ottos and the early Salic emperors—tried to impose their imperial liturgy on Rome. Charlemagne had planned to bind his empire together with liturgical bonds: Christ the holy King, as Judge, Guardian of Peace, King of Peace in the liturgy of Advent and Christmas, was to direct the subject peoples into the way of *fides*—political-religious allegiance to Charlemagne, the King.

Byzantine glorification of the role of the king had been introduced into Europe by the Franks. Theodolf of Orleans, for example, was the author of that imperial salute, the *Gloria Laus et Honor*. The warrior spirit of the Franks found the Roman breviary deplorably lacking in good solid selections from the Books of Maccabees. The Roman liturgy was gradually perverted into a ritual homage to barbarian emperors and kings and their sacred laws of blood and race. Humbert and Gregory wanted to purify and restore it to the classical simplicity of old Rome. It was no longer to serve the Holy Emperor, but St Peter. The emperor was not the only opponent. The Humbert-Gregory front soon faced the terrible antagonism of the archaic, tribal culture of the clerical aristocracy. The imperial and princely bishops, Manasses of Rheims and the German hierarchy, bitterly opposed Gregory's attempts to liberate them from blood and soil, from principality and power. These were men for whom the pomp and splendour of the liturgy was a proclamation and celebration of their own empire—(*riche*). With bitter irony Humbert explained to them that it is not the art of singing which makes a good priest, but 'a good life'.

As representatives of the Roman Renaissance in its struggle against the barbarians, Humbert and Gregory proceeded to solidify the position of the Roman pope. In 1046 Pope Clement II proclaimed himself the successor of the early Roman Pope Clement I. For the next hundred years, till Lucius II (1144–5), each reforming pope celebrated in himself the rebirth of a pope of the primitive Roman Church, whose name he bore. It was a counter-demonstration against the reborn Charleses and Ottos, and the Hohenstaufen Fredericks. This self-proclamation was one of the most remarkable demonstrations in history. It gave the Christian rebirth its setting within the realm of grace, the clerical *civitas*, and denied the sacral-political rebirth within the archaic community and in the emperor's *sacrum imperium*. Their campaign was not confined to the names of the emperors. Gregory VII stripped the ancient community of *all* its sacred names—i.e., of all the bases of its law and its very existence—and transferred them to his own empire of grace. Otto III had sought to regard himself as a new Paul. Gregory, the Pauline Pope, was the first to put Paul side by side on his coins (as later popes did on their seals). Henceforward the Roman Church was the Church of Peter and Paul, the presence on earth of the power of God, of law and of the spirit.

Gregory was able to achieve his initial success in this colossal 'expropriation of the Expropriators', to use Marx's phrase, only because he himself was *filius fabri*, a man of the common people who was at the deepest level both bound to and estranged from the magical bonds of that people. Damian described his great friend as 'a holy Satan', a union of extreme opposites. Like the magicians of archaic society, Gregory tells us that he heard every thought in the mind of Odilo of Cluny, though travelling far behind him on the road. He was a wizard of the ancient world when he laid upon the Emperor Henry IV the ban of his bulls of excommunication and deposition: 'Victory do we take from his weapons; not only in the spirit do we bind him, but even in this natural world . . .' 'No (sacred) power in battle shall he have, nor any victory, to the end of his days.' To his contemporaries this act seemed demonic. Gregory stripped the sacred power from the old world with the old world's own weapons. When that world had recourse to its saints, Gregory confronted it with his holy patrons and

protectors, Peter and Paul, and solemnly declared that there had been
in all history very few truly holy kings and emperors. History was
a record of endless persecution of the true Church of God by the evil
sovereigns of the world. Hrotsvith, the Ottonian nun, had timidly
hinted at the idea of *mala consuetudo;* now it became the ideology of a
revolution. Five thousand years of 'evil custom', declared Anselm of
Lucca, 'cannot turn injustice into justice'. The whole outlook of archaic
society and its medieval heirs was mortally wounded by this blow. The
'good, old law' was stripped of its power to save.

Only a few years before, the 'holy emperor' had been deposing
unholy popes. Now Gregory declared that any priest, the very least
of clerics in the lowest degree of orders in the new spiritual Church
of spiritual men, possessed more saving power than all the kings and
emperors on earth. A later canonist, Hugo Hostiensis, was to establish
that the dignity of a priest was precisely 7,644½ times higher than that
of a king, for such is the proportion, by Ptolemy's reckoning, between
the sun and the moon. It was vain henceforth for the emperors to array
themselves in the sun-mantle, and—as did Frederick I and Frederick II
—to have their propagandists hail them as the true sun and the in-
vincible sun. The ban and the solemn excommunications of Gregory VII
reduced Henry IV, the 'holy Emperor by blood and by rite' to the
naked man of sin. The de-sacralization of the ancient ruling power
formed the definitive basis for Europe's great dualities. It set Church
and state, religious and secular, materialist and spiritualist against
each other. At the same time, it created a polarized field of tension in
which the liberties of modern Europe, heirs of the *libertas ecclesiae,*
found room to grow. The violence of this attack led, in turn, to the
fifty-year battle over Investiture between the pope and the Salic emperors. The Gregorian reform was, in a sense, a triumph over the
East. The remarkable document of 1075 known as the *Dictatus Papae,*
records that 'the Pope alone shall bear the imperial insignia'. 'All
princes shall kiss the Pope's foot.' 'He alone shall be spoken of by name
in the liturgical prayer of all churches.' 'He can depose Emperors.'
'None can judge him.' 'Every Pope is sanctified by the merits of St
Peter.' 'The Pope can himself, without a synod, condemn bishops.'
*Unicum nomen est papae.* 'The Pope is the one representative of God
on earth; he bears the keys of heaven and hell.'

These world-shattering propositions were directed not only against
Constantinople and Aix but against all hitherto self-sufficient saviour-

rulers of the archaic world. The secular nobility, in communion with all their comrades living and dead, had also dispensed salvation, each in his own realm, *riche* or *regnum*. If modern Europe* was to be created as a union of secular and spiritual realms (*regna*) under the patronage of the pope, the bishops had to be detached from the governmental order of the ancient folk-community and the clergy from the world of their kindred and from the ties of marriage, blood and soil. Like all revolutionaries, Gregory was not afraid of such a utopian undertaking, even if it involved centuries of protracted struggle. The behaviour of the bishops of the period after the Council of Trent indicates that as late as the seventeenth and eighteenth centuries very little progress had been made. But the foundation was laid, in principle, by the imposition of celibacy upon the clergy. The demand that the secular clergy, and not only the small band of universally admired ascetics, should lead a purely spiritual life appeared to the ancient world as unnatural, even monstrous. Gregory was forced, in order to carry it out, to burden his renovated papacy with a series of highly perilous alliances. He supported the radical, popular movement of the *Pataria* in Milan, the enemy of all 'great, rich lords' who attempted to make an adulterous union between the world and the priesthood, and adopted the revolutionary spiritualism of the later Augustine, and the no less revolutionary rationalism of the dialecticians associated with Berengar of Tours.

The consequences of Gregorian celibacy for Europe's spiritual history were far-reaching. A special realm of the spirit was detached from the world. An entirely new field of tension was created in which pioneers of the mind and of the heart were to set about constructing a new set of relationships between God and the world and between man and woman. A new kind of purely intellectual labour was made possible, out of which the pure research and pure science of a later age was to grow. At the same time a remarkable culture of the heart evolved. Not only were priests and nuns new men and women in a literal sense, but all men and women were related in a new, spiritual way. Whereas the archaic world had regarded marriage and sex entirely in terms of legal status, the post-Gregorian Church spoke of spiritual and sacramental union. Love was possible outside of marriage, and there were marriages of the spirit like those of Abélard and

* It was the reforming popes who began again to speak of Europe!

Héloïse, or Francis de Sales and Jeanne Françoise de Chantal. The
single man, who lived a life of celibacy, resisted nature and the world
and the tension generated by this resistance was inherently creative.

Gregory and his successors won the support of only one genuine
ally, the young nobility. As a result, this nobility was the first to reap
for itself the fruits of the quarrel. It rejected its old fathers for its new
father, the pope, and by handing over to him its (reformed) monasteries, it went on to receive an education. For the first time, a thoroughly reformed, coherent class took shape, which expressed its ripen-
ing self-consciousness in the new religious orders: Cistercians (1098),
Premonstratensians (1120), Carthusians and Carmelites. In the secular
world the courtly culture of the Christian knight of the twelfth and
thirteenth centuries began to emerge. The knight received the consecration and anointing which were formerly reserved for king and emperor. He was the new king and emperor, who built himself a kingdom
of grace in monastery and court (Gottfried of Strasbourg's *minne-
grotte*). From 1096 on, he waged the new wars, the crusades, against
Islam in the East and in Spain, against Byzantium, against the Albigensian heretics, against primitive peasant leagues (the Stedingers) and
pagans (Prussians). He lived the new life (Dante's *Vita Nuova*).

The iron law of the spiritual dialectic was to bind Europe for the
next thousand years in the tension of spirit and matter. Gregory VII
won his final personal victory while suffering his last defeat. His last
words, while he lay dying, after fleeing from Rome, denied the claims
of the kings of the ancients. 'I have loved righteousness and hated
injustice,' he said, 'therefore, I die in Exile.' The psalmist of the Old
Testament had sung: 'Thou hast loved justice and hated iniquity,
therefore God the Lord anoints thee with the oil of salvation.' The
psalm belonged to the old world. The king or bishop of the psalmist
was the man blessed with the power of grace, who achieved earthly
and heavenly dominion, saving power and victory. Heaven and earth
were united in a single, continuous order of law and fate. Gregory's
last words spoke of the new world: heaven and earth confronting one
another. The servant of God could triumph on earth only in persecution and death.

From the late eleventh century until the thirteenth century, all the
symbols of power (throne, crown, royal robe), the rites and formulas,
and the worldly status of emperor and king were transferred to the
papal Church. Innocent III sat as judge upon the kings of the earth, as
once Otto the Great and Henry III had upon popes. Imperial law was

broken by canon law; the Papal University suppressed the emperor's palace and monastic schools; scholasticism triumphed over the symbolic, universal lore of the old world. In the long run, there were other consequences for Europe. . . .

In its attempts to free itself from the leading-reins of the early Middle Ages the revolutionary Papacy found allies who later revealed themselves as enemies: the spiritually awakened masses, new monastic reformers, and even lay princes, both within the Empire and without, who saw alliance with Rome as a means of reducing the Emperor to a position where he was at most an impotent *primus inter pares*.

Roman Catholicism still bears some of the scars of the battle fought by Gregory VII and his reforming allies against the 'laicization' of the Church and against Henry IV, that 'unchaste king'. Gregory aimed at making celibacy the rule for all the clergy: free of the 'flesh', unhampered by a family and the demands of kindred and clan, a clerk could devote himself wholly to the service of God and St Peter, which meant in practice St Peter's successor, the Pope in Rome. The impact of this proclamation of a unique fatherhood was revolutionary: at a stroke all temporal fatherhood and lordship were desanctified and rendered powerless, including the specific authority of the 'Lord Emperor': as *christus domini*, the Lord's anointed (in virtue of his unction and coronation), he had hitherto possessed quasi-episcopal rank and through the device of the honorary diaconate had had a seat in numerous cathedral chapters, including that of Rome, all of which had given him a secure and consecrated position within the sacerdotal hierarchy itself.

The Gregorian reformers had initiated a programme which was to be systematically extended during the twelfth and thirteenth centuries. The dismantling of the Emperor's sacerdotal powers was paralleled by the Pope's accumulation of the titles, ranks, offices and duties of the Emperor and the Empire. The Roman curia was using formulae of the imperial chancery as early as the eleventh century. The Pope assumed (or usurped) sacred vestments which surpassed the Emperor's in magnificence; and he trumped the imperial crown, that symbol of universal dominion, with the ace of the three-tiered papal tiara, abandoning in its favour the simple cap which had been the Pope's traditional headgear. The canonists now brought increasing precision to the juridical theory which was the ideological basis of Papal claims: the Roman Church was the unique legitimate successor of the Roman Empire, the Empire of ancient Rome. Only Rome, Papal Rome, could be Rome's heir. The Pope was the only lawful inheritor of the rights and authority

of the Roman Emperors. He was entitled to choose who should afford
him temporal assistance and bear the sword of temporal power, which
meant that he was free to appoint the ruler of Germany and of all
Christian principalities. It is understandable that lay princes, both
within the Empire and in Europe at large, were wholly agreeable to
this emasculation of imperial power and were willing to offer the Pope
their assistance, so long as they were not themselves drawn into a
similar conflict with the Curia over the control of their own 'territorial'
churches. It will also be appreciated that the Emperor resisted this
development with all the resources at his disposal. An attempt at com-
promise was finally successful, and a concordat was reached at Worms
in 1122, thanks to the legal ingenuity of a French churchman and the
weariness of both parties after a struggle which had already lasted half
a century. The terms were that the Emperor, as King of the Germans,
was to be left a free hand in Germany proper, even in church matters,
but that in Italy the Pope's primacy should be acknowledged when it
came to appointing bishops, which in effect gave him control of the
Church there.

Each renewed attempt at an accommodation between Emperor and
Pope foundered, because both parties were driven by their conception
of their task and status to make fresh inroads on each other's position;
they always confronted each other in Italy, the field of battle which
neither could avoid. Whenever an Emperor was strong in Germany, his
thoughts always turned to the recovery of former greatness, to *reno-
vatio imperii*, which above all else meant recovering his authority over
imperial possessions in Italy, whose connection with the Empire was
becoming more and more tenuous. The Popes knew that in the long
run they had no chance of withstanding the military and political pressure which would be applied once the Emperor had a firm foothold in
Italy. The marriage between Constance, heiress to the Norman kingdom of Sicily and southern Italy, and Henry VI, the son of the Emperor Frederick I, a hard, cunning and ruthless politician cast in the
true Norman mould, offered a grave threat to the Papacy. The Hohenstaufen eagle was soaring with unerring aim to the empyrean heights
of world domination, and its beating pinions cast their shadows over
Rome from both North and South. All lesser lords, both lay and ecclesiastical, who dared resist its rise had reason to fear the sharpness
of its talons. Rome lay helpless in the trap.

Frederick II, Henry's youthful son, had been the ward of Pope Innocent III. Shortly before his death Innocent made Frederick promise that

once he was crowned Emperor he would renounce Sicily in favour of his own infant son Henry, who should rule it with the Pope as regent. Frederick in fact had no intention of surrendering Sicily, the island kingdom where he had been brought up, and whose cosmopolitan society of Saracens, Greeks and Normans and distinguished élite of professional administrators and technologists was admirably suited to his purpose. Sicily, with its Norman administrative system as a foundation, was the one place where Frederick could build up his ideal state of the future: a fool-proof state, governed and regulated by officials, experts, judges, policemen and a highly-developed system of taxes, and whose material wealth would be exploited to the full. On the mainland of Italy, where Frederick was hemmed in by powerful city states and the lordships of his allies and adversaries, there was little room for experiment. In Germany, where the lay and ecclesiastical princes had gained the initiative, there seemed no room to build up a direct imperial lordship. It was not until the last years of his reign that such a chance presented itself in the eastern part of the *Reich*, when the last Babenberg duke of Austria died. Frederick planned to create an Austrian kingdom which would combine with the old Hohenstaufen territories to form a bastion of independent power in the south-eastern part of his Empire, stretching from Alsace across south-west Germany via Eger to Vienna. It was in precisely this region that the Hapsburgs started building up their power some thirty years later.

Excommunicated, outlawed—killing Frederick was not merely permissible but a Christian duty—proclaimed as anti-Christ by papal emissaries up and down Italy, battling his way from one place to the next, harried by traitors and would-be assassins, often defeated, briefly victorious, the Emperor died exhausted in 1250. This was the end of an epoch in world history. In Germany the Holy Empire collapsed in a welter of civil war: the time of terror had come, the 'age without an Emperor'.

Conradin, Frederick's grandson and the last of the Hohenstaufen, met his death by execution in 1268. The sentence was carried out in the market-place of Naples, where Frederick II had founded his imperial 'anti-papal' university, to be a centre of 'enlightenment' and an advanced training school for administrators from all over Europe. Conradin, attempting to recover his Sicilian inheritance, had fallen into the hands of the kingdom's new master, Charles of Anjou. The papal party in Italy was jubilant: the last of the eaglets had been blotted out and the devil's brood exterminated.

The public execution of the last of the Hohenstaufen in the market-place of Naples was a revolutionary event, without precedent in the history of Europe; until it had happened anyone would have said it was unthinkable. In terms of 'the logic of history' it may seem the 'right' conclusion to the papal revolt against the Emperor. It was only papal approval and the tenor of papal propaganda over the past two centuries that made the deed possible. The Popes, by diminishing the status of imperial descent, had prepared the scaffold for future princes of noble birth (or of 'divine descent', according to popular belief): for the execution of Charles I and Louis XVI. It was fruitless for Popes of more modern times, from the sixteenth to the nineteenth centuries, to set themselves up as the sworn allies of 'Christian princes' in the task of crushing 'infamous rebellions' instigated by heretics and 'the scum of society'; it was fruitless for papal ideologists to try to breathe fresh life and meaning into post-revolutionary attempts at restoration. The Papacy had encompassed the destruction of the Empire only by a revolutionary breach of the continuity of European history; the transformation of the popular image of the Christian monarch from a sacred and sacrosanct figure into a diabolical object of execration had called for the most blatant techniques of propaganda and political manoeuvring. Scarcely a generation elapsed after the execution of Conradin before the Pope was forced to pay the first instalment of the penalty for having degraded and dishallowed the highest office in Christendom apart from his own. In 1303 Boniface VIII [pope, 1294–1303] was taken prisoner at Anagni by William of Nogaret, Councillor to Philip IV of France. Subjected to all manner of ignominy, the Pope's pride and self-confidence were mortally wounded and he died in Rome only a few weeks after his release.

Only a short time before Boniface had excommunicated the King of France. This 'splendid autocrat' (as Previté-Orton described him) had attempted to take over the role assumed a century earlier by Innocent III as overlord of all Christian princes and arbiter of the nations. Long before he became Pope, Boniface had been convinced that the papal mission was to lead mankind, the whole of mankind, to God. In his great Bulls (*Clericis Laicos, Ausculta Fili*, and above all *Unam Sanctam*) he proclaimed to the world his sacred conviction that the laity were subject to the clergy, that the Pope had the right to command Christian kings and was supreme judge over them, and that all Christians owed him political and religious obedience. The Bull *Unam Sanctam* could be described as a programme of universal domination; it was never amended from the papal side until the late nineteenth century, in the time of Leo XIII.

Boniface, a highly-trained jurist, commanded an organization capable of making mass propaganda and staging spectacular attractions. The invention of the Jubilee Year, proclaimed in 1300, provided an excuse for bringing all Christendom to his feet in Rome, a spectacle which satisfied his own inner yearnings. The decrees of indulgence proclaimed for the Holy Year attracted the common folk to Rome in their thousands. Mass demonstrations of this kind are usually thought to be a phenomenon of a later period of European history, but this assembling of the people at Rome is perhaps the first example of the manipulation of the masses for a political end, in this case the demonstration of the power of the papal theocracy and the full authority of papal rule over all Christian people.

The invention and staging of the Holy Year throws into relief some other features of this 'new Church' of the 'new age'. This was a Church in which the lay masses were strictly controlled by the clergy; it was centred on Rome, it was absolutist in tendency, governed by Canon Law and moulded by the exigencies of litigation and finance. The organization of the Holy Year was itself a financial operation of some magnitude. This vast extension of the Church's activity on the material plane went hand in hand with other manifestations which reveal just how false, anachronistic and altogether unreal was the whole image of the Church as it moved into its new age in the later medieval and early modern periods.

Proceedings were opened against Boniface in France in 1303, and Philip's legal advisers prolonged them over the next ten years, in fact long after the accused was dead. The deposition of the Pope was demanded on grounds of heresy. The prosecutors included French prelates and crown lawyers, always ready to curry favour with the king, and the Cardinals of the Colonna family, implacably hostile to Boniface. The supporting 'evidence' they produced is of little interest today. What is interesting is the historical situation in which such proceedings were even possible. Boniface, who fancied himself as a realist, had completely overlooked the substantial transformation in the religious and political climate which had occurred since the time of Innocent III: new states, France and England, were emerging in the West, and they were not at all disposed to surrender control over 'their' territorial churches to Rome. The people, when they looked towards Rome, felt disillusioned and cheated; Rome's misfortunes were a matter of indifference, malicious pleasure, or even positive distaste, evoking only anger or sorrow. We can now see that a highly significant process was at work. The Church was out of step with the times, and was continually at odds with the new states of the West. The Church of the later Middle Ages was becoming completely institutionalized and completely clerical: the laity were regarded as little more than serfs, as slaves even, 'instruments' whose function was to yield willing obedience. (It is interesting that this word 'instrument', used by Aristotle with reference to slaves, is still retained, for example by Catholic Action, to describe the distinctive role of the laity.)

While the Popes were finding it in practice increasingly difficult, even impossible, to coerce the rising nation states into recognition of papal rights and claims, canon lawyers and other papal theorists were redoubling the Pope's claim to possess 'fullness of power' over the Church and all Christendom. This *plenitudo potestatis* made him the fountain of law and justice, whose secrets were locked in his own bosom, '*omne jus in scrinio sui pectoris habet*'. 'He rules and disposes all things, orders and governs everything as he pleases. . . . He can deprive anyone of his right, as it pleases him . . . for with him his will is right and reason; whatever pleases him has the force of law.' This account of the Pope's *plenitudo potestatis* was written in 1332 by a Spanish Franciscan, Alvarez Pelayo. Another tract emanating from curial circles at much the same date ridicules the Emperor for his impotence: 'it is said that the Emperor possesses all things; but in reality he possesses virtually nothing.'

But much the same could be said of the Popes. When steel struck on steel, as in the struggle between the Popes and the monarchs of the West, particularly the kings of France and England, it became appallingly evident how little real power the Pope possessed, except when he could play one prince off against another.

It is not difficult for us to pick out the weaknesses and self-delusions in the personality of Boniface VIII, whose pontificate was such a decisive turning-point in the history of the medieval Church. It is more difficult to recognize in him the traits of greatness, of inner strength and of courage (which was not merely a matter of pride). These traits only become obvious when we are bold enough to admit that many of the anachronistic features of Boniface's policy and outlook are already to be found in the pontificate of the man who is commonly regarded as representing the highest point of achievement reached by the medieval papacy and as the greatest Pope of his age: Innocent III [1198–1216].

Innocent, while admitting that the Pope was inferior to God, nevertheless held that he was something more than man: God spoke and acted through the Pope, hence whatever the Pope proclaimed as law was divine law. The Pope interpreted the will of God. In political terms this meant that Innocent saw himself as the one true *Imperator;* the superior of kings and Emperor, he had the right to arbitrate in all important disputes between the peoples. In ecclesiastical terms this meant that bishops were subject to the Pope and had no autonomous power, that they were papal officials; through his legates the Pope could intervene in the Church government of the various countries.

Many of Innocent's much-lauded triumphs (still much admired) can be shown to have been precarious, accidental or empty, while other policies he initiated were to prove disastrous for the Church and Christendom as their effect became plain over the centuries. For example, the Pope saw himself as the head of a league of Christian states. True, a number of weak kings and pretenders owed their crowns to him and declared themselves his vassals to gain a political advantage. The rulers of Portugal, Aragon, Poland, Hungary, Galicia and Lodomeria, Serbia, Croatia and Bulgaria were all indebted to him in this way. But these were momentary and vulnerable successes. Innocent's intervention in English affairs shows how seriously he could overreach himself. Although he could force John to receive back England as a papal fief, his opposition to Magna Carta was quite unavailing. His meddling in the affairs of France and Germany only aroused implacable hostility, expressed in the political songs of Walther von der Vogelweide and long nursed in France, whose thirteenth and fourteenth century kings revenged themselves by their anti-papal policy for the interdicts and excommunications and other coercive measures heaped on their predecessors in time of weakness. Innocent's cherished project, the Fourth Crusade, met with complete disaster; he was responsible for the barrage of propaganda which accompanied its launching and for its finances, but completely lost control of its direction, since he could not lead it in person, though many of his contemporaries pleaded that he should. The sack of Constantinople and the conquest of the Byzantine Empire aroused the undying hatred of the Greeks and the Eastern Church. No less disastrous was the injury inflicted on Western Europe by the Albigensian Crusade and the subsequent extermination of Provençal culture. Admittedly, the Fourth Lateran Council of 1215 brought a moment of triumph. But it was also the occasion on which Innocent publicly acknowledged the weakness and corruption within the Church, the venality of the bishops, the illiteracy of the clergy and the impiety of the laity.

The key to the Pope's steadfast urging of his absolutist claims may be found in the title of one of Innocent's best-known works, *De Contemptu Mundi* [contempt of the world]. Although Innocent's successors were not all his equal as personalities, they shared his pessimistic view of man as a creature so debilitated by sin that his salvation could be achieved only by coercion; unless they submitted to that perfect government which the Church alone could offer, the masses were doomed to damnation. The Church was the world's supreme court, *ecclesia judiatrix*, the judge of kings, nations and individuals. The comforting image of Mother Church, indulgent of her children's whims and aberrations, was receding, to be replaced by the forbidding figure of a prosecuting tribunal made up of lawyers and financiers.

Admittedly, theologians like Godfrey of Fontaines and Augustinus Triumphus of Ancona (both died early in the fourteenth century) could still debate the question whether the Church was better governed by a lawyer or a theologian and decide in favour of the latter. But during the thirteenth and fourteenth centuries the Papacy was being remorselessly turned over to the lawyers, and the Church as a whole was declining into a state of 'canonist petrifaction', to use an expression coined by Heimpel, one of the greatest authorities on the later Middle Ages. It became generally accepted that the leadership of the Church was best entrusted to lawyers, preferably those learned in both Canon and Roman Law, to administrative officials, and most important of all, to men with a talent for finance.

Throughout the thirteenth and fourteenth centuries canon lawyers were bringing further refinement to the doctrine of the fullness of papal power, on which the Pope based his claim to be the Church's ruler and law-giver. Clerks of all nations were involved, though the leading canon lawyers were mainly Italians, Spaniards and Englishmen: Boniface VIII relied on the authority of Alanus the Englishman and English canon lawyers and jurists were prominent at Rome in his time. 'The Pope can do whatever God can do.' As the 'Emperor sent by heaven', *coelestis imperator*, the Pope could absolve men from binding oaths and depose kings and emperors. Heresy was *lèse-majesté* and resistance to papal policies, whether political or religious, was heresy and rebellion. The 'rebels' were excommunicated and papal armies sent to do battle with them. It was on this pretext that papal troops fought in and for Italy.

During the fourteenth century the Popes entrenched themselves within the massive and uncompromising walls, several feet thick, of their fortified palace on the chalk cliffs above the Rhône at Avignon. Philip the Fair of France, victor over Boniface VIII, was mainly responsible for this removal, which took place in 1309, and Avignon remained the seat of the Curia until 1377. There were contributory influences from the papal side: the Pope's anxiety over the trial of his predecessor, which was still in progress with the object of unmasking Boniface as a heretic, and his hope of quashing the scandalous proceedings initiated by the French king against the Templars.

Here at Avignon the Papal Church put on the armour of stone walls, whose chilly angularity symbolized the triumph of undeviating correctness and of overweening dominion. But this was all external. In the great hall within, lightness and luxury abounded. The frescoes and tapestries which contributed to this effect have now almost vanished, with the exception of the graceful and delicate sylvan frescoes adorning the Pope's robing room in the Tour de la Garde-Robe: with their frankly sensuous portrayal of earthly pleasures, they remain as witness that the hard outer shell concealed a soft centre.

St Bridget of Sweden had a vision of Avignon in which it was revealed to her as a 'field of tares'. 'It must first be weeded with an iron hoe, then purified by fire and finally smoothed again with the plough.' The 'tares' were pride, envy, ambition, lust and simony; everything at Avignon had its price. Other contemporary writers describe Avignon in the most opprobrious terms. It was a 'sink of iniquity', Hell, Babylon.

The streets of medieval Avignon, squatting beneath the papal residence which was palace and fortress in one, were narrow and filthy. The stench was such as to cause at least one foreigner, an ambassador from Aragon, to swoon. Rents were high, accommodation limited (few houses had more than one storey) and the city thronged with people: petitioners, envoys, money-changers (by 1327 there were already forty-three Italian money-changers in Avignon), notaries, lawyers, officials of the Curia and of other European courts, craftsmen, painters, builders, and a host of adventurers—thieves, money-lenders, prostitutes, astrologers, sorcerers, necromancers and men taken prisoner. The papal administration was growing at a prodigious rate and provided employment for a large staff. One of the main departments was the *camera apostolica*, under its director the *camerarius*, who was always a cardinal; as the Pope's finance minister and most intimate adviser, he was the most important personage of the Curia. The *camerarius* had under his control the secretaries who conducted political correspondence, the treasurer, and the papal mint, in fact the whole financial apparatus in all its ramifications.

Another important department was the chancery, made up of seven distinct offices, all under the direction of a vice-chancellor. Yet another department was that of justice, which in the last resort was directly under the control of the Pope and cardinals in Consistory, though there were occasional courts presided over by cardinals and a series of inferior courts. The energies of the Church were increasingly concentrated on litigation and raising money. The upkeep of the court and its army of officials, together with the wars in Italy (which dragged on throughout the fourteenth century), ate up huge sums of money. It was essential to find and build up new sources of income to replace the crusading tithes formerly paid to finance those wars officially designated as Crusades and which most states now refused to pay. Supplying this financial need presented no problem to a centralizing Church, and taxation and centralization marched forward hand in hand. Anyone who needed anything from the Church had to pay for it, and go to the Curia to do so. Bishops and other high church dignitaries had to pay *servitia* on appointment to their offices; churches and abbeys had to pay a tax for recognition; every document and privilege cost something; annates, the first year's income from a benefice, was a further new source of revenue; however, the clerical tax known as 'tenths' often had to be shared with the lay ruler of the country concerned. John XXII was the chief architect of this comprehensive system. Chroniclers of many nations, Italian, German, English and French, not to mention Petrarch and Dante, were loud in their complaints over this financial machine, and the harshness with which it was operated aroused general hostility. Anyone who failed to pay was excommunicated. On July 5, 1328, for example, there was a mass excommunication on these grounds of a patriarch, five archbishops, thirty bishops and forty-six abbots.

The men at the head of the papal bureaucracy were largely French in origin. Of the 134 cardinals created by the Avignon Popes, thirteen were Italians, five Spanish, two English, one was a native of Geneva, and the remaining 113 were French. There was thus not a single German among them. The exclusion of Germans dated from the time of Gregory IX [1227–1241], and was only brought to an end under the stress of the Great Schism [1378–1417], when Urban needed the help of the Emperor. The Avignon papacy, generally suspected of being anti-German and pro-French, sowed some of the seeds which were to germinate in the German and English Reformations.

As individuals the Avignon Popes were often more attractive than their reputation allows. The first of them, Clement V (1305–14), formerly Archbishop of Bordeaux, was a man of culture and learning; he ordered the institution of chairs in Hebrew, Syriac and Arabic at Paris, Bologna, Oxford and Salamanca, and his friends included doctors of medicine and some early humanists. But he was dogged by ill-health and incapable of meeting the political challenge presented by so formidable an adversary and master as Philip the Fair; it was he who moved the Papacy to Avignon. His successor, John XXII (1316–34), who came of a wealthy bourgeois family from Cahors in Provence, made the Curia the world's leading financial power. Reserved, avaricious and irascible in his personal character, in his policy John showed himself the determined enemy of the Emperor and of heterodoxy. He excommunicated not only the Spiritual Franciscans (for their stand in the matter of poverty) but also Waldensians, Cathars and Beguines; he censured twenty-eight propositions of Meister Eckhart and sixty of Johannis Petrus Olivi. But he himself came close to heresy in the views he propounded concerning the fate of the soul after death. He set out these ideas in three sermons. The souls of the righteous, he maintained, will not enjoy the Beatific Vision of God until the time comes for the general resurrection of the body; nor will Hell have any occupants until the Last Day. This confused doctrine was a gift to the Emperor's theologians, Michael of Cesena, Ockham and Bonagrazia of Bergamo, who were quick to expose the heresy of this heresy-hunting Pope. The choleric and tenacious old man (he was already seventy-two when he became Pope) half-recanted of his heresy before he died; he had been generally hated and a great nepotist.

His successor Benedict XII (1334–42) was one of his protégés and as professor at Paris and later as Bishop had helped him by writing pamphlets attacking Franciscans, Joachimites, Meister Eckhart, Ockham and Olivi. As Pope, Benedict was renowned as 'the scourge of heretics'; those whom he so relentlessly persecuted, Waldensians and Albigensians, execrated him as a 'devil', 'the spirit of evil'. A man of lowly birth, his aim as Pope was to eradicate all wickedness from the Church. His drastic measures of reform and his campaign against the Mendicant Orders (he himself was a Cistercian) brought him some partial success. Harsh and uncompromising in character, he was castigated by contemporaries for his avarice, his hardness of heart and his egotism. When he died the cardinals showed their desire to bring about a change of atmosphere at Avignon by the election as Pope of Pierre Roger, Archbishop of Rouen, an open-handed and affable *grand sei-*

*gneur,* who ruled as Clement VI from 1342 to 1352. During his pontificate the number of clerks seeking papally provided benefices rose to a
hundred thousand. His court was the acknowledged centre of high
society in Europe, attracting the pleasure-loving and cultured aristocracy by jousts and grand parties; his three immediate successors were
all to complain of his inroads on the papal treasury. Clement VI was
also a patron of learning and the arts; in some ways he foreshadows
the Popes of the Renaissance, for he gathered round him painters from
Germany and Italy, poets and architects from France, and physicians
and scientists from all over Europe. But if he was open-minded he was
also open-handed; during the peak period of the Black Death he dispensed charity on a grand scale. Under Innocent VI (1352–62), the
wind shifted to a different quarter. The new Pope had been an Inquisi-
tor, a remorseless persecutor of Spiritual Franciscans.

In the early years of the fourteenth century Pierre Dubois, one of
Philip the Fair's propagandists, wrote: 'It would be salutary for the
whole world to submit to France, for the French make better use of the
power of rational judgment than do any other people.' Dubois argued
in favour of a European federation under the hegemony of France. For
him the supremacy of France was equivalent to the supremacy of
political reason; and to France had fallen the task of diminishing the
pretensions of the Holy Roman Empire and the papalized Church.
Dubois describes the Empire as German, not Roman, and the Church
as the *secta catholicorum* [sect of Catholics]. He thus robs the two
great powers of their old and hallowed titles, a fact highly significant
of the altered temper of the times. The Crusades he regarded as a
means of promoting trade and colonization, of making Oriental
products cheaper in the West and of securing the Mediterranean trade-
routes. He had some interesting ideas for the reform of teaching and
about education generally, which is seen as one of the important tasks
to be undertaken by the projected federation. Dubois in fact anticipated UNESCO by some six centuries. The supremacy of the West in the
world at large could be secured only by education, superior knowledge
and a rationally ordered way of life. Dubois specifically mentions the
education of women as being something in need of attention.

*Secta catholicorum:* Dubois' casual use of this expression simply put
into words an idea which had long been held as axiomatic by politicians and officials, not excluding ecclesiastics, who served the state in
France and England. The 'Church' meant on the one hand the Curia,
with which one must continually bargain or quarrel, particularly over

the steepness of its financial demands (though there was always the chance of keeping the lion's share for oneself). But the 'Church' also meant the church and clergy in one's own country, slowly but surely becoming subject to the political authority of the national monarch. The centralized, bureaucratic, autocratic administration characteristic of the Curia at this period was being duplicated in France, where the royal bureaucrats were 'making the Civil Law their gospel'. In the light of what was happening in France and England, the apparently aggressive papal policies and the ideological propaganda which went with them should be seen as a defensive reflex. Rome and Avignon adopted the maxim that attack was the best form of defence in order to maintain the *status quo*. But it was becoming increasingly difficult for the towering façade of papal and curial claims to conceal the harsh realities of political events. The kings continually gained ground at the expense of the Pope, building up their new states with the help of a corps of officials, in France known as the *chevaliers du roi*, drawn from the petty aristocracy and the bourgeoisie.

## Suggestions for Further Reading

BARRACLOUGH, GEOFFREY, *The Medieval Papacy*. London: Thames and Hudson, 1968.

BARRACLOUGH, GEOFFREY, *The Origins of Modern Germany*. Oxford: Basil Blackwell, 1936.

CANTOR, N. F., *Church, Kingship and Lay Investiture in England, 1089–1135*. New York: Octagon, 1969.

COHN, NORMAN, *The Pursuit of the Millennium*. Fair Lawn, N. J.: Essential Books, 1957.

KERN, FRITZ, *Kingship and Law in the Middle Ages*. Oxford: Basil Blackwell, 1948.

STRAYER, JOSEPH R., *On the Medieval Origins of the Modern State*. Princeton: Princeton University Press, 1970.

TELLENBACH, GERD, *Church, State, and Christian Society at the Time of the Investiture Contest*. Oxford: Basil Blackwell, 1940.

ULLMANN, WALTER, *The Growth of Papal Government*, London: Methuen & Co., Ltd., 1955.

ULLMANN, WALTER, *Origins of the Great Schism*. Hamden, Conn.: Shoe String Press, 1967.

WHITNEY, J. P., *Hildebrandine Essays*, Cambridge, England: Cambridge University Press, 1932.

A. C. CROMBIE

# Medieval Science and Technology

≈§§≈ Historical insight is a function of the social situation which the historian himself experiences. The questions that historians ask of the past and the assumptions which provide the models for organizing the historical continuum arise out of contemporary experience. In the nineteenth century, politics seemed to be the conditioning force in western life, and to some extent also economics. Hence the emphasis—which continued well into the twentieth century—on political and economic interpretations of European history. But in recent years it has begun to appear that what distinguishes the West from non-western societies is not Europe's political effectiveness or institutions or even its wealth, but rather its science and technology. At least, it is claimed, all that the non-West has to learn from Europe is science and technology; consequently there has been a great effort to establish the history of European theoretical and applied science and to account for Europe's uniqueness in this regard.

The task of discovering the main lines of European scientific development has not been easy, and the role of

FROM A. C. Crombie, *Science in the Middle Ages and Early Modern Times*, Vol. I, *Augustine to Galileo* (London: Mercury Books, Heinemann Educational Books Ltd., 1964; Cambridge, Mass.: Harvard University Press), 2d ed., pp. 175–183, 186–189, 196–213; and A. C. Crombie, *Science in the Middle Ages and Early Modern Times*, Vol. II (London: Mercury Books, Heinemann Educational Books Ltd., 1964; Cambridge, Mass.: Harvard University Press), 2d ed., pp. 106–110.

medieval culture is a particularly complicated one, not yet entirely resolved. Historians of science placed the Scientific Revolution, which they made virtually equivalent to The New Physics stretching from Galileo to Newton, in the seventeenth century. They identified the idea and strategy of the quantification of nature as the essence of the Scientific Revolution. At this point medieval historians began to ask some awkward questions. They pointed to thirteenth- and fourteenth-century thinkers such as Robert Grosseteste, William of Occam, Roger Bacon, Albertus Magnus, and Jean Burdan—hitherto regarded as "scholastics"—and claimed that these late medieval philosophers had conceived of the quantification of nature, had made serious efforts in this direction, had anticipated Galileo's physics in several respects, and had a pretty clear idea of the experimental method.

The common view today is to regard the late medieval scientific development as an abortive or partial intellectual revolution that did not quite manage to achieve the great breakthrough accomplished in the seventeenth century. The reasons given are usually: Late medieval knowledge of algebra was too primitive actually to effect the quantification of nature that was envisioned. Medieval technology, while it did make some significant advances, did not establish to a sufficient degree that exciting and mutually interacting symbiosis with theoretical science that occurred in the seventeenth and eighteenth centuries.

A. C. Crombie, holder of the Chair in the History of Science at Oxford, has written an excellent study of Robert Grosseteste as a scientist. Here, from another insightful work, he succinctly summarizes the present state of our general knowledge about medieval science and technology —but research has only gotten under way in this field in recent years, and ten or twenty years from now we may have a quite different understanding of the relationship between the science of 1300 and that of 1700.

&#9986;&#11825;

## TECHNICS AND EDUCATION

It has often been pointed out that science develops best when the speculative reasoning of the philosopher and mathematician is in closest touch with the manual skill of the craftsman. It has been said also that the absence of this association in the Greco-Roman world and in medieval Christendom was one reason for the supposed backwardness of science in those societies. The practical arts were certainly despised by the majority of the most highly educated people in classical antiquity, and were held to be work for slaves. In view of such evidence as the long series of Greek medical writings, stretching from the first members of the so-called Hippocratic corpus to the works of Galen, the military devices and the 'screw' attributed to Archimedes, the treatises on building, engineering and other branches of applied mechanics written during Hellenistic and Roman times by Ctesibius of Alexandria, Athenæus, Apollodorus, Hero of Alexandria, Vitruvius, Frontinus and Pappus of Alexandria, and the works on agriculture by the elder Cato, Varro and Columella, it may be doubted whether even in classical antiquity the separation of technics and science was as complete as has been sometimes supposed. In the Middle Ages there is much evidence to show that these two activities were at no period totally divorced and that their association became more intimate as time went on. This active, practical interest of educated people may be one reason why the Middle Ages was a period of technical innovation, though most of the advances were probably made by unlettered craftsmen. And certainly it was this interest of many theoretical scientists in practical results that encouraged them to ask concrete and precise questions, to try to get answers by experiment and, with the aid of technics, to develop more accurate measuring instruments and special apparatus.

From the early Middle Ages, Western scholars showed an interest in getting certain kinds of results for which some technical knowledge was necessary. Medicine was studied in the earliest Benedictine monasteries, and the long series of medical works written during the Middle Ages, and continuing without a break into the 16th century and modern times, is one of the best examples of a tradition in which empirical observations were increasingly combined with attempts at rational and theoretical explanation, with the results that definite medical and surgical problems were solved. Another long series of treatises was written on astronomy by scholars from the time of Bede in the 7th century for purely practical purposes such as determining the date of Easter, fixing latitude, and showing how to determine true North and tell the time with an astrolabe. Even a poet such as Chaucer could write an excellent practical treatise on the astrolabe. Another series of practical treatises is that on the preparation of pigments and other chemical substances, which includes the 8th-century *Compositiones ad Tigenda* and *Mappæ Clavicula*, of which Adelard of Bath later produced an edition, the early 12th-century *Diversarum Artium Schedula* of Theophilus the Priest, who lived probably in Germany, the late 13th-century *Liber de Coloribus Faciendis* by Peter of Saint Omer, and the early 15th-century treatises of Cennino Cennini and John Alcherius. Technical treatises were among the first to be translated out of Arabic and Greek into Latin, and this was the work of educated men. It was, in fact, chiefly for their practical knowledge that Western scholars, from the time of Gerbert at the end of the 10th century, first began to take an interest in Arabic learning. The 13th century encyclopædias of Alexander Neckam, Albertus Magnus and Roger Bacon contained a great deal of accurate information about the compass, chemistry, the calendar, agriculture, and other technical matters. Other contemporary writers composed special treatises on these subjects: Grosseteste and later writers on the calendar; Giles of Rome in *De Regimine Principum* on the art of war; Walter of Henley and Peter of Crescenzi on agriculture; Peregrinus, in the second part of *De Magnete*, on the determination of azimuths. It took a scholar to write about arithmetic, yet most of the advances that followed Fibonacci's treatise on the Hindu numerals were made in the interests of commerce.

In the 14th century, the Italian Dominican friar, Giovanni da San Gimignano (d. 1323), wrote an encyclopædia for preachers in which he gave for use as examples in sermons descriptions of numerous technical subjects: agriculture, fishing, cultivation of herbs, windmills and watermills, ships, painting and limning, fortifications, arms, Greek fire, smithing, glass making, and weights and measures. The names of two other Dominicans, Alessandro della Spina (d. 1313) and Salvino degl' Armati (d. 1317), are associated with the invention of spectacles. In the 15th century, a most interesting series of treatises was written on military technology. Beginning with Konrad Kyeser's *Bellifortis*, written between 1396 and 1405, this included a treatise by Giovanni de' Fontana (*c.* 1410–20), the *Feuerwerksbuch* (*c.* 1422), a treatise by an anonymous engineer in the Hussite wars (*c.* 1430), and the so-called

'Mittelalterliches Hausbuch' (*c.* 1480). The series went on in the 16th century with the treatises of Biringuccio and Tartaglia. These contained descriptions of how to make guns and gunpowder as well as problems of military engineering, which were discussed also by other contemporary writers such as Alberti and Leonardo da Vinci. Some of these treatises dealt also with general technical matters such as the construction of ships, dams and spinning-wheels. The series of practical chemical treatises which, in the earlier Middle Ages, had consisted mainly of recipes for pigments, continued in the 14th and 15th centuries with accounts of distillation and other practical techniques and went on in the 16th century with Hieronymus Brunschwig's books on distillation, the metallurgical *Probierbüchlein*, and Agricola's *De Re Metallica*. Examples of the interest shown by medieval scholars in technics could, in fact, be multiplied considerably. They show not only that they had an abstract desire for power over nature such as Roger Bacon had expressed, but also that they were capable of getting the kind of knowledge that would lead to results useful in practice.

One reason for this interest of the learned in technics is to be found in the education they received. The popular handbook on the sciences by Hugh of St. Victor (d. 1141), *Didascalicon de Studio Legendi*, shows that by the 12th century the seven liberal arts [grammar, rhetoric, dialectic, geometry, arithmetic, astronomy, and music] had been extended and specialised so as to include various kinds of technical knowledge. The mathematical subjects forming the *quadrivium* had, of course, had a practical object at least since the time of Bede, but from the early 12th century there was a tendency to increasing specialisation. In the *Didascalicon* Hugh of St. Victor followed a modified version of the classification of science in the tradition coming from Aristotle and Boethius; he divided knowledge in general into theory, practice, mechanics and logic. Giving a pseudo-historical account of the origin of the sciences, he said that they arose first in response to human needs as a set of customary practices, which were later reduced to formal rules. These practices began by man imitating nature: for example, he made his own clothes in imitation of the bark with which nature covered trees or the shell with which she covered shellfish. Each of the 'mechanical' arts, forming the 'adulterine' science of mechanics which provided for those things necessary because of the weakness of the human body, arose in this way. In mechanics Hugh included seven sciences: the manufacture of cloth and of arms, and navigation, which ministered to the extrinsic needs of the body; and agriculture, hunting, medicine and the science of theatrical performances, which ministered to intrinsic needs. He gave a brief description of each of these activities.

Later in the 12th century another popular classification of the sciences was written by Dominicus Gundissalinus, his *De Divisione Philosophiæ*. This was based partly on Arabic sources, in particular on Alfarabi, whereas Hugh had used only the traditional Latin sources. Gundissalinus, following another form of the Aristotelian tradition, classified the sciences into theoretical and practical. He subdivided the former into physics, mathematics and metaphysics and the latter into politics, or the art of civil government, the art of family government, which included giving instruction in the liberal and mechanical arts, and ethics or the art of self-government. The 'fabrile' or 'mechanical' arts were those concerned with making out of matter something useful to man, and the matter used could come either from living things, for example wood, wool, linen or bones, or from dead things, for example gold, silver, lead, iron, marble or precious stones. Through the mechanical arts resources were acquired which provided for the needs of the family. To each of the mechanical arts there corresponded a theoretical science which studied the basic principles which the mechanical art put into practice. Thus theoretical arithmetic studied the basic principles of numbers used in reckoning by the abacus, as in commerce; theoretical music studied in the abstract the harmonies produced by voices and instruments; theoretical geometry considered the basic principles put into practice in measuring bodies, in surveying, and in using the results of observing the motions of the heavenly bodies with the astrolabe and other astronomical instruments; the science of weights considered the basic principles of the balance and lever. Finally, the science of 'mathematical devices' turned the results of all the other mathematical sciences to useful purposes, for stone-masonry, for instruments for measuring and lifting bodies, for musical and optical instruments, and for carpentry.

In the 13th century, these ideas were taken up by a number of well-known writers, for example Roger Bacon, Thomas Aquinas and Giles of Rome. The treatises of Michael Scot and Robert Kilwardby are of special interest. Michael Scot held that each of the practical sciences was related to a theoretical science and was the practical manifestation of the corresponding theoretical science. Thus to different branches of theoretical 'physics' there corresponded such practical sciences as medicine, agriculture, alchemy, the study of mirrors, and navigation; to the different branches of theoretical mathematics there corresponded such practical arts as business concerned with money, carpentry, smithing and stone-masonry, weaving, shoemaking. Robert Kilwardby's treatise, *De Ortu Scientiarum*, very widely read for generations, expressed the same conviction of the importance of the practical side of science concerned with getting useful results. Of special significance is Kilwardby's pseudo-historical account of the theoretical sciences as arising out of particular, concrete problems encountered in attempting to satisfy the physical needs of the body as, for example, his version of the ancient Greek tradition that geometry arose first as a practical art among the Egyptians because they had to survey the land after the flooding of the Nile, and was transformed into a theoretical and demonstrative science by Pythagoras. Among the 'mechanical' sciences he included agriculture, viticulture, medicine, cloth-making, armouring, architecture and commerce. Roger Bacon gave elaborate descriptions of various practical sciences, asserted emphatically that the jusification of the theoretical sciences was their useful results, and stressed the need to include the study of the practices of artisans and of practical alchemists in any scheme of education.

Though it was only in guilds of artisans that any sort of practical training in the mechanical arts was received, the utilitarian aims of medieval writers on education were reflected, often to a surprising extent, in the courses that might be taken at a university. This was the case, for example, in the 12th-century medical school at Salerno, where the regulations of King Roger II of Sicily and the Emperor Frederick II required that the medical student should take a course lasting five years and including human anatomy and surgery. After passing an examination at the end of this course he was not allowed to practise until he had spent a further year learning from a trained practitioner. From the end of the 13th century, attendance at an 'anatomy' at least once a year was prescribed for medical students at Bologna, and in the 14th century the medical school in the university devoted itself increasingly to surgery. Some practical instruction in anatomy seems, in fact, to have been required in most medical schools from the end of the 13th century.

In the 'arts' courses in most universities the mathematical subjects very often had some practical object in view. In 12th-century Chartres a list of books recommended for study by Thierry of Chartres included a high proportion of works on surveying, measuring and practical astronomy; a list of text-books in use at Paris at the end of the 12th century shows that the same utilitarian tradition was continued there.

At the beginning of the 13th century the arts course at Paris took six years, a Licence in Arts not being granted before the age of 20, though at Paris and most other universities the six years were later reduced, sometimes to as little as four. The course usually consisted of a study of the seven liberal arts followed by the 'three philosophies,' natural philosophy (that is, natural science), ethics and metaphysics. At Paris during the 13th century there was a tendency to reduce the time spent on mathematical subjects in favour of the other arts subjects such as metaphysics. At Oxford a considerable emphasis was placed on the mathematical subjects, the text-books prescribed including, for example, not only Boethius' *Arithmetic* and Euclid's *Elements*, but also Alhazen's *Optica*, Witelo's *Perspectiva*, and Ptolemy's *Almagest*. The arts course at Oxford is also of interest for including the study of Aristotle's *De Animalibus* as well as the more usual *Physica, Meteorologica, De Cælo*, and other works on 'natural philosophy.' A similar emphasis on mathematics is seen in the arts course at Bologna, where the subjects prescribed included a book on arithmetic known as *Algorismi de Minutis et Integris*, Euclid, Ptolemy, the *Alfonsine Tables*, a book of rules by Jean de Linières for using astronomical tables to determine the motions of the heavenly bodies, and a work on the use of the quadrant. Some of the German universities seem also seriously to have cultivated the study of arithmetic, algebra, astronomy, optics, music, and other mathematical sciences. It seems unlikely that any actual practical or laboratory instruction was included in the arts course at any medieval university, but there is evidence that special courses in astronomy were given at Oxford in the 14th century. According to its preface, Chaucer wrote his treatise on the astrolabe to explain to his son how to use the instrument which he gave him when he went up to Oxford. Certainly the Fellows of Merton College made astronomical observations, and in at least one case, that of Richard of Wallingford and his planetarium, a scholar is known actually to have made his own instruments.

An important result of this mathematical training received in medieval education was that it encouraged the habit of expressing physical events in terms of abstract units and emphasised the need for the standardisation of systems of measurement. Without this habit of thought mathematical physics would be impossible. Lewis Mumford has vividly described how it developed first in connection with the purely practical regulation of affairs. The need to measure time for the orderly institutions of the Church and the routine of the monastery led to the sustained medieval interest in the calendar and to the division of

the day into the unequal canonical hours, while the secular requirements of government and commerce led to the prevalence in civil life
of the system of 24 equal hours in the day. The invention at the end
of the 13th century of the mechanical clock, in which the hands translated time into units of space on the dial, completed the replacement
of 'organic,' growing, irreversible time as experienced, by the abstract
mathematical time of units on a scale, belonging to the world of
science. Space also underwent abstraction during the later Middle Ages.
The symbolic arrangement of subjects in paintings according to their
importance in the Christian hierarchy gave way, from the middle of the
14th century in Italy, to the division of the canvas into an abstract
checkerboard according to the rules of perspective. Besides the symbolic maps, like the Hereford *Mappa Mundi* of 1314, there appeared
maps by cartographers in which the traveller or mariner could find his
position on an abstract system of co-ordinates of latitude and longitude. Commerce changed during the Middle Ages from a barter
economy based on goods and services to a money economy based on
abstract units, first of gold or silver coinage, and later also of letters of
credit and bills of exchange. The problems arising from the dissolution
of partnerships (some discussed in Italy as early as the 12th century)
and in connection with interest, discount and exchange were among
the chief incentives to mathematical research. Problems of currency
reform became the subject of treatises by academic mathematicians
like Nicole Oresme in the 14th century and Copernicus two centuries
later. This process of abstraction concentrated attention on the systems
of units used. Attempts were made from as early as Anglo-Saxon times
in England to standardise weights and measures and later (in legislation
during the reign of Richard I) to replace units based on the human
body like the foot and span by standard measures made of iron.
Attempts were made also to establish the relationship between the
different systems existing in different countries and even within the
same country. A series of treatises was written by doctors interested
in standardising units of weight and volume for drugs.

\*     \*     \*     \*     \*

## TECHNOLOGICAL PROGRESS

Most of the fundamental techniques on which both classical and
medieval economic life were based had been invented in prehistoric

times. Prehistoric man discovered the use of fire, tools and agriculture, bred, domesticated, and harnessed animals, invented the plough, pottery, spinning and weaving and the use of organic and inorganic pigments, worked metals, made ships and wheeled carts, invented the arch in building, devised such machines as the windlass, pulley, lever, rotary quern, bow-drill and lathe, invented numbers, and laid the empirical foundations of astronomy and of medicine.

To this basic practical knowledge some important additions were made in the Greco-Roman world. Though the chief contribution of classical civilisation to science was not in technics but in speculative thought, one of the most important contributions ever made to technology was made by the Greeks. This was their attempt to give rational explanations of the machines and other inventions and discoveries of their predecessors, which made it possible to generalise and extend their use. Thus it was the Greeks who first converted the practical, technological methods of reckoning and measuring, as developed in Mesopotamia and Egypt, into the abstract sciences of arithmetic and geometry, and who first attempted to give rational explanations of the facts observed in astronomy and medicine. By combining observation and theory they greatly extended the practical use of these sciences. Greek writers, from the author or authors of the Aristotelian *Mechanica* and Archimedes down to Hero of Alexandria, attempted to explain the lever and other mechanisms. Hero gave a full account of the five 'simple' machines by which a given weight might be moved by a given force and of some of their combinations: the wheel and axle, lever, pulley, wedge and endless screw. These were held to be the basis of all machinery until the 19th century. The Greeks developed also the elementary principles of hydrostatics. Some Hellenistic and Roman writers were the first to give descriptions of the various kinds of machinery then in practical use. Some of the most important of these were the crossbow, catapults and other ballistic devices, watermills involving the important method of transmitting power through geared wheels and perhaps a windmill, the screw press and trip hammer, syphons, vacuum pumps, force pumps and Archimedes' screw, the bellows organ and water organ, a steam turbine and a puppet theatre driven by falling weights, the water clock and such important measuring instruments as the cyclometer or hodometer, surveying instruments such as the dioptra ( a theodolite without telescope described by Hero), and the cross-staff, astrolabe and quadrant which remained the basic astronomical instruments until the invention of the telescope in the

17th century. Most of these devices were, in fact, Greek inventions. In other technical fields as, for example, in medicine and in agriculture (where the Romans seem to have introduced legume rotation), important improvements were introduced in the classical world. But whether they were describing new techniques or simply ones inherited from the less expressive Egyptian, Babylonian and Assyrian civilisations, these Greco-Roman technical writings were to have a very important influence as a source of technical knowledge in both the Moslem and the Christian worlds in the Middle Ages. In Western Christendom these classical technical works exerted an influence right down into the 17th century.

In the period that followed the collapse of the Roman Empire in the West there was a considerable loss of technical knowledge, though this was compensated to a slight extent by some new techniques introduced by the invading Germanic tribes. From about the 10th century, however, there was a gradual improvement of technical knowledge in Western Christendom. This was brought about partly by learning from the practices and writings (often of classical origin) of the Byzantine and Arabic worlds, and partly by a slow but increasing activity of invention and innovation within Western Christendom itself. The gains thus made during the Middle Ages were never lost, and it is characteristic of medieval Christendom that it put to industrial use technical devices which in classical society had been known but left almost unused or regarded simply as toys. The result was that, as early as 1300, Western Christendom was using many techniques either unknown or undeveloped in the Roman Empire. By the year 1500 the most advanced countries of the West were in most aspects of technics distinctly superior to any earlier society.

\*    \*    \*    \*    \*

## THE MECHANIZATION OF INDUSTRY

The great expansion of the use of watermills and windmills that took place during the later Middle Ages, in association with the growth of manufacturing, brought in an essentially new stage in mechanical technique. From this period must be dated that increasing mechanisation of life and industry, based on the ever-increasing exploitation of new forms of mechanical power, which characterises modern civilisation. The initial stages of the industrial revolution, before the use of steam, were brought about by the power of the horse and ox, water and wind. The mechanical devices and instruments invented in classical times, pumps, presses and catapults, driving wheels, geared wheels and trip hammers, and the five kinematic 'chains' (screw, wheel, cam, ratchet and pulley) were applied in the later Middle Ages on a scale unknown in earlier societies. The remaining kinematic 'chain,' the crank, was known in its simple form in late classical times. It was used in such simple mechanisms as the rotary grindstone depicted in the mid-9th-century *Utrecht Psalter*. The combined crank and connecting-rod was a medieval invention. Though it is difficult to trace its later history, this mechanism had certainly come into general use by the 15th century. With the crank it became possible for the first time to convert reciprocating into rotary motion and *vice versa*, a technique without which modern machinery is inconceivable.

The earliest water-driven mills were used for grinding corn, though before them waterwheels operating chains of pots had been used in ancient Sumeria for raising water. These early cornmills were of three kinds. Horizontal millstones on a vertical shaft turned by water flowing past vanes attached to the bottom of the shaft are known from the 5th century A.D. from Ireland, Norway, Greece and other places, though there is no direct evidence for this kind of mill in antiquity. A second type of mill, in which a vertical undershot waterwheel operated a pestle by a trip hammer mechanism, is described by Pliny. An undershot waterwheel driving a millstone by means of geared wheels is described by Vitruvius [first century B.C.]. This is the first instance known of the use of geared wheels for transmitting power. Four centuries later Pappus of Alexandria described a toothed wheel rotating on a helix or worm gearing. There is evidence that the Romans used also overshot wheels, which had the mechanical advantage that they were driven by the weight of the water as well as the force of the current. From the Mediterranean, watermills spread northwestward and, by the 4th century A.D., they were in general use throughout Europe for grinding corn and pressing olives. In the 4th century Ausonius describes a water-driven saw in use on the Moselle for cutting marble. In the 11th century Domesday Book records 5,000 watermills in England alone. The first evidence as to the type of mill in use in medieval Christendom comes from the 12th century, by which time the vertical undershot wheel was the common type. Overshot wheels do not appear in illustrations before the 14th century and even by the end of the

16th century they had by no means entirely displaced the undershot type.

With the spread of watermills came improvements in methods of transmitting power and of converting their rotary motion for special purposes. As early as the 12th century, illustrations show that the proportions of the crown and pinion wheels forming the gear were adjusted to give the millstone a high speed of rotation even in slow streams, and the general mechanism of the geared wheel was adapted to mills worked by other forms of power. Illustrations from the end of the 13th century to the 16th show such mechanisms in mills worked by horses or oxen or by hand, and 15th-century illustrations show them in windmills. By the end of the 12th century the rotary motion of the waterwheel was being converted to operate trip hammers for fulling and for crushing woad, oak bark, for tanning leather, and other substances, and by the 14th century the same mechanism was used for forge hammers. In the 14th century the treadle hammer, the English 'oliver,' appeared, and in the 15th century a stamping mill was described for crushing ore. In the late 13th century the waterwheel was adapted also to drive forge bellows and, if a device sketched by Villard de Honnecourt represents something actually used, sawmills for cutting wood. Water-driven sawmills certainly existed in the next century. By the 14th century waterwheels and also horse-driven wheels were used to drive grindstones for making edged tools; by the 15th century they were in use for pumping in mines and salt pits, for hoisting in mines with crank or windlass, and for driving iron-rolling mills and wire-drawing mills; by the 16th century they were used to drive silk mills.

Windmills came into use much later than watermills. The first certain knowledge of windmills comes from the writings of Arab geographers travelling in Persia in the 10th century, though mills may have existed there before that time. These writings describe windmills with horizontal sails operating a vertical axle, to the lower end of which was attached a horizontal millstone. Windmills may have come to the West from Persia through the Arabs of Spain, through the Crusades, or through trade between Persia and the Baltic known to have passed through Russia. Certainly when windmills first appear in Christendom in the 12th century it is in the northwest, though these had vertical sails driving a horizontal axle. But whatever its early history in the West, by the end of the 12th century the windmill was widespread in England, the Netherlands and northern France; it was used especially in those regions where there was no water. The chief mechanical problem introduced by the windmill arose out of the need to present the sails to the wind, and in the earlier mills the whole structure was rotated about a pivot or post. This meant that mills had to remain small, and only from the end of the 15th century did the windmill increase in size and develop in a really efficient form. The axle was then set at a slight angle to the ground, the sails adjusted to catch every breath of wind, a brake was fitted, and there were levers to adjust the position of the millstones. The 'turret' type of windmill with only the top section rotating, which was developed in Italy towards the end of the 15th century, was the last significant addition to the list of prime movers before the invention of the steam engine.

The development and application of these forms of power produced the same kind of social and economic changes and dislocations in the Middle Ages as were to occur again on a larger scale in the 18th and 19th centuries. As early as the 10th century the lords of the manor began to claim a monopoly for their cornmills, which were a source of money-income, and this led to a long struggle between the lords and the commune. The monks of Jumièges, as lords of the manor, destroyed the hand mills at Viville in 1207; the monks of St. Albans carried on a campaign against hand mills from the end of the 13th century until the so-called Peasants' Revolt, the great rising of the English communities led by Wat Tyler in 1381. The mechanisation of fulling in the 13th century led to a wholesale shift of the English cloth industry from the plains of the southeast to the hills of the northwest where water was available. Colonies of weavers settled round the fulling mills in the Lake District, the West Riding and the Stroud valley, and the cloth industry decayed in towns like York, Lincoln, London and Winchester which had provided the broadcloth that was the staple of English industry in the 12th century. The insistence of the landowners who erected these mills that cloth should be brought to them, and not fulled by hand or foot at home, led to a long struggle, aspects of which are vividly described in *Piers Plowman,* and this action by the owners of mills was certainly also one of the causes of the Peasants' Revolt.

Though the other processes involved in the manufacture of cloth did not, until the 18th century, reach the complete mechanisation achieved in fulling in the 13th, the first steps towards this also were made during the Middle Ages. The main stages in early cloth making were carding and combing by hand, spinning by hand from a distaff on to a loose spindle, and weaving of the yarn thus prepared into a loose 'web' on a loom worked by hand and foot. The 'web' was then fulled in water and so felted. After fulling the cloth went to the 'rower' who raised the nap with teasels and to the shearsman who cut off the loose threads, after which, when small blemishes had been repaired, it was ready for sale. The mechanisation of spinning began in the 13th century when the spinning wheel turned by hand made its appearance. The processes of twisting silk and winding it on reels are said to have been mechanised in Bologna in 1272. Certainly various kinds of thread were being spun with wheels by the end of the 13th century and about the same time the quilling wheel came in, by means of which the spun yarn was wound regularly on to the quill or bobbin which was set in the shuttle for weaving. There are several 14th-century illustrations of this wheel in use. It is interesting from the mechanical point of view as one of the earliest attempts to use continuous rotary motion. At the end of the 15th century further improvements in mechanisms for spinning and winding were envisaged by Leonardo da Vinci, who drew a sketch of a 'flyer' by means of which these two processes could go on simultaneously; he seems to have had in mind large-scale machinery driven by water power or a horse winch. He designed also a power-driven gig wheel for raising the nap on cloth with teasels. In fact no satisfactory substitute has ever been discovered for teasels, though unsuccessful attempts to use iron combs were made as early as the mid-15th century. The flyer actually came into use about 1530 in a wheel incorporating also another innovation, the drive by treadle and crank. Power-driven spinning wheels and gig mills seem to have been used on a considerable scale in the Italian silk industry from the end of the 16th century, and full descriptions of them are given by Zonca (1607).

In weaving, the improvements that took place between the end of the Roman Empire and the revival of Western silk manufacture in the 14th century occurred mainly outside the West in Byzantium, Egypt, Persia and China, though they were rapidly taken over in the West in the later Middle Ages. These improvements were introduced mainly to make possible the weaving of patterned silk materials, for which it was necessary to be able to select the particular threads of the warp to be moved. This was done by two distinct improvements to the loom: first, a loom worked by pedals with better heddles, and later with a reed frame to provide a runway for the shuttle; and secondly, the draw loom. Both these devices seem to have been in existence in Egypt by about the 6th century A.D. and they probably entered Christendom through Italy, perhaps as early as the 11th century. From the silk industry their use spread to other branches of textile manufacture. Some further minor improvements were made in weaving technique in Europe in the 14th and 15th centuries; a knitting machine or stocking frame was invented in the 16th century, hand knitting having been invented a century earlier; and a ribbon loom was introduced about 1621. But the major improvements in weaving were not to come until the invention of the flying shuttle and power loom which, with the contemporaneous advances in the mechanisation of spinning, were to transform the textile industry, particularly in England, in the 18th and early 19th centuries.

Another industry which became rapidly mechanised at the end of the Middle Ages was the production of books. Of the different elements involved in printing, the manufacture of linen paper seems to have begun in China in the 1st century A.D., whence it spread westwards through the countries dominated by Islam, to enter Christendom through Spain and southern France in the 12th century. This was a more suitable material for printing than the older costly parchment and brittle papyrus. The inks with an oil base used in printing were developed first by painters rather than calligraphers. Presses were already known in the manufacture of wine and the printing of cloth. The most essential element, the type itself, was made possible by skills acquired by wood engravers and by goldsmiths who had developed a technique for casting metal. Type developed in three main stages, first in China and then in Europe, though since the techniques used in these two regions were very different it is difficult to say to what extent the one influenced the other. In China, printing from wooden blocks, a separate block being cut for each page, appeared in the 6th century A.D., printing from movable wooden characters in the 11th century, and from movable metal type (in Korea) in the 14th century. In Europe the use of wood cuts for the elaborate initial letters of manuscripts first appeared in a monastery at Engelberg in 1147; block printing appeared at Ravenna in 1289 and was common throughout Europe by the 15th century; movable metal type came in at the end of the 14th century, appearing at Limoges in 1381, Antwerp in 1417, and Avignon in 1444. The advantage of cast metal type was that hundreds of copies of each letter could be cast from a single mould instead of having to be carved separately as with wooden type. Though the first record of it in Europe is in the Netherlands, it was at Mainz that the use of accurately set movable type was brought to perfection. At Mainz, between 1447 and 1455, Gutenberg and his associates introduced, in place of the older method of casting type in sand, first the adjustable metal type-mould for making lead type, then the improvement of punches and the preparation of copper type. These were the strategic inventions in printing and with them the multiplication of books on a large scale became possible.

Perhaps the most spectacular result of medieval mechanical techniques is to be seen in the buildings, and many of the devices employed by the medieval mason to solve the statical problems arising in the construction of large churches were altogether original. It is impossible to say to what extent the medieval builder was being purely empirical and to what extent he was able to use the results of theoretical work in statics, but it is significant that during the late 12th and 13th centuries, just when the erection of the great cathedrals was producing the most difficult practical problems, Jordanus Nemorarius and others were making important additions to theoretical statics; at least one 13th-century architect, Villard de Honnecourt, showed a knowledge of geometry. The original developments in Gothic architecture arose from the attempt to put a stone roof on the thin walls of the central aisle of a basilica, the usual form of Christian church since Roman times. The Romans never had to face the problems which arose for the medieval mason because they built the barrel or groined vaults over their baths in concrete, and domes, like that of the Pantheon, in horizontally coursed brickwork with mortar; when the concrete or mortar had set, the thrust of the roof on the wall was very small. This was not the case with medieval buildings, in which no such concrete or mortar was used.

The masons of 10th- and 11th-century Burgundy tried to roof their naves with barrel vaults in the Roman style, but they found that the enormous thrust on the side walls tended to push them out even though they were made very thick. The first attempt to overcome this difficulty was to make the side aisles nearly the same height as the nave and roof them by means of groined vaults formed by two barrel vaults intersecting at right angles. These groined vaults of the aisles counteracted the thrust of the barrel vault of the nave and themselves exerted very little thrust except at the corners, which could be supported by massive pillars. This arrangement had the disadvantage that it left the church lighted only by the aisle windows, and when, as in many Cluniac churches, the roof of the nave was raised to get windows above the aisles, the walls collapsed from lack of support. A solution was found at Vézelay and Langres by using groined vaults for the nave, two semicircular wooden centrings being used on which to construct the diagonals of the vault. By this means the 11th-century builder could construct a vaulted roof to cover any space, square or oblong, with a separate vault over each bay resting on semicircular transverse arches separating the bays.

This arrangement still had serious defects. The form of the semi-circular arch, in which the height must be half the span, was quite inelastic and there was still a formidable outward thrust so that the transverse arches tended to drop. Considerable elasticity of design was introduced and the outward thrust reduced by adopting the pointed arch which appeared in Christendom first in Vézelay and other Cluniac churches in the late 11th century, and later in the Île de France. It is thought to have been brought to Europe from Asia Minor, where it had become common by the 9th century. Half-arches of this kind were used in the 12th century to buttress the walls of several French churches, flying buttresses, in fact, in all respects except that they were hidden under the triforium roof.

A further step which completed the change from the Roman to the Gothic vaulted roof was to build diagonal arches over the wooden centrings used in constructing the groins, and to use these as per-manent ribs (sprung from columns) on which to build the vault sur-face. This seems to have been done in various parts of Europe during the 11th and early 12th centuries, and it was this invention which gave rise to the wonderful Gothic of the Île de France in the 12th century. It gave great elasticity of design to the vault and meant that any space of any shape could be vaulted with ease, so long as it could be divided up into triangles, and that the summits of all the arches and vaults could be kept at any level desired. This freedom was increased still further when it was realised that the diagonal ribs need not be com-plete arches, but that three or more half-ribs could be used butting against each other at the summit of a pointed roof. Following the intro-duction of the permanent rib, differences in the method of filling in the vault surface led to a striking divergence in roof design between France and England. The French method was to make each vaulting panel arched and self-supporting. The English, on the other hand, did not make their panels self-supporting, so that further ribs had to be added to keep them up and this led to the fan vaulting of which good examples are Exeter Cathedral and the Chapel of King's College, Cambridge.

Perhaps the most striking of all the devices invented to solve the problems created by stone vaulting was the flying buttress introduced in the Île de France in the 12th century. In contrast with English builders, who at first retained the Norman tradition of thick walls, the French reduced their walls to little else than frames for the stained-glass windows, and in so doing they had to devise some means of counteracting the thrust of the nave roof. This they did, at Poissy in 1135 and later at Sens and St. Germain des Près, by carrying up a half-arch above the roof of the side aisle to the junction of the roof and wall of the nave. Later it was realised that the roof thrust extended some way down the wall, and the flying buttress was doubled to meet this thrust as at Chartres and Amiens. This method of counteracting roof thrust created another problem, for it exposed the building to a considerable strain from east to west. To tie it together in this direction the wall arches and the gables over the windows were made specially strong. This gave the windows in French churches like La Sainte Chapelle in Paris a prominence they never had in England.

Probably many of the devices invented by the 12th- and 13th-century architects were based on rule of thumb, and the great period of medieval building is singularly lacking in treatises on the subject. But the notebook of Villard de Honnecourt, who designed parts of Laon, Rheims, Chartres and other French cathedrals, shows that the 13th-century architect could possess a greater ability to generalise the problems of stress and weight lifting involved than the poverty of theoretical writings might suggest. The *Architettura* of Alberti shows that certainly by the 15th century architects had a good knowledge of mechanics. This knowledge becomes even more evident in the late 15th and early 16th centuries, when Leonardo da Vinci calculated the weight that a pillar or a cluster of pillars of any given diameter could safely carry and tried also to determine the greatest weight that could be borne by a beam of any given span. By the 16th century, Vitruvius had begun to have a great influence on building, but his admirers, such as Palladio, whose *Architettura* was published in 1570, far surpassed him in scientific knowledge. By the 17th century, problems such as the strength of materials and the stability of arches had become a subject of research by professional mathematicians like Galileo, Wren and Hooke; Wren and Hooke were also employed as architects.

Another branch of construction in which considerable progress was made during the Middle Ages, with the object of making better use of wind power, was ship building. The two common types of medieval European ship derived, respectively, from the Roman galley and the Norse long ship. They had a number of features in common: both were long, narrow and flat-bottomed, with a single mast and a square sail; both were steered by an oar on the side at the stern of the ship. The first improvement on this arrangement was the fore-and-aft rig as seen in the lateen sail which appears suddenly in Greek miniatures in the 9th century. By the 12th century lateen sails were common in the Mediterranean, and from there they spread to northern Europe. At the same time ships grew larger, got higher out of the water, the number of masts increased, and in the 13th century the modern rudder fixed to the stern post, itself an extension of the keel, made its appearance. These improvements made it possible to tack effectively against the wind, made oarsmen unnecessary, and extended the range of exploration. An early exercise in the mechanisation of ships, not necessarily representing anything actually built, appeared at the beginning of the 15th century with the drawings of ships with paddle-wheels by Konrad Kyeser and by the Sienese engineer, Jacopo Mariano Taccola. Ramelli also gave an illustration of a paddle boat in 1588 and another innovation, a submarine, was actually built and successfully used in the Thames in 1614.

An improvement to inland water transport was brought about in the 14th century by the introduction of lock gates on canals; new possibilities for transport on land were introduced by making roads of stone cubes set in a bed of loose earth or sand and by improvements in wheeled vehicles, including (in the 13th century) the invention of the wheelbarrow. Mechanisation was attempted also with land vehicles as early as 1420, when Fontana described a velocipede. At the end of the 16th century wagons propelled by man-driven machinery and by sails were apparently constructed in the Low Countries. Flight had attracted attention in the West at least since the 11th century, when Oliver of Malmesbury is said to have broken his legs in an attempt to glide from a tower with wings fitted to his hands and feet. Roger Bacon was also interested in flight. Leonardo da Vinci actually designed a mechanical flying-machine which flapped its wings like a bird.

An important advance associated with these improvements in methods of transport was the appearance of the first good maps in the West since Roman times. When accurate maps were added to the rudder and the compass, which came into use in the 12th century, ships could be navigated effectively away from sight of land and, as Mumford has put it, exploration was encouraged in an attempt to fill in the gaps suggested by the rational expectations of space. The first true medieval maps were the *portolani*, or compass-charts, for mariners. The earliest known *portolano* is the late 13th-century *Carte Pisane*, but its relative technical excellence suggests that others which have disappeared were made before it. Genoese sailors are said to have shown St. Louis of France his position on a map when he was crossing to Tunis in 1270. Some of the evidence might seem to suggest a Scandinavian origin for *portolani*, but the Arabs certainly had charts from an early date, and charts were developed also by the Byzantines, Catalans and Genoese. The use of the Catalan *legua* for distances in all the known *portolani* perhaps supports the Catalan claim to primacy, but this use may have come in later as a matter of convenience. In fact, the question of the origin of *portolani* is undecided. The novel feature of the *portolani*, as compared with the old traditional symbolic *mappæ mundi*, is that they were made for use as guides to a specific area. Made by practical men and based on the direct determination of distances and azimuths by using log and compass, they were generally restricted to the coastline. They contained no indications of longitude and latitude. They were covered with networks of rhumb-lines giving the compass bearing of the places on the map. The rhumb-lines radiated from a number of points arranged in a circle, corresponding to the points marked on a compass-card.

Other accurate maps showing inland regions as well as the coastline were produced by men of education from the 13th century, by which time scholars like Roger Bacon were taking an interest in real geography. Bacon himself made no practical contributions to cartography, though his belief that there was no great width of ocean between Europe and China is said to have influenced Columbus, who found it repeated in works by Pierre d'Ailly and Aeneas Sylvius. As early as about 1250 Matthew Paris drew four recognisable maps of Great Britain showing details such as the Roman Wall, roads and towns. Between 1325 and 1330 an unknown cartographer produced a remarkably detailed and accurate map of England, the so-called 'Gough Map,' now in the Bodleian Library in Oxford, which shows roads with mileages probably as estimated by travellers. About the same time good maps showing northern Italy were made by Opicinus de Canistris, who died about 1352, and in 1375 the so-called Majorcan school of cartographers produced for Charles V of France the famous *Catalan Mappemonde*, which combined the virtues of the *portolani* and the land maps and included North Africa and parts of Asia. This Majorcan centre had collected an enormous amount of marine and commercial information and was the forerunner of the colonial and naval institute founded by Prince Henry the Navigator at Sagres about 1437. These early maps showed no indication of latitude and longitude, though the latitude of many towns had been determined with the astrolabe. But in his *Geographia* Ptolemy had drawn maps on a complete network of parallels and meridians. This work, as it has come down to us, seems to be at least partly a later compilation, and the maps in the existing manuscripts were probably made by Byzantine artists in the 13th and 14th centuries. It was recovered and translated into Latin by Giacomo d'Angelo, who dedicated his translation, with some excellent maps redrawn from the Greek original by a Florentine artist, to Pope Gregory XII in 1406 and Pope Alexander V in 1409. After this, cartographers began to adopt Ptolemy's practice. Good examples are Andrea Bianco's map of Europe in 1436, and the map of central Europe found among the manuscripts of Nicholas of Cusa (1401–64) and printed in 1491. Ptolemy's own atlas of the world was printed in numerous editions from 1477, when the *Geographia* was published, at Bologna, for the first time with Ptolemy's maps. These were redrawn by Italian cartographers. It gradually transformed cartography by emphasising the need for an accurate linear measure of the arc of the meridian, the essential requirement for accurate terrestrial cartography.

Until the end of the 18th century the most important material for machinery and construction generally was wood. Most of the parts of watermills and windmills, spinning wheels, looms, presses, ships and vehicles were of wood, and wood was used for geared wheels in much machinery as late as the 19th century. Thus it was that the first machine tools were developed for working wood, and even in the tools themselves only the cutting edge was of metal. Of the boring machines, the bow-drill known since Neolithic times, in which the drill was driven rapidly by a string wound round it and attached at each end to a bow which was moved back and forth, was replaced during the later Middle Ages by the brace and bit, and a machine for boring pump barrels from solid tree trunks was also known. The most important of the machine tools for accurate work, the lathe, may have been known in some form in antiquity, but the pole-lathe was probably a medieval invention. The first known illustrations of pole-lathes appear only in sketches by Leonardo da Vinci, but they must have been in use before that time. The spindle was driven by a cord wound round it as in the bow-drill, and attached at the bottom to a treadle and at the top to a springy pole which flexed the cord back on taking the foot off the treadle. Leonardo shows also a rotary lathe driven by bands from a wheel, though rotary lathes with crank and treadle drive became common only from the 17th century. In these early lathes the work was turned between fixed centres, but in the mid-16th century Besson designed a mandrel lathe in which the work was fixed to a chuck to which power was applied. Besson designed also a crude screw-cutting lathe, to which further improvements were made in the 17th century, in particular the change introduced by the clockmakers from traversing the work over a stationary tool to traversing the tool itself while the work merely rotated. Thus, from the early machine tools designed for working wood, were developed tools capable of accurate work with metals.

The earliest machines made entirely of metal were firearms and the mechanical clock, and the mechanical clock in particular is the prototype of modern automatic machinery in which all the parts are precisely designed to produce an accurately-controlled result. In the mechanical clock the use of geared wheels, the main point of interest in early machinery, was completely mastered.

Water clocks, like the clepsydra, measuring time by the amount of water dripping through a small hole, had been used by the ancient Egyptians, and the Greeks had improved them by fitting devices to indicate the hours by a pointer on a scale, and to regulate the movement. The water clocks developed by the Arabs and Latin Christians were based on these Greek devices and also on the devices of the automatic puppet theatre, which was popular in the Middle Ages. They were so successful that water clocks remained in use as late as the 18th century. These water clocks were worked by a float suspended in a basin filled and emptied by a regulating mechanism, and the motion of the float was communicated to the indicator, usually some kind of puppet show, by ropes and pulleys. In Islam, they were sometimes very large and were set up where the public could see them; and in Christendom smaller clocks were used in monasteries where they were looked after by a special keeper, one of whose duties was to adjust the clock at night by taking observations on a star. One such clock is said to have been made by Gerbert for the monastery at Magdeburg. Other early clocks were worked by a burning candle, and a mid-13th-century work prepared for Alfonso X of Castile describes a clock operated by a falling weight controlled by the resistance created by the passage of mercury through small apertures. Similar devices were developed in the long series of astronomical mechanisms—planetaria, mechanically rotated star-maps, etc.—which are as essential a part of the ancestry of the mechanical clock as time-keepers proper. In none of the devices were there any gears.

The essential features of the mechanical clock were a drive by a falling weight which set in motion a train of geared wheels, and an oscillatory escapement mechanism which prevented the weight accelerating as it fell, by stopping it at frequent intervals. The earliest illustration of an escapement mechanism, at least in the West, appears in the mid-13th century in a device drawn by Villard de Honnecourt for making an angel rotate slowly so that its finger always pointed towards the sun. It is possible that the first mechanical clocks were made shortly afterwards. There are references to what seem to have been mechanical clocks of some kind in London, Canterbury, Paris and other places during the second half of the 13th century and in Milan, St. Albans, Glastonbury, Avignon, Padua and elsewhere during the first half of the 14th century. Some of these were planetaria, for showing the motions of the heavenly bodies, rather than clocks. Probably the earliest true clocks of which the mechanism is definitely known are the Dover Castle clock, usually dated 1348 but probably later, and Henri de Vick's clock set up in Paris at the Palais Royal, now the Palais de Justice, in 1370. These clocks were regulated by a verge escapement with a foliot balance. The essential components of this mechanism were a crown wheel with saw-like teeth, which were engaged alternatively by two small plates or pallets on a rod, so that the wheel was intermittently stopped and released. The foliot was a mechanism for regulating the speed of rotation of the crown or 'escape' wheel, and therefore of the whole train of wheels ending with the axle carrying the hands of the clock. The perfection of this verge escapement and foliot balance marks a limit in clock design on which, in point of accuracy, no real advance was made until the application of the pendulum to clocks in the 17th century, though before that time considerable refinements were made in construction. The early clocks were, in fact, mostly very large and the parts were made by a blacksmith. De Vick's clock was moved by a weight of 500 lbs. which fell 32 feet in 24 hours and had a striking weight of nearly three-quarters of a ton. In the

15th century, clocks became smaller and were used in houses, screws were used to hold the parts together, and the end of the century saw the first 'clock-watches' driven by a spring.

These early clocks were reasonably accurate if set nightly by observing a star, and by 1500 most towns had public clocks on the outside walls of monasteries or cathedrals or on special towers. They either simply struck the hours or also showed them on a circular face marked in divisions of 12 or 24. The effect of placing them in public places was to bring about the complete replacement of the seven variable liturgical hours by the 24 equal hours of the clock. From an early date in antiquity astronomers had, in fact, divided the day into 24 equal hours, taking the hours of the equinox as standard, and throughout the early Middle Ages this system had existed, particularly in civil life, side by side with the ecclesiastical system. A decisive step was taken in 1370 by Charles V of France when he ordered all churches in Paris to ring the hours and quarters according to time by de Vick's clock, and from that time the equal hours became more common. The division of the hour into 60 minutes and of the minute into 60 seconds also came into general use in the 14th century and was fairly common as early as 1345. The adoption of this system of division completed the first stages in the scientific measurement of time, without which the later refinements of both physics and machinery would scarcely have been possible.

*   *   *   *   *

## BASIC CONTRIBUTIONS OF MEDIEVAL SCIENCE AND TECHNOLOGY

In the field of scientific method, the recovery of the Greek idea of theoretical explanation in science, and especially of the 'Euclidean' form of such explanation and its use in mathematical physics, raised the problems of how to construct and to verify or falsify theories. The basic conception of scientific explanation held by the medieval natural scientists came from the Greeks and was essentially the same as that of modern science. When a phenomenon had been accurately described so that its characteristics were adequately known, it was explained by relating it to a set of general principles or theories connecting all similar phenomena. The problem of the relation between theory and experiment presented by this form of scientific explanation was analysed by the scholastics in developing their methods of 'resolution and composition.' Examples of the use of the scholastic methods of induction and experiment are seen in optics and magnetics in the thirteenth and fourteenth centuries. The methods involved everyday observations as well as specially devised experiments, simple idealisations, and 'thought experiments,' but also mention of imaginary and impossible experiments.

Another important contribution to scientific method was the extension of mathematics to the whole of physical science, at least in principle. Aristotle had restricted the use of mathematics, in his theory of the subordination of one science to another, by sharply distinguishing the explicative roles of mathematics and 'physics.' The effect of this change was not so much to destroy this distinction as to change the kind of question scientists asked. One principal reason for the change was the influence of the Neoplatonic conception of nature as ultimately mathematical, a conception exploited in the notion that the key to the physical world was to be found in the study of light. Certainly the medieval scientists did not press this conception to the limit, but they did begin to show less interest in the 'physical' or metaphysical question of cause and to ask the kind of question that could be answered by a mathematical theory within reach of experimental verification. Examples of this method are seen in mechanics, optics and astronomy in the 13th and 14th centuries. It was through the mathematicisation of nature and of physics that the inconvenient classical concept of pairs of opposites was replaced by the modern concept of homogeneous linear measures.

Besides these ideas on method, though often closely connected with them, a radically new approach to the question of space and motion began at the end of the 13th century. Greek mathematicians had constructed a mathematics of rest, and important advances in statics had been made during the 13th century, progress assisted by Archimedean methods of manipulating ideal quantities such as the length of the weightless arm of a balance. The 14th century saw the first attempts to construct a mathematics of change and motion. Of the various elements contributing to this new dynamics and kinematics, the ideas that space might be infinite and void, and the universe without a centre, undermined Aristotle's cosmos with its qualitatively different directions and led to the idea of relative motion. Concerning motion, the chief new idea was that of *impetus*, and the most significant characteristic of this concept was that a measure was given of the quantity of *im-*

*petus* in which this was proportional to the quantity of matter in the body and the velocity imparted to it. Also important was the discussion of the persistence of *impetus* in the absence of resistance from the medium and of the action of gravity. *Impetus* was still a 'physical' cause in the Aristotelian sense; in considering motion as a state requiring no continuous efficient causation, Ockham made another contribution perhaps related to the 17th-century idea of inertial motion. The theory of *impetus* was used to explain many different phenomena, for instance the motion of projectiles and falling bodies, bouncing balls, pendulums and the rotation of the heavens or of the earth. The possibility of the last was suggested by the concept of relative motion, and objections to it from the argument from detached bodies were met by the idea of 'compound motion' advanced by Oresme. The kinematic study of accelerated motion began also in the 14th century, and the solution of one particular problem, that of a body moving with uniform acceleration, was to be applied later to falling bodies. Discussion of the nature of a continuum and of maxima and minima began also in the 14th century.

In the field of technology, the Middle Ages saw some remarkable progress. Beginning with new methods of exploiting animal-, water- and wind-power, new machines were developed for a variety of purposes, often requiring considerable precision. Some technical inventions, for instance the mechanical clock and magnifying lenses, were to be used as scientific instruments. Measuring instruments such as the astrolabe and quadrant were greatly improved as a result of the demand for accurate measurement. In chemistry, the balance came into general use. Empirical advances were made and the experimental habit led to the development of special apparatus.

In the biological sciences, some technical advances were made. Important works were written on medicine and surgery, on the symptoms of diseases, and descriptions were given of the flora and fauna of different regions. A beginning was made with classification, and the possibility of having accurate illustrations was introduced by naturalistic art. Perhaps the most important medieval contribution to theoretical biology was the elaboration of the idea of a scale of animated nature. In geology observations were made and the true nature of fossils understood by some writers.

Concerning the question of the purpose and nature of science, two medieval contributions may be singled out. The first is the idea, first explicitly expressed in the 13th century, that the purpose of science was to gain power over nature useful to man. The second is the idea insisted on by the theologians, that neither God's action nor man's speculation could be constrained within any particular system of scientific or philosophical thought. Whatever may have been its effects in other branches of thought, the effect of this idea on natural science was to bring out the relativity of all scientific theories and the fact that they might be replaced by others more successful in fulfilling the requirements of the rational and experimental methods.

Thus the experimental and mathematical methods were a growth, developing within the medieval system of scientific thought, which was to destroy from within and eventually to burst out from Aristotelian cosmology and physics. Though resistance to the destruction of the old system became strong among certain of the late scholastics, and especially among those whose humanism had given them too great a devotion to the ancient texts and those by whom the old system had been too closely linked with theological doctrines, there can be little doubt that it was the development of these experimental and mathematical methods of the 13th and 14th centuries that at least initiated the historical movement of the Scientific Revolution culminating in the 17th century.

But when all is considered, the science of Galileo, Harvey and Newton was not the same as that of Grosseteste, Albertus Magnus and Buridan. Not only were their aims sometimes subtly and sometimes obviously different and the achievements of the later science infinitely the greater; they were not in fact connected by an unbroken continuity of historical development. Towards the end of the 14th century, the brilliant period of scholastic originality came to an end. For the next century and a half all that Paris and Oxford produced on astronomy, physics, medicine or logic were dreary epitomes of the earlier writings. One or two original thinkers like Nicholas of Cusa and Regiomontanus appeared in Germany in the 15th century. Italy fared better but rather with the new group of 'artist-engineers' like Leonardo da Vinci than in the universities. Interest and intellectual originality were directed towards literature and the plastic arts rather than towards natural science.

Apart from anything else, the enormously greater achievements and confidence of the 17th-century scientists make it obvious that they were not *simply* carrying on the earlier methods though using them better. But if there is no need to insist on the historical fact of a Scientific Revolution in the 17th century, neither can there be any doubt about the existence of an original scientific movement in the 13th and 14th centuries.

## Suggestions for Further Reading

BUTTERFIELD, H., *Origins of Modern Science*. London: G. Bell and Sons, 1949.

CIPOLLA, C. N., *Clocks and Culture 1300–1700*. New York: Walker and Co., 1967.

CLAGETT, M., *The Science of Mechanics in the Middle Ages*. Madison, Wisconsin: University of Wisconsin Press, 1959.

EASTON, STEWART, *Roger Bacon and His Search for a Universal Science*. Westport, Conn.: Greenwood Press, 1952.

KLEMM, FRIEDRICH, *A History of Western Technology*, New York: Scribner's, 1959.

MUMFORD, L., *Technics and Civilization*. New York: Harcourt Brace Jovanovich, Inc., 1934.

PALTER, R. M., ed., *Toward Modern Science*, Vol. I: *Studies in Ancient and Medieval Science*. New York: Noonday Press, 1961.

PANOFSKY, ERWIN, *Gothic Architecture and Scholasticism*. New York: Meridian, 1957.

SARTON, GEORGE, *Introduction to the History of Science*, Vols. I–III. Baltimore: Williams and Wilkins, 1927, 1931.

THORNDIKE, LYNN, *History of Magic and Experimental Science*, Vols. I–IV. New York: Columbia University Press, 1923–1934.

THORNDIKE, LYNN, *Science and Thought in the Fifteenth Century*. New York: Hafner, 1929.

WHITE, LYNN, *Medieval Technology and Social Change*. Oxford: Clarendon Press, 1962.

# JOHAN HUIZINGA

# The Waning of Medieval Culture

࿔ Our knowledge of the fourteenth and fifteenth centuries is less certain and less firmly grounded than that of any era except the seventh century A.D. It is not likely that historians will ever improve upon their meager knowledge of the pattern of events in the seventh century because the surviving sources for this age of barbarian turmoil and violence are extremely sparse. Precisely the opposite condition prevails with the fourteenth- and fifteenth-century material: the sources are too voluminous and unmanageable. Down to the latter part of the thirteenth century the sources for medieval history are sufficiently limited in volume to have facilitated publication of nearly all of them by the indefatigable scholars of the late nineteenth century, and twentieth-century historians have mined these published sources to build up a quite clear picture of the main lines of development for the period from 750 to about 1275. But after that date, because of a great increase in literacy and the proliferation of records by governments and corporations at all levels, the sources increase in a fantastic geometric progression. There are, for instance, several dozen volumes of English judicial records for the fourteenth and fifteenth centuries which

FROM Johan Huizinga, *The Waning of the Middle Ages* (Garden City, N.Y.: Doubleday & Company, Inc., 1954), pp. 136–159, 206–242, 308. This is a reprint of the English translation first published in 1924 by Edward Arnold and Company, London.

have never been analyzed, and the archives of the north Italian cities for the same period are extremely rich and detailed in information on all aspects of political, economic, and social life. It is only since 1945 that the massive archival resources for fourteenth- and fifteenth-century history have begun to be systematically exploited, and many monographic studies remain to be completed before the contours of change during the period can be determined with confidence by scholars.

Historical insight into the fourteenth and fifteenth centuries has been hampered by intellectual as well as source problems. For the era which stretches from the eighth to the thirteenth century, scholars have been able to follow the universally held assumption that they are examining the rise and transformation of feudal society—the process of transition from ruralism, disorder, and ignorance to political and legal order, the entrenchment of ecclesiastical leadership, and the achievement of intellectual creativity. No such commonly agreed-upon interpretation exists to guide historians through the sources for the paradoxical and confused two centuries after 1275. Not only are the sources voluminous and difficult to work with, but also historians have had a very difficult time trying to decide exactly what they are looking for in the primary material. It is relatively easy to do detailed institutional studies on particular aspects of fourteenth- and fifteenth-century government and economy, but it has required the highest and most subtle exercise of the historical imagination to bring the general pattern of development for this period into meaningful focus.

A half century ago, because there was a carry-over of the old notion that the Middle Ages was simply an era of barbarism and stagnation, it was possible to identify the fourteenth and fifteenth centuries as "the age of the Renaissance," in which European society supposedly advanced from dark disorder and superstition and ruralism into enlightened government and intellectual and artistic progress. This convenient thesis was shown to be false, at least as pertained to Europe north of the Alps, by the Dutch historian Johan Huizinga in the early 1920's.

Huizinga's seminal interpretive work, *The Waning of the Middle Ages*, demonstrated that in northern France and the Netherlands the fourteenth and fifteenth centuries were an era of spiritual and moral decay and cultural ossification, and he thereby inaugurated a fundamental revision of the assumptions which historians brought to bear on the materials of fourteenth- and fifteenth-century history. Leaving aside Italy, which may have been a special case and where there may indeed have taken place a great change in values and attitudes that we can designate as the Renaissance, it became clear from Huizinga's work that the fourteenth and fifteenth centuries marked not the beginning of the modern world but rather the breakdown of medieval culture and the dissolution of the medieval social order.

Johan Huizinga came from a distinguished Dutch academic family; he became a professor at the University of Leiden in 1915 at the age of 43 and pursued a normally successful and outwardly uneventful academic career until the Nazi occupation, when as an old man he bitterly resisted the new forces of darkness and was harshly treated by the German conquerors. He died in 1945.

Huizinga was a member of that great generation of original and creative thinkers of the late nineteenth century who exploded the smug rigidity of nineteenth-century thought and in the study of human nature and in art and literature revealed the hitherto unknown facets of human experience. The keynote of all the new art and literature of the *fin de siècle* was the creative power of human experience, the central place of the human mind in fashioning the world of consciousness. This movement has generally been called relativism; it casts doubt on the existence of an objective absolute world outside of human consciousness and in any case makes the real world, the only world that matters to us, the one that is created by human imagination. The experiences of each individual create for him a special world which is the only one that can have meaning and significance for him. It is this primacy of the creative power of human consciousness which runs through all the literature, art, and higher thought of the generation that came to maturity in the 1890's. To place Huizinga in his historiographical context and intellectual background, we have to remember that he was the almost exact contemporary of Freud and James Joyce and that he tried to do for historical understanding what they did for psychology and literature.

In several works that are masterpieces of the historian's art, Huizinga explored the subtle and complex relationship between human consciousness and its environment. All his works are arguments in favor of the thesis that the only true history is the history of human consciousness and imagination, of how men at various times have reacted to their environment and built up a world of beauty and terror in their attempts to understand it and to come to terms with it. When Huizinga's work first began to appear about 1920 his underlying methodology was almost totally misunderstood and ignored by academic historians who were still imbued with the naive realism of mid-nineteenth-century thought. It was in fact only after the tremendous impact of Freudian psychology and of impressionism in art and literature that Huizinga's main point was evident to a new generation of scholars after 1945, and he was seen to be not only a historian of great learning and insight and not only a literary craftsman of the highest excellence, but one of the most original historical minds of all time.

*The Waning of the Middle Ages* is Huizinga's masterpiece. For his material he went to no archives and he discovered no hitherto unknown records. On the contrary he used material available to almost anybody, such as might be found in any good public library. He studied the literature and art and descriptions of court life principally in the Duchy of Burgundy (Flanders) in the fourteenth and fifteenth centuries. He showed that the precise imagery in literature and the naturalism in art characteristic of the age are not the qualities of an emerging, but rather of a decaying, civilization. The vitality of the medieval spirit is gone; its symbols have become "crystallized" and ossified into empty images and uninspired description. The spontaneity, the inner creative life of the culture has departed and the failure of nerve, the terrible malaise of a disintegrating society, has set in.

All the work that has been done on the late Middle Ages in the past four decades, partial and limited as it is, has confirmed the brilliance and truth of Huizinga's perception. We now know that a far-reaching economic depression, which began in the late thirteenth century, for nearly two centuries frustrated all the efforts of the hitherto successful medieval governments and engendered a persistent and bitter class conflict. We know too that—as in fact Huizinga himself suggested—the effects of the Black Death went far beyond the economic and social turmoil produced by the plague's decimation of a third of Europe's population. This catastrophe undermined the morale of medieval society and made the Dance of Death, one of the favorite motifs of late medieval art, medieval culture's obituary on its own extinction.

·ᥱᐧᏱᐧᥱ·

Towards the end of the Middle Ages two factors dominate religious life: the extreme saturation of the religious atmosphere, and a marked tendency of thought to embody itself in images.

Individual and social life, in all their manifestations, are imbued with the conceptions of faith. There is not an object nor an action, however trivial, that is not constantly correlated with Christ or salvation. All thinking tends to religious interpretation of individual things; there is an enormous unfolding of religion in daily life. This spiritual wakefulness, however, results in a dangerous state of tension, for the presupposed transcendental feelings are sometimes dormant, and whenever this is the case, all that is meant to stimulate spiritual consciousness is reduced to appalling commonplace profanity, to a startling worldliness in other-worldly guise. Only saints are capable of an attitude of mind in which the transcendental faculties are never in abeyance.

The spirit of the Middle Ages, still plastic and naïve, longs to give concrete shape to every conception. Every thought seeks expression in an image, but in this image it solidifies and becomes rigid. By this tendency to embodiment in visible forms all holy concepts are constantly exposed to the danger of hardening into mere externalism. For in assuming a definite figurative shape thought loses its ethereal and vague qualities, and pious feeling is apt to resolve itself in the image.

\* \* \* \* \*

The specific forms of the thought of an epoch should not only be studied as they reveal themselves in theological and philosophic speculations, or in the conceptions of creeds, but also as they appear in practical wisdom and everyday life. We may even say that the true character of the spirit of an age is better revealed in its mode of regarding and expressing trivial and commonplace things than in the high manifestations of philosophy and science. For all scholarly speculation, at least in Europe, is affiliated in a very complicated way to Greek, Hebrew, even Babylonian and Egyptian origins, whereas in everyday life the spirit of a race or of an epoch expresses itself naïvely and spontaneously.

The mental habits and forms characteristic of the high speculation of the Middle Ages nearly all reappear in the domain of ordinary life. Here, too, as we might expect, primitive idealism, which the schools called realism, is at the bottom of all mental activity. To take every idea by itself, to give it its formula, to treat it as an entity, next to combine the ideas, to classify them, to arrange them in hierarchic systems, always to build cathedrals with them, such, in practical life also, is the way in which the medieval mind proceeds.

All that acquires a fixed place in life is considered as having a reason for existence in the divine scheme. The most commonplace customs share this honour with the most exalted things. A very plain instance of this may be found in the treatment of rules of court etiquette, which we have touched upon already in another connection. Aliénor de Poitiers and Olivier de la Marche considered them wise laws, judiciously instituted by ancient kings and binding for all centuries to come. Aliénor speaks of them as of sacred monuments of the wisdom of ages: "And then I have heard it said by the ancients who knew . . ." etc. She sees with sorrow signs of decline. For a good many years the ladies of Flanders have been putting the bed of a woman newly delivered of a child before the fire, "at which people mocked a good deal," because formerly this was never done. What are we coming to? "But at present everybody does what he pleases: because of which we may well be afraid that all will go badly."—La Marche gravely asks the following question: Why has the "fruit-master," also the "wax-department" (le mestier de la cire), that is to say, illumination, among his attributes?—He answers, not less gravely: Because wax is extracted from flowers whence the fruit comes too: "so that this matter is very well ordained thus."

In matters of utility or of ceremony medieval authority creates a special organ for every function, because it regards the function as an idea and considers it as an actual thing. The "grand sergeanty" of the king of England comprised a dignitary whose office it was to hold the king's head when he crossed the Channel and was suffering with seasickness. A certain John Baker held this office in 1442, and after his death it passed to his two daughters.

Of the same nature is the custom, very ancient and very primitive, of giving a proper name to inanimate objects. We witnessed a revival of this usage when the big guns during the late war got names. During the Middle Ages it was much more frequent. Like the swords of the heroes in the *chansons de geste,* the stone mortars in the wars of the fourteenth and fifteenth centuries had names of their own: "Le Chien d'Orléans, la Gringade, la Bourgeoise, Dulle Griete." A few very celebrated diamonds are still known by proper names: this, too, is a survival of a widely spread custom. Several jewels of Charles the Bold had their names: "le sancy, les trois frères, la hôte, la balle de Flandres." If, at the present time, ships still have names, but bells and most houses have not, the reason lies in the fact that the ship preserves a sort of personality, also expressed in the English usage of making ships feminine. In the Middle Ages this tendency to personify things was much stronger; every house and every bell had its name.

In the minds of the Middle Ages every event, every case, fictitious or historic, tends to crystallize, to become a parable, an example, a proof, in order to be applied as a standing instance of a general moral truth. In the same way every utterance becomes a dictum, a maxim, a text. For every question of conduct, Scripture, legends, history, literature furnish a crowd of examples or of types, together making up a sort of moral clan, to which the matter in question belongs. If it is desired to make someone to pardon an offence, all the Biblical cases of pardon are enumerated to him; if to dissuade him from marrying, all the unhappy marriages of antiquity are cited. In order to free himself from blame for the murder of the duke of Orleans, Jean sans Peur compares himself to Joab and his victim to Absalom, rating himself as less guilty than Joab, because he had not acted in open defiance of a royal warning. "Ainsy avoit le bon duc Jehan attrait ce fait à moralité."[1]

In the Middle Ages everyone liked to base a serious argument on a text, so as to give it a foundation. In 1406, at the national council of Paris, where the question of the schism was debated, the twelve propositions for and against renouncing obedience to the pope of Avignon, all started from a Biblical quotation. Profane orators, too, no less than preachers, choose their text.

All the traits indicated are found united in striking fashion in the famous plea delivered on the 8th of March, 1408, at the hôtel de Saint Pol before a princely audience, by Master Jean Petit, divine, preacher and poet, in order to clear the duke of Burgundy of the charge of the murder which the latter repented of having confessed. It is a real masterpiece of political wickedness, built up with perfect art and in a severe style on the text: *Radix omnium malorum cupiditas* (the root of all evil is covetousness). The whole is cunningly arranged in a scheme of scholastic distinctions and complementary Biblical texts, illustrated by Scriptural and historical examples and animated by a fiendish verve. After having enumerated twelve reasons obliging the duke of Burgundy to honour, love and avenge the king of France, Maître Petit draws two applications from his text: covetousness makes apostates and it makes traitors. Apostasy and treason are divided and subdivided, and then illustrated by three examples. Lucifer, Absalom and Athalia rise up before the imagination of the hearers as the archetypes of a traitor. Eight truths are brought forward to justify tyrannicide. Referring to one of the eight, he says: "I shall prove this truth by twelve reasons in honour of the twelve apostles." And he cites three sentences of the doctors, three of the philosophers, three of the jurists and three from Scripture. From the eight truths eight corollaries are derived, completed by a ninth. By the aid of allusions or insinuations he revives all the old suspicions which hung over the memory of the ambitious and debauched prince: his responsibility for the disaster of the "bal des ardents," where the young king's company, disguised as wild men, miserably perished by fire, while the king himself narrowly escaped; his plans of murder and poisoning, hatched in the Celestine monastery, in the course of his conversations with "the sorcerer," Philippe de Mézières. The notorious leaning of the duke towards necromancy

---

[1] Thus good duke John had drawn the moral inference of the case.

furnished an opportunity for describing very picturesque scenes of horror. Maître Petit is even familiar with the demons whom Orleans consulted; he knows their names and the way in which they were dressed. He goes so far as to ascribe a sinister meaning to the delirious utterances of the mad king.

All this makes up the major term of the syllogism. The minor follows it, point by point. Grounding themselves on the general propositions which had raised the case to the plane of fundamental ethics and had artfully roused a sentiment of shuddering horror, the direct accusations burst out in a flood of passionate hatred and defamation. The pleading lasted for four hours, and at the end Jean sans Peur pronounced the words: "I avouch you" (Je vous avoue). The justification was written out in four costly copies for the duke and his nearest relations, ornamented with gilding and miniatures, and bound in pressed leather. It was also for sale.

The tendency to give each particular case the character of a moral sentence or of an example, so that it becomes something substantial and unchallengeable, the crystallization of thought, in short, finds its most general and natural expression in the proverb. In the thought of the Middle Ages proverbs have performed a very living function. There were hundreds in current use in every nation. The greater number are striking and concise. Their tone is often ironical, their accent always that of bonhomie and resignation. The wisdom we glean from them is sometimes profound and beneficent. They never preach resistance. "Les grans poissons mangent les plus petis." "Les mal vestus assiet on dos ou vent." "Nul n'est chaste si ne besongne." "Au besoing on s'aide du diable." "Il n'est si ferré qui ne glice."[2] To the laments of moralists about the depravation of man the proverbs oppose a smiling detachment. The proverb always glozes over iniquity. Now it is naïvely pagan and now almost evangelical. A people which has many proverbs in current use will be less given to talking nonsense, and so will avoid many confused arguments and empty phrases. Leaving arguments to cultured people, it is content with judging each case by referring to the authority of some proverb. The crystallization of thought in proverbs is therefore not without advantage to society.

Proverbs in their crude simplicity were thoroughly in accordance with the general spirit of the literature of the epoch. The level reached

[2] The big fishes eat the smaller. The badly dressed are placed with their back to the wind. None is chaste if he has no business. At need we let the devil help us. No horse is so well shod that it never slips.

by authors was but little higher than that of the proverbs. The dicta
of Froissart often read like proverbs gone wrong. "It is thus with feats
of arms: sometimes one loses, another time one wins." "There is
nothing of which one does not tire." It is therefore safer, instead of
hazarding moral sentences of one's own, to use well-established proverbs like Geffroi de Paris, who lards his rhyming chronicle with them.
The literature of the time is full of ballads of which each stanza ends
with a proverb, as, for instance, the *Ballade de Fougères* of Alain
Chartier, the *Complaincte de Eco* of Coquillart, and several poems by
Jean Molinet, not to mention Villon's well-known ballad which was
entirely composed of them. The 171 stanzas of the *Passe Temps
d'Oysiveté*, by Robert Gaguin, nearly all end in some phrase looking
like a proverb, although the greater number are not found in the best-
known collections. Did Gaguin invent them, then? In that case we
should have a still more curious indication of the vital function of the
proverb at this epoch, if we see them here arising in an individual
mind, *in statu nascendi*, as it were.

In political speeches and in sermons, proverbs are in frequent use.
Gerson, Jean de Varennes, Jean Petit, Guillaume Fillastre, Olivier
Maillard, take pains to strengthen their arguments by the most common ones. "Qui de toute se tait, de toute a paix.—Chef bien peigné
porte mal bacinet.—Qui commun sert, nul ne l'en paye."[3]

Related to the proverb, in so far as it is a crystallized form of
thought, is the motto, which the declining Middle Ages cultivated with
marked predilection. It differs from it in that it is not, like the proverb,
a wise adage of general application, but a personal maxim or exhorta-
tion. To adopt a motto is, to say, to choose a text for the sermon of
one's life. The motto is a symbol and a token. Marked in golden letters
on every article of the wardrobe and of the equipment, it must have
exercised a suggestive influence of no mean importance. The moral tone
of these mottoes is mostly that of resignation, like that of the proverbs,
or that of hope. The motto should be mysterious. "Quand sera ce?—
Tost ou tard vienne.—Va oultre.—Autre fois mieulx.—Plus deuil que
joye."[4] The greater number refer to love. "Aultre naray.—Vostre

[3] He who is silent about all things, is troubled by nothing.—A well-
groomed head wears the helmet badly.—He who serves the common weal,
is paid by none for his trouble.

[4] When will it be?—Soon or late it may come.—Onward.—Better next
time.—More sorrow than joy.

plaisir.—Souvienne vous.—Plus que toutes."[5] When of such a nature they were worn on armour and caparisons. Those engraved in rings have a more intimate note: "Mon cuer avez.—Je le desire.—Pour toujours.—Tout pour vous."[6]

A complement to mottoes is found in the emblem, like the knotty stick of Louis of Orleans with the motto "Je l'envie," a gambling term meaning "I challenge," to which Jean sans Peur replied with a plane and the words "Ic houd," that is to say, "accepted." Another instance is the flint-and-steel of Philip the Good. With the emblem and the motto we enter the sphere of heraldic thought, of which the psychology is yet to be written. To the men of the Middle Ages the coat of arms was undoubtedly more than a matter of vanity or of genealogical interest. Heraldic figures in their minds acquired a value almost like that of a *totem*. Whole complexes of pride and ambition, of loyalty and devotion, were condensed in the symbols of lions, lilies or crosses, which thus marked and expressed intricate mental contexts by means of an image.

The spirit of casuistry, which was greatly developed in the Middle Ages, is another expression of the same tendency to isolate each thing as a special entity. It is another effect of the dominant idealism. Every question which presents itself must have its ideal solution, which will become apparent as soon as we have ascertained, by the aid of formal rules, the relation of the case in question to the eternal verities. Casuistry reigns in all the departments of the mind: alike in morals and in law, and in matters of ceremony, of etiquette, of tournaments and the chase, and, above all, of love. We have already spoken of the influence which chivalrous casuistry exercised on the origins of the laws of war. Let us quote some more examples from the *Arbre des Batailles* of Honoré Bonet. Should a member of the clergy aid his father or his bishop? Is one bound to make good borrowed armour which one has lost during a battle? May one fight a battle on festal days? Is it better to fight fasting or after a meal?

No subject lent itself better to the distinction of casuistry than that of prisoners of war. To take noble and rich prisoners was, at that time, the main point of the military profession. In what circumstances may one escape from captivity? What is a safe conduct worth? To whom

---

[5] I shall have no other.—Your pleasure.—Remember.—More than all.
[6] You have my heart.—I desire it.—For ever.—All for you.

does an escaped and recaptured prisoner belong? May a prisoner on parole fly, if his victor puts him in chains? Or may he do so, if his captor forgot to ask his parole? In *Le Jouvencel* two captains dispute for a prisoner before the commander-in-chief. "I seized him first," says one, "by the arm and by the right hand, and tore his glove from him." "But to me," says the other, "he gave that same hand with his parole."

Besides idealism, a strong formalism is at the bottom of all the traits enumerated. The innate belief in the transcendental reality of things brings about as a result that every notion is strictly defined and limited, isolated, as it were, in a plastic form, and it is this form which is all-important. Mortal sins are distinguished from venial sins according to fixed rules. In law, culpability is established in the first place by the formal nature of the deed. The ancient judicial adage, "The deed judges the man," had lost nothing of its force. Although jurisprudence had been long ago freed from the extreme formalism of primitive law, which knew no difference between the intentional and the involuntary deed and did not punish an attempt that had miscarried, yet traces of a severe formalism existed in great number at the close of the Middle Ages. Thus, there was a rule of long standing that a slip of the tongue in the formula of an oath rendered it null and void, the oath being a sacred thing. In the thirteenth century an exception was made in favour of foreign merchants who only knew the language of the country imperfectly, and it was conceded that their incorrect language in taking the oath should not lose them their rights.

The extreme sensibility to everything touching honour is an effect of the general formalism. A nobleman is blamed for having the caparison of his horse ornamented with his armorial bearings, because, if the horse, "a brute beast," should stumble at the joust, the coat of arms would be dragged through the sand and the whole family dishonoured.

The formal element occupied a large place in everything connected with vengeance, expiations, reparations for wounded honour. The right of vengeance, a very vital element in the customs of France and the Netherlands in the fifteenth century, was exercised more or less according to fixed rules. It is not always furious anger which urges people to acts of violence in pursuit of vengeance; amends for offended honour are sought according to a well-regulated plan. It is, above all, a question of shedding blood, not of killing; sometimes care is taken to wound the victim only in the face, the arms, or the thighs.

The satisfaction sought for, being formal, is symbolic. In political reconciliations in the fifteenth century, symbolic actions have a very large share: demolition of houses which recall the crime, erection of commemorative crosses or chapels, injunctions to block up a doorway, etc., not to mention expiatory processions and masses for the dead. After his reconciliation with his brother at Rouen in 1469, Louis XI's first care is to have the ring which the bishop of Lisieux gave to Charles in marrying him to Normandy as its duke, broken on an anvil in the presence of the notables.

The chronicle of Jean de Roye records a striking instance of this craving for symbols and forms. One Laurent Guernier had been hanged by mistake at Paris in 1478; he had obtained a reprieve, but his pardon arrived too late. A year later his brother obtained permission to have the body honourably buried. "And before this bier went four town criers of the aforesaid town sounding their rattles, and on their breasts were the arms of the aforesaid Guernier, and around that bier were four tapers and eight torches, carried by men dressed in mourning and bearing the aforesaid crest. And in this way it was carried, passing through the aforesaid city of Paris . . . as far as the gate of Saint Anthony, where the aforesaid corpse was placed on a cart draped in black to take it to Provins to be buried. And one of the aforesaid criers who walked before the aforesaid corpse, cried: 'Good people, say your pater nosters for the soul of the late Laurent Guernier, in his life an inhabitant of Provins, who was lately found *dead under an oak-tree!'* "

The mentality of the declining Middle Ages often seems to us to display an incredible superficiality and feebleness. The complexity of things is ignored by it in a truly astounding manner. It proceeds to generalizations unhesitatingly on the strength of a single instance. Its liability to wrong judgment is extreme. Inexactitude, credulity, levity, inconsistency, are common features of medieval reasoning. All these defects are rooted in its fundamental formalism. To explain a situation or an event, a single motive suffices, and, for choice, the most general motive, the most direct or the grossest. To Burgundian party-feeling, for example, there could be but a single ground which could have urged the duke of Burgundy to compass the murder of the duke of Orleans: he wished to avenge the (assumed) adultery of the queen with Orleans. In every controversy people would disregard all the features of the case save a few, whose significance they exaggerated at pleasure. Thus the presentment of a fact, in the minds of the epoch, is always like a primitive woodcut, with strong and simple lines and very clearly marked contours.

So much for "simplistic" habits of mind. As to ill-considered generalization, it manifests itself on every page of the literature of that
time. From a single case of impartiality reported of the English of olden
time, Olivier de la Marche concludes that at that period the English
were virtuous, and because of that had been able to conquer France.
The importance of a particular case is exaggerated, because it is seen
in an ideal light. Moreover, every case can be paralleled in sacred
history, and so be exalted to higher significance. In 1404 a procession
of students at Paris was assaulted: two were wounded, the clothes of a
third were torn. This was enough for the chancellor of the University,
carried away by the heat of his indignation, and by a simple conso-
nance, "Les enfants, les jolis escoliers comme agneaux innocens,"[7] to
launch into comparison of the incident to the massacre of Bethlehem.

If for every particular case an explanation is so easily admitted, and,
once admitted, takes root in the mind without meeting with resistance,
then the danger of wrong judgments is extremely great. Nietzsche said
that abstaining from wrong judgments would make life impossible, and
it is probable that the intense life which we sometimes envy past
centuries, was partly due to the facility of false judgments. In our own
day too, in times which require the utmost exertion of national force,
the nerves need the help of false judgment. The men of the Middle
Ages lived in a continual mental crisis. They could not for a moment
dispense with false judgments of the grossest kind. If, in the fifteenth
century, the cause of the dukes of Burgundy could persuade so many
Frenchmen first to breach of fealty and next to hostility to their country, this political sentiment can only be explained by a whole tissue of
emotional conceptions and confused ideas.

It is in this light that the general and constant habit of ridiculously
exaggerating the number of enemies killed in battle should be considered. Chastellain gives a loss of five nobles on the side of the duke
at the battle of Gavre, as against twenty or thirty thousand of the
Ghent rebels.

What are we to say, lastly, of the curious levity of the authors of
the close of the Middle Ages, which often impresses us as an absolute
lack of mental power? It sometimes seems as if they were content to
present to their readers a series of vague pictures, and felt no need
whatever of really hard thinking. Superficial description of outward
circumstances—this is all we get from writers like Froissart and Mon-

[7] The children, the pretty scholars, like innocent lambs.

strelet. Compared with Herodotus, to say nothing of Thucydides, their narrative is disjointed, empty, without pith or meaning. They do not distinguish the essential from the accidental. Their lack of precision is deplorable. Monstrelet was present at the interview of the duke of Burgundy with Joan of Arc, when a prisoner: he does not remember what was said. Thomas Basin himself, who conducted the process of rehabilitation, says in his chronicle that Joan was born at Vaucouleurs instead of Domremy, and that she was conducted to Tours by Baudricourt himself, whom he calls lord of the town instead of captain, while he is mistaken by three months as to the date of her first interview with the dauphin. Olivier de la Marche, master of the ceremonies and an impeccable courtier, constantly muddles the genealogy of the ducal family and goes so far as to make the marriage of Charles with Margaret of York take place after the siege of Neuss in 1475, though he was present at the wedding festivities in 1468. Even Commines is not exempt from surprising inexactitudes.

The credulity and the lack of critical spirit are too general and too well known to make it necessary to cite examples. It goes without saying that here the degree of erudition makes a great difference. Basin and Molinet treated the popular belief that Charles the Bold would come back as a fable. Ten years after the battle of Nancy, people were still lending money which was to be reimbursed on his return.

> J'ay veu chose incongneue:
> Ung mort ressusciter,
> Et sur sa revenue
> Par milliers achapter.
> L'un dit: il est en vie,
> L'autre: ce n'est que vent.
> Tous bons cueurs sans envie
> Le regrettent souvent.[8]

A mentality, dominated like that of the declining Middle Ages by a lively imagination, by naïve idealism and by strong feeling, easily believes in the reality of every concept which presents itself to the mind. When once an idea has received a name and a form, its truth is presumed; it glides, so to say, into the system of spiritual figures and shares in their credibility.

[8] I have seen an unknown thing: A dead man coming to life. And on his return Buy for thousands. The one says: he is alive. The other: it is but wind. All good hearts, void of envy, Regret his loss often.

On the one hand, their clear outlines and frequently anthropomorphic character give ideas a marked degree of fixity and immobility; on the other hand, the *meaning* of a conception runs a constant risk of being lost in the too vivid *form*. The principal person of the long allegorical and satirical poem of Eustache Deschamps, *Le Miroir de Mariage*, is called Franc Vouloir. Folly and Desire advise him to marry, Repertory of Science dissuades him. Now, if we ask ourselves what Deschamps wanted to express by the abstraction Franc Vouloir, it appears that the idea oscillates between the careless liberty of the bachelor and free will in a philosophic sense. The personification has more or less absorbed the idea which gave it birth. As undecided as the character of the central figure is the moral tone of the poem. The pious praise of the spiritual marriage and of the contemplative life contrasts strangely with the customary and rather vulgar mockery of women and of female virtue. The author sometimes puts exalted truths into the mouth of Folly and Desire, though their part is that of the devil's advocate. It is very hard to decide what was the personal conviction of the poet, and to what degree he was serious.

To distinguish clearly the serious element from pose and playfulness, is a problem that crops up in connection with nearly all the manifestations of the mentality of the Middle Ages. We saw it arise in connection with chivalry, and with the forms of love and of piety. We always have to remember that in more primitive cultural phases than ours, the line of demarcation between sincere conviction and "pretending" often seems to be wanting. What would be hypocrisy in a modern mind, is not always so in a medieval one.

The general want of balance, characterizing the soul of this epoch, in spite of the clear-cut form of its ideas, is especially felt in the domain of superstition. On the subject of sorcery, doubt and rationalistic interpretations alternate with the blindest credulity. We can never tell precisely to what degree this belief was sincere. Philippe de Mézières, in the *Songe du Vieil Pelerin*, tells that he himself learned the magic arts from a Spaniard. During more than ten years he did not succeed in forgetting his infamous knowledge. "A sa volenté ne povoit pas bien extirper de son cuer les dessusdits signes et l'effect d'iceulx contre Dieu."[9] At last, "through the grace of God, by dint of confessing and resisting, he was delivered from this great folly, which is an enemy to the Christian soul."

[9] He could not voluntarily extirpate from his mind the aforesaid signs and their effect against God.

During the horrible campaign of persecution against sorcerers in 1461, known as the "Vauderie d'Arras," both the people and the magistrates gravely doubted the reality of the alleged crimes. Outside the town of Arras, says Jacques du Clercq, "not one person in a thousand believed that it was true that they practised the aforesaid sorcery. Such things were never before heard of happening in these countries." Nevertheless, the town suffered severely in consequence: people would no longer shelter its merchants or give them credit, for fear that, accused of witchcraft, on the morrow, perhaps, they might lose all their possessions by confiscation. One of the inquisitors, who claimed to be able to discover the guilty at sight, and went so far as to declare that it was impossible for a man to be wrongly accused of sorcery, afterwards went mad. A poem full of hatred accused the persecutors of having got up the whole affair out of covetousness, and the bishop himself called the persecution "a thing intended by some evil persons." Philip the Good having asked the advice of the Faculty of Louvain, several of its members declared that the sorcery was not real. Upon which the duke, who, in spite of the archaic turn of his mind, was not superstitious, sent the king-at-arms of the Golden Fleece to Arras. Then the executions and the imprisonments ceased. Later on, all the processes were annulled, which fact the town celebrated by a joyful feast with representations of edifying "moralities."

The opinion that the rides through the air and the orgies of the witches' sabbath were but delusions which the devil suggested to the poor foolish women, was already rather widely spread in the fifteenth century. Froissart, describing the striking case of a Gascon nobleman and his familiar demon called Horton (he surpasses himself here in exactness and vividness of narrative), treats it as an "error." But it is an error caused by the devil, so the rationalizing interpretation, after all, goes only half-way. Gerson alone goes so far as to suggest the notion of a cerebral lesion, the others confine themselves to the hypothesis of diabolical illusions. Martin Lefranc, provost of the church of Lausanne, in the *Champion des Dames*, which he dedicated to Philip the Good in 1440, defended this opinion.

> Je ne croiray tant que je vive
> Que femme corporellement
> Voit par l'air comme merle ou grive,
> —Dit le Champion prestement.—

\* \* \* \* \*

Quant la pourelle est en sa couche,
Pour y dormir et reposer,
L'ennemi qui point ne se couche
Se vient encoste allé poser.
Lors illusions composer
Lui scet sy tres soubtillement
Qu'elle croit faire ou proposer
Ce qu'elle songe seulement.
Force la vielle songera
Que sur un chat ou sur un chien
A l'assemblée s'en ira;
Mais certes il n'en sera rien:
Et sy n'est baston ne mesrien
Qui le peut ung pas enlever.[10]

In general the mental attitude towards supernatural facts was a vacillating one. Rational interpretation, timid credulity, or the suspicion of diabolical ruses, have the upper hand by turns. The Church did its best to combat superstitions. Friar Richard, the popular preacher at Paris, has the mandrakes brought to him to be burned, "which many foolish people kept in safe places, having such great faith in this ordure, that, indeed, they firmly believed, that so long as they had it (provided it were very neatly wrapped up in silk or linen folds) they would never be poor so long as they lived."

Dogmatic theology was always studious to inculcate the exact distinction between matters of faith and of superstition. Benedictions and conjurations, says Denis the Carthusian in his treatise *Contra vitia superstitionum*, have no effect in themselves. They operate only in so far as they are pronounced as humble prayers, with pious intention and placing one's hope in God. Since popular belief, nevertheless, attributes magical virtue to them, it would be better that the clergy forbade these practices altogether.

Unhappily, the zeal of the Church for the purity of the faith did not affect demonomania. Its own doctrine prevented it from uprooting

[10] As long as I live I shall not believe That a woman can bodily Travel through the air like blackbird or thrush, Said the Champion forthwith. . . . When the poor woman lies in her bed, In order to sleep and to rest there, The enemy who never lies down to sleep Comes and remains by her side. Then to call up illusions Before her he can so subtly, That she thinks she does or proposes to do What she only dreams. Perhaps the gammer will dream That on a cat or on a dog She will go to the meeting; But certainly nothing will happen; And there is neither a stick nor a beam Which could lift her a step.

belief in it. For it kept to the norm, fixed by the authority of Saint Augustine and Saint Thomas: *Omnia quae visibiliter fiunt in hoc mundo, possunt fieri per daemones.*[11] Conjurations, says Denis continuing the argument we have just cited, often take effect in spite of the absence of a pious intention, because then the devil has taken a hand in it. This ambiguity left room for a good deal of uncertainty. The fear of sorcery and the blind fury of persecution continued to darken the mental atmosphere of the age. The official confirmation of both the theory and the practice of persecution was effected in the last quarter of the fifteenth century by the *Malleus maleficarum*, the Hammer for Witches, by two German Dominicans, which appeared in 1487, and by the bull, *Summis desiderantes*, of Pope Innocent VIII, of 1484.

So towards the end of the Middle Ages this dark system of delusion and cruelty grew slowly to completion. All the deficiencies of medieval thinking and its inherent tendencies to gross error had contributed to its building. The fifteenth century transmitted it to the coming age like a horrible disease, which for a long time neither classical culture nor Protestant reformation nor the Catholic revival were able or even willing to cure.

If a man of culture of 1840 had been asked to characterize French civilization in the fifteenth century in a few words, his answer would probably have been largely inspired by impressions from Barante's *Histoire des Ducs de Bourgogne* and Hugo's *Notre Dame de Paris*. The picture called up by these would have been grim and dark, scarcely illuminated by any ray of serenity and beauty.

The experiment repeated to-day would yield a very different result. People would now refer to Joan of Arc, to Villon's poetry, but above all to the works of art. The so-called primitive Flemish and French masters—Van Eyck, Rogier van der Weyden, Foucquet, Memling, with Claus Sluter, the sculptor, and the great musicians—would dominate their general idea of the epoch. The picture would altogether have changed its colour and tone. The aspect of mere cruelty and misery as conceived by romanticism, which derived its information chiefly from the chronicles, would have made room for a vision of pure and naïve beauty, of religious fervour and profound mystic peace.

It is a general phenomenon that the idea which works of art give us of an epoch is far more serene and happy than that which we glean

[11] All that happens visibly in this world, can be done by demons.

in reading its chronicles, documents, or even literature. Plastic art does
not lament. Even when giving expression to sorrow or pain it transports
them to an elegiac sphere, where the bitter taste of suffering has passed
away, whereas the poets and historians, voicing the endless griefs of
life, always keep their immediate pungency and revive the harsh realities of bygone misery.

Now, our perception of former times, our historical organ, so to say,
is more and more becoming visual. Most educated people of to-day owe
their conception of Egypt, Greece, or the Middle Ages, much more to
the sight of their monuments, either in the original or by reproductions,
than to reading. The change of our ideas about the Middle Ages is
due less to a weakening of the romantic sense than to the substitution
of artistic for intellectual appreciation.

Still, this vision of an epoch resulting from the contemplation of
works of art is always incomplete, always too favourable, and therefore
fallacious. It has to be corrected in more than one sense. Confining
ourselves to the period in question, we first have to take into consideration the fact that, proportionately, far more of the written documents
than of the monuments of art have been preserved. The literature of
the declining Middle Ages, with some few exceptions, is known to us
fairly completely. We have products of all genres: the most elevated
and the most vulgar, the serious and the comic, the pious and the profane. Our literary tradition reflects the whole life of the epoch. Written
tradition, moreover, is not confined to literature: official records, in
infinite number, enable us to augment almost indefinitely the accuracy
of our picture.

Art, on the contrary, is by its very nature limited to a less complete
and less direct expression of life. Moreover, we only possess a very
special fraction of it. Outside ecclesiastical art very little remains. Profane art and applied art have only been preserved in rare specimens.
This is a serious want, because these are just the forms of art which
would have most clearly revealed to us the relation of artistic production to social life. The modest number of altar-pieces and tombs
teaches us too little in this respect; the art of the epoch remains to us
a thing apart from the history of the time. Now, really to understand
art, it is of great importance to form a notion of the function of art in
life; and for that it does not suffice to admire surviving masterpieces,
all that has been lost asks our attention too.

Art in those times was still wrapped up in life. Its function was to
fill with beauty the forms assumed by life. These forms were marked

and potent. Life was encompassed and measured by the right efflores-
cence of the liturgy: the sacraments, the canonical hours of the day and
the festivals of the ecclesiastical year. All the works and all the joys
of life, whether dependent on religion, chivalry, trade or love, had their
marked form. The task of art was to adorn all these concepts with
charm and colour; it is not desired for its own sake, but to decorate life
itself, as the expression of life's significance. Whether it served to
sustain the flight of piety or to be an accompaniment to the delights of
the world, it was not yet conceived as mere beauty.

Consequently, we might venture the paradox that the Middle Ages
knew only applied art. They wanted works of art only to make them
subservient to some practical use. Their purpose and their meaning always preponderated over their purely æsthetic value. We should add
that the love of art for its own sake did not originate in an awakening
of the craving for beauty, but developed as a result of superabundant
artistic production. In the treasuries of princes and nobles, objects of
art accumulated so as to form collections. No longer serving for practical use, they were admired as articles of luxury and of curiosity; thus
the taste for art was born which the Renaissance was to develop consciously.

In the great works of art of the fifteenth century, notably in the
altar-pieces and tombs, the nature of the subject was far more important than the question of beauty. Beauty was required because the subject was sacred or because the work was destined for some august
purpose. This purpose is always of a more or less practical sort. The
triptych served to intensify worship at the great festivals and to preserve the memory of the pious donors. The altar-piece of the Lamb by
the brothers Van Eyck was opened at high festivals only. Religious
pictures were not the only ones which served a practical purpose. The
magistrates of the towns ordered representations of famous judgments
to decorate the law courts, in order to solemnly exhort the judges to do
their duty. Such are the judgment of Cambyses, by Gerard David, at
Bruges; that of the Emperor Otto, by Dirk Bouts, at Louvain; and the
lost pictures by Rogier van der Weyden, once at Brussels.

The following example may serve to illustrate the importance attached to the subjects represented. In 1384 an interview took place at
Lelinghem for the purpose of bringing about an armistice between
France and England. The duke of Berry had the naked walls of the old
chapel, where the negotiating princes were to meet, covered with tapestry representing battles of antiquity. But John of Gaunt, duke of

Lancaster, as soon as he saw them on entering, demanded that these pictures of war should be removed, because those who aspire to peace ought not to have scenes of combat and of destruction before their eyes. The tapestries were replaced by others representing the instruments of the Passion.

The importance of the subject is closely connected with the artistic value in the case of portraits, which even now preserve some moral significance, as souvenirs or heirlooms, because the sentiments determining their use are as vital as ever. In the Middle Ages portraits were ordered for all sorts of purposes, but rarely, we may be certain, to obtain a masterpiece of art. Besides gratifying family affection and pride, the portrait served to enable betrothed persons to make acquaintance. The embassy sent to Portugal by Philip the Good in 1428, to ask for the hand of a princess, was accompanied by Jan van Eyck, with orders to paint her portrait. Court chroniclers liked to keep up the fiction that the royal fiancé had fallen in love with the unknown princess on seeing her portrait—for instance, Richard II of England when courting the little Isabelle of France, aged six. Sometimes it is even said that a selection was made by comparing portraits of different parties. When a wife had to be found for the young Charles VI, according to the *Religieux de Saint Denis*, the choice lay between a Bavarian, an Austrian and a Lorraine duchess. A painter of talent was sent to the three courts; three portraits were submitted to the king, who chose the young Isabella of Bavaria, judging her by far the most beautiful.

Nowhere was the practical use of works of art weightier than in connection with tombs, by far the most important domain of the sculpture of the epoch. The wish to have an effigy of the deceased was so strong that it claimed satisfaction even before the construction of the tomb. At the burial of a man of rank, he is represented either by a living man or by an effigy. At the funeral service of Bertrand du Guesclin, at Saint Denis, "four men-at-arms, armed cap-à-pie, mounted on four chargers, well appointed and caparisoned, representing the dead man as he was alive," entered the church. An account of the Polignacs of 1375 relating to a funeral ceremony shows the item: "Six shillings to Blaise for representing the dead knight at the funeral." At royal interments a figure of leather, in state dress, represented the deceased. Great pains were taken to obtain a good likeness. Sometimes there is more than one of these effigies in the cortège. Visitors to Westminster Abbey know these figures. Perhaps the origin of making funeral masks, which began in France in the fifteenth century, is to be found here.

As all art was more or less applied art, the distinction between artists and craftsmen did not arise. The great masters in the service of the courts of Flanders, of Berry, or of Burgundy, each of them an artist of a very marked personality, did not confine themselves to painting pictures and to illuminating manuscripts; they were not above colouring statues, painting shields and staining banners, or designing costumes for tournaments and ceremonies. Thus Melchior Broederlam, court painter to the first duke of Burgundy, after holding the same position in the household of his father-in-law, the count of Flanders, puts the finishing touches to five sculptured chairs for the palace of the counts. He repairs and paints some mechanical apparatus at the castle of Hesdin, used for wetting the guests with water by way of a surprise. He does work on a carriage for the duchess. He directs the sumptuous decoration of the fleet which the duke had assembled at Sluys in 1387 for an expedition against the English, which, however, did not take place. So, too, at wedding festivities and funeral ceremonies court painters were laid under contribution. Statues were painted in Jan van Eyck's workshop. He himself made a sort of map of the world for Duke Philip, on which the towns and the countries were painted with marvellous delicacy. Hugo van der Goes designed posters advertising a papal indulgence at Ghent. When the Archduke Maximilian was a prisoner at Bruges in 1488, the painter Gerard David was sent for, to decorate with pictures the wickets and shutters of his prison.

Of all the handiwork of the masters of the fifteenth century, only a portion of a very special nature has survived: some tombs, some altarpieces and portraits, numerous miniatures, also a certain number of objects of industrial art, comprising vessels used in religious worship, sacerdotal dress and church furniture, but of secular work, except woodwork and chimneys, scarcely anything is left. How much more should we know of the art of the fifteenth century if we could compare the bathing and hunting pieces of Jan van Eyck and Rogier van der Weyden with their *pietàs* and madonnas. It is not only profane pictures we lack. There are whole departments of applied art of which we can hardly even form a conception. For this we lack the power to compare with the priestly vestments that have been preserved, the court costumes with their precious stones and tiny bells, that have perished: we lack the actual sight of the brilliantly decorated war-ships of which miniatures give us but a conventional and clumsy representation. Froissart, who, as a rule, is little susceptible to impressions of beauty, fairly exults in his descriptions of the splendours of a decked-out fleet, with its streamers, gay with blazonry, floating from the mast-heads, and some reaching the water. The ship of Philippe le Hardi, decorated by Broederlam, was painted azure and gold; large heraldic shields surrounded the pavilion of the castle; the sails were studded with daisies and the initials of the duke and the duchess, and bore the motto *Il me tarde*. The nobles vied with each other in lavishing money on the decoration of their vessels. Painters had a good time of it, says Froissart; there were not enough of them to go round, and they got whatever prices they asked. According to him, many nobles had their ship-masts entirely covered with goldleaf. Guy de la Trémoïlle spent £ 2,000 on decorations. "And all this was paid by the poor people of France. . . ."

These lost products of decorative art would have revealed to us, above all, extravagant sumptuousness. This trait is characteristic of the epoch; it is to be found equally in the works which we do possess, but as we study these only for the sake of their beauty, we pay little attention to this element of splendour and of pomp, which no longer interests us, but which was just what people of that time prized most.

Burgundo-French culture of the expiring Middle Ages tends to oust beauty by magnificence. The art of this period exactly reflects this spirit. All that we cited above as characteristic of the mental processes of the epoch: the craving to give a definite form to every idea, and the overcrowding of the mind with figures and forms systematically arranged—all this reappears in art. There, too, we find the tendency to leave nothing without form, without figure, without ornament. The flamboyant style of architecture is like the postlude of an organist who cannot conclude. It decomposes all the formal elements endlessly; it interlaces all the details; there is not a line which has not its counter-line. The form develops at the expense of the idea, the ornament grows rank, hiding all the lines and all the surfaces. A *horror vacui* reigns, always a symptom of artistic decline.

All this means that the border-line between pomp and beauty is being obliterated. Decoration and ornament no longer serve to heighten the natural beauty of a thing; they are overgrowing it and threaten to stifle it. The further we get away from pure plastic art, the more this rankness of formal decorative motifs is accentuated. This may be very clearly observed in sculpture. In the creation of isolated figures this overgrowth of forms does not occur: the statues of Moses' well and the "plourants" of the tombs are as sober as the figures of Donatello. But where sculpture is performing a decorative function we at once find the overgrowth. In looking at the tabernacle of Dijon, everyone will be struck by a lack of harmony between the sculpture of Jacques de Baerze and the painting of Broederlam. The picture, painted for its own sake, is simple and sober; the reliefs, on the contrary, in which the purpose is decorative, are complicated and overloaded. We notice the same contrast between painting and tapestry. Textile art, even when representing scenes and figures, remains limited by its technique to decorative conception and expression; hence we find the same craving for excessive ornamentation.

In the art of costume, the essential qualities of pure art, that is to say, measure and harmony, vanish altogether, because splendour and adornment are the sole objects aimed at. Pride and vanity introduce a sensual element incompatible with pure art. No epoch ever witnessed such extravagance of fashion as that extending from 1350 to 1480. Here we can observe the unhampered expansion of the æsthetic sense of the time. All the forms and dimensions of dress are ridiculously exaggerated. The female head-dress assumes the conical shape of the "hennin," a form evolved from the little coif, keeping the hair under the kerchief. High and bombed foreheads are in fashion, with the temples shaved. Low-necked dresses make their appearance. The male dress had features still more bizarre—the immoderate length of the points of the shoes, called "poulaines," which the knights at Nicopolis had to cut off, to enable them to flee; the laced waists; the balloon-shaped sleeves standing up at the shoulders; the too long "houppelandes" and the too short doublets; the cylindrical or pointed bonnets; the hoods draped about the head in the form of a cock's comb or a flaming fire. A state costume was ornamented by hundreds of precious stones.

The taste for unbridled luxury culminated in the court fêtes. Every one has read the descriptions of the Burgundian festivities at Lille in 1454, at which the guests took the oath to undertake the crusade, and at Bruges in 1468, on the occasion of the marriage of Charles the Bold with Margaret of York. It is hard to imagine a more absolute contrast than that of these barbarous manifestations of arrogant pomp and the pictures of the brothers Van Eyck, Dirk Bouts and Rogier van der Weyden, with their sweet and tranquil serenity. Nothing could be more insipid and ugly than the "entremets," consisting of gigantic pies enclosing complete orchestras, full-rigged vessels, castles, monkeys and whales, giants and dwarfs, and all the boring absurdities of allegory. We find it difficult to regard these entertainments as something more than exhibitions of almost incredible bad taste.

Yet we must not exaggerate the distance separating the two extreme forms of the art of the fifteenth century. In the first place, it is important to realize the function of festivals in the society of that time. They still preserved something of the meaning they have in primitive societies, that of the supreme expression of their culture, the highest mode of a collective enjoyment and an assertion of solidarity. At epochs of great renovations of society, like that of the French Revolution, we see that festivals resume this social and æsthetic function.

Modern man is free, when he pleases, to seek his favourite distractions individually, in books, music, art or nature. On the other hand, at a time when the higher pleasures were neither numerous nor accessible to all, people felt the need of such collective rejoicings as festivals. The more crushing the misery of daily life, the stronger the stimulants that will be needed to produce that intoxication with beauty and delight without which life would be unbearable. The fifteenth century, profoundly pessimistic, a prey to continual depression, could not forgo the emphatic affirmation of the beauty of life, afforded by these splendid and solemn collective rejoicings. Books were expensive, the country was unsafe, art was rare; the individual lacked the means of distraction. All literary, musical and artistic enjoyment was more or less closely connected with festivals.

Now festivals, in so far as they are an element of culture, require other things than mere gaiety. Neither the elementary pleasures of gaming, drinking and love, nor luxury and pomp as such, are able to give them a framework. The festival requires style. If those of modern times have lost their cultural value, it is because they have lost style. In the Middle Ages the religious festival, because of its high qualities of style founded on the liturgy itself, for a long time dominated all the forms of collective cheerfulness. The popular festival, which had its own elements of beauty in song and dance, was linked up with those of the Church. It is towards the fifteenth century that an independent form of civil festival with a style of its own disengages itself from the ecclesiastical one. The "rhetoricians" of Northern France and the Netherlands are the representatives of this evolution. Till then only princely courts had been able to equip secular festivals with form and style, thanks to the resources of their wealth and the social conception of courtesy.

Nevertheless, the style of the courtly festival could not but remain greatly inferior to that of religious festivals. In the latter worship and rejoicing in common were always the expression of a sublime thought, which lent them a grace and dignity that even the excesses of their frequently burlesque details could not affect. On the other hand, the ideas glorified by the secular feast were nothing more than those of chivalry and of courtly love. The ritual of chivalry, no doubt, was rich enough to give these festivities a venerable and solemn style. There were the accolade, the vows, the chapters of the orders, the rules of the tournaments, the formalities of homage, service and precedence, all the dignified proceedings of kings-at-arms and heralds, all the brightness of blazonry and armour. But this did not suffice to satisfy all aspirations. The court fêtes were expected to visualize in its entirety the dream of the heroic life. And here style failed. For in the fifteenth century the apparatus of chivalrous fancy was no longer anything but vain convention and mere literature.

The staging of the amazing festivities of Lille or of Bruges is, so to say, applied literature. The ponderousness of material representation destroyed the last remainder of charm which literature with the lightness of its airy reveries had hitherto preserved. The unfaltering seriousness with which these monstrous pageants were organized is truly Burgundian. The ducal court seems to have lost, by its contact with the North, some qualities of the French spirit. For the preparation of the banquet of Lille, which was to crown and conclude a series of banquets which the nobles provided, each in his turn, vying with each other in magnificence, Philip the Good appointed a committee, presided over by a knight of the Golden Fleece, Jean de Lannoy. The most trusted counsellors of the duke—Antoine de Cory, the chancellor Nicolas Rolin himself—were frequently present at the sessions of the committee, of which Olivier de la Marche was a member. When the latter in his memoirs comes to this chapter, a feeling of awe still comes over him. "Because great and honourable achievements deserve a lasting renown and perpetual remembrance . . . ," thus he begins the narrative of these memorable things. It is needless to reprint it here, as it belongs to the *loci communes* of historical literature.

Even from across the sea people came to view the gorgeous spectacle. Besides the guests, a great number of noble spectators were present at the feast, disguised for the most part. First every one walked about to admire the fixed show-pieces; later came the "entremets," that is to say, representations of "personages" and tableaux vivants. Olivier himself played the important part of Holy Church, making his appearance in a tower on the back of an elephant, led by a gigantic Turk. The tables were loaded with the most extravagant decorations. There were a rigged and ornamented carack, a meadow surrounded by trees with a fountain, rocks and a statue of Saint Andrew, the castle of Lusignan with the fairy Mélusine, a bird-shooting scene near a windmill, a wood in which wild beasts walked about, and, lastly, a church with an organ and singers, whose songs alternated with the music of the orchestra of twenty-eight persons, which was placed in a pie.

The problem for us is to determine the quality of taste or bad taste to which all this bears witness. It goes without saying that the mythological and allegorical tenor of these "entremets" cannot interest us. But what was the artistic execution worth? What people looked for most was extravagance and huge dimensions. The tower of Gorcum represented on the table of the banquet of Bruges in 1468 was 46 feet high. La Marche says of a whale, which also figured there: "And certainly this was a very fine entremets, *for* there were more than forty persons in it." People were also much attracted by mechanical marvels: living birds flying from the mouth of a dragon conquered by Hercules, and such-like curiosities, in which, to us, any idea of art is altogether lacking. The comic element was of a very low class: boars blow the trumpet in the tower of Gorcum; elsewhere goats sing a motet, wolves play the flute, four large donkeys appear as singers—and all this in honour of Charles the Bold, who was a good musician.

I would not, however, suggest that there may not have been many an artistic masterpiece among these pretentious and ridiculous curiosities. Let us not forget that the men who enjoyed these Gargantuan decorations were the patrons of the brothers Van Eyck and of Rogier van der Weyden—the duke himself, Rolin, the donor of the altars of Beaune and of Autun, Jean Chevrot, who commissioned Rogier to paint "The Seven Sacraments," now at Antwerp. What is more, it was the painters themselves who designed these show-pieces. If the records do not mention Jan van Eyck or Rogier as having contributed to similar festivities, they do give the names of the two Marmions and Jacques Daret. For the fête of 1468 the services of the whole corporation of painters were requisitioned; they were summoned in haste from Ghent, Brussels, Louvain, Tirlemont, Mons, Quesnoy, Valenciennes, Douai, Cambray, Arras, Lille, Ypres, Courtray, Oudenarde, to work at Bruges. It is impossible to believe that their handiwork was ugly. The thirty vessels decorated with the arms of the duke's domains, the sixty images of women dressed in the costume of their country, "carrying fruit in baskets and birds in cages. . . ." I should be ready to give more than one mediocre church-picture to see them.

We may go further, at the risk of being thought paradoxical, and affirm that we have to take this art of show-pieces, which has disappeared without leaving a trace, into account, if we would thoroughly understand the art of Claus Sluter.

Of all the forms of art, sepulchral sculpture is most fettered by the exigencies of its purpose. The sculptors charged with making the ducal tombs were not left free to create beautiful things; they had to exalt the glory of the deceased prince. The painter can always give free rein to his imagination; he is never obliged to limit himself strictly to commissioned work. It is probable, on the other hand, that the sculptor of this epoch rarely worked except on specified tasks. The motifs of his art, moreover, are limited in number and fixed by a rigorous tradition. It is true that painters and sculptors are equally servants of the ducal household; Jan van Eyck, as well as Sluter and his nephew, Claus de Werve, bore the title of "varlet de chambre," but for the two latter, the service is far more real than for the painters. The two great Dutchmen whom the irresistible attraction of French art life drew for good from their native country were completely monopolized by the duke of Burgundy. Claus Sluter inhabited a house at Dijon which the duke placed at his disposal; there he lived as a gentleman, but at the same time as a servant of the court. His nephew and successor, Claus de Werve, is the tragic type of an artist in the service of princes: kept back at Dijon year after year, to finish the tomb of Jean sans Peur, for which the financial means were never forthcoming, he saw his artistic career, so brilliantly begun, ruined by fruitless waiting.

Thus the art of the sculptor at this epoch is a servile art. On the other hand, sculpture is generally little influenced by the taste of an epoch, because its means, its material and its subjects are limited and little subject to change. When a great sculptor appears, he creates everywhere and always that *optimum* of purity and simplicity which we call classic. The human form and its drapery are susceptible of few variations. The masterpieces of carving of the different ages are very much alike, and, for us, Sluter's work shares this eternal identity of sculpture.

Nevertheless, on examining it more closely, we notice that especially the art of Sluter bears the marks of being influenced by the taste of the time (not to call it Burgundian taste) as far as the nature of sculpture permits. Sluter's works have not been preserved as they were, and as the master intended them to be. We must picture the well of Moses as it was in 1418, when the papal legate granted an indulgence to whosoever should come to visit it in a pious spirit. It must be remembered that the well is but a fragment, a part of a calvary with which the first duke of Burgundy of the house of Valois intended to crown the well of his Carthusian monastery of Champmol. The principal part, that is to say, the crucified Christ with the Virgin, Saint John and Mary Magdalen, had almost completely disappeared before the French Revolution. There remains only the pedestal, surrounded by the statues of the six prophets who predicted the death of the Savior, with a cornice supported by angels. The whole composition is in the highest degree a representation, "une œuvre parlante," a show, closely related as such to the tableaux vivants or the "personnages" of the princely entries and of the banquets. There, too, the subjects were borrowed, for choice, from the prophecies relating to the coming of Christ. Like these "personnages," the figures surrounding the well hold scrolls containing the text of their predictions. It rarely happens in sculpture that the written word is of such importance. We can only fully realize the marvellous art here displayed in *hearing* these sacred and solemn words. *Immolabit eum universa multitudo filiorum Israel ad vesperum;* this is Moses' sentence. *Foderunt manus meas et pedes meos, dinumeraverunt omnia ossa mea;* this is David's. Jeremiah says: *O vos omnes qui transitis per viam, attendite et videte si est dolor sicut dolor meus.*[12] Isaiah, Daniel, Zachariah, all announce the death of the Lord. It is like a threnody of six voices rising up to the cross. Now in this feature lies the essence of the work. The gestures of the hands by which the attention is directed to the texts are so emphatic, and there is an expression of such poignant grief on the faces, that the whole is in some danger of losing the *ataraxia* which marks great sculpture. It appeals too directly to the spectator. Compared with the figures of Michelangelo, those of Sluter are too expressive, too personal. If more had come down to us of the calvary supported by the prophets than the head and the torso of Christ, or a stark majesty, this expressive character would be still more evident.

The spectacular character of the calvary of Champmol also came into prominence in the luxurious decorations of the work. We must picture it in all its polychrome splendour, for Jean Malouel, the artist, and Herman of Cologne, the gilder, were not sparing of vivid colours and brilliant effects. The pedestals were green, the mantles of the

---

[12] Exodus xii. 6: "And the whole assembly of the congregation of Israel shall kill it in the evening." Psalm xxii. 16, 17: "They pierced My hands and My feet. They told all My bones." Lamentations of Jeremiah i. 12: "All ye that pass by, behold, and see if there be any sorrow like unto My sorrow."

prophets were gilt, their tunics red and azure with golden stars. Isaiah, the gloomiest of all, wore a dress of gold-cloth. The open spaces were filled with golden suns and initials. The pride of blazonry displayed itself not only round the columns below the figures, but on the cross itself, which was entirely gilt. The extremities of the arms of the cross, shaped like capitals, bore the coats of arms of Burgundy and Flanders. Can one ask for better proof of the spirit in which the duke conceived this great monument of his piety? As a crowning "bizarrerie," a pair of spectacles of gilded brass, the work of Hannequin de Hacht, were placed on Jeremiah's nose.

This serfdom of a great art controlled by the will of a princely patron is tragic, but it is at the same time exalted by the heroic efforts of the great sculptor to shake off his shackles. The figures of the "plourants" around the sarcophagus had for a long time been an obligatory motif in Burgundian sepulchral art. These weeping figures were not meant to express grief in general; the sculptor was bound to give a faithful representation of the funeral cortège with the dignitaries present at the burial. But the genius of Sluter and his pupils succeeded in transforming this motif into the most profound expression of mourning known in art, a funeral march in stone.

Is it so certain, after all, that we are right in thinking of the artist as struggling with the lack of taste and refinement of his patron? It is quite possible that Sluter himself considered Jeremiah's spectacles a very happy find. In the men of that epoch artistic taste was still blended with the passion for what is rare or brilliant. In their simplicity they could enjoy the bizarre as if it were beauty. Objects of pure art and articles of luxury and curiosity were equally admired. Long after the Middle Ages the collections of princes contained works of art mixed up indiscriminately with knick-knacks made of shells and of hair, wax statues of celebrated dwarfs and such-like articles. At the castle of Hesdin, where side by side with art treasures the "engins d'esbatement" (contrivances for amusement) usual in princely pleasure-grounds were found in abundance, Caxton saw a room ornamented with pictures representing the history of Jason, the hero of the Golden Fleece. The artist is unknown, but was probably a distinguished master. To heighten the effect, a "machinerie" was annexed which could imitate lightning, thunder, snow and rain, in memory of the magic arts of Medea.

In the shows at the entries of princes inventive fancy stuck at nothing. When Isabella of Bavaria made her entry into Paris in 1389, there was a white deer with gilt antlers, and a wreath round its neck, stretched out on a "lit de justice," moving its eyes, antlers, feet, and at last raising a sword. At the moment when the queen crossed the bridge to the left of Notre Dame, an angel descended "by means of well-constructed engines" from one of the towers, passed through an opening of the hangings of blue taffeta with golden fleurs-de-lis which covered the bridge, and put a crown on her head. Then the angel "was pulled up again as if he had returned to heaven of his own accord." Philip the Good and Charles VIII were treated to similar descents. Lefèvre de Saint Remy greatly admired the spectacle of four trumpeters and twelve nobles on artificial horses, "sallying forth and caracoling in such a way that it was a fine thing to see."

Time the destroyer has made it easy for us to separate pure art from all these gewgaws and bizarre trappings, which have completely disappeared. This separation which our æsthetic sense insists upon, did not exist for the men of that time. Their artistic life was still enclosed within the forms of social life. Art was subservient to life. Its social function was to enhance the importance of a chapel, a donor, a patron, or a festival, but never that of the artist. Fully to realize its position and scope in this respect is now hardly possible. Too little of the material surroundings in which art was placed, and too few of the works of art themselves, have come down to us. Hence the priceless value of the few works by which private life, outside courts and outside the Church, is revealed to us. In this respect no painting can compare with the portrait of Jean Arnolfini and of his wife, by Jan van Eyck, in the National Gallery. The master, who, for once, need not portray the majesty of divine beings nor minister to aristocratic pride, here freely followed his own inspiration: it was his friends whom he was painting on the occasion of their marriage. Is it really the merchant of Lucca, Jean Arnoulphin, as he was called in Flanders, who is represented? Jan van Eyck painted this face twice (the other portrait is at Berlin); we can hardly imagine a less Italian-looking physiognomy, but the description of the picture in the inventory of Margaret of Austria, "Hernoul le fin with his wife in a chamber," leaves little room for doubt. However this may be, the persons represented were friends of Van Eyck; he himself witnesses to it by the ingenious and delicate way in which he signs his work, by an inscription over the mirror: *Johannes de Eyck fuit hic*, 1434.

"Jan van Eyck was here." Only a moment ago, one might think. The sound of his voice still seems to linger in the silence of this room. All that tenderness and profound peace, which only Rembrandt was to recapture, emanate from this picture. That serene twilight hour of an age, which we seemed to know and yet sought in vain in so many of the manifestations of its spirit, suddenly reveals itself here. And here at last this spirit proves itself happy, simple, noble and pure, in tune with the lofty church music and the touching folk-songs of the time.

So perhaps we imagine a Jan van Eyck escaping from the noisy gaiety and brutal passions of court life, a Jan van Eyck of the simple heart, a dreamer. It does not require a great effort of fancy to call up the "varlet de chambre" of the duke, serving the great lords against his will, suffering all the disgust of a great artist obliged to belie his sublime ideal of art by contributing to the mechanical devices of a festival.

Nothing, however, justifies us in forming such a conception of his personality. This art, which we admire, bloomed in the atmosphere of that aristocratic life, which repels us. The little we know of the lives of fifteenth-century painters shows them to us as men of the world and courtiers. The duke of Berry was on good terms with his artists. Froissart saw him in familiar conversation with André Beauneveu in his marvellous castle of Mehun sur Yevre. The three brothers of Limburg, the great illuminators, come to offer the duke, as a New Year's present, a surprise in the shape of a new illuminated manuscript, which turned out to be "a dummy book, made of a block of white wood painted to look like a book, in which there were no leaves and nothing was written." Jan van Eyck, without doubt, moved constantly in court circles. The secret diplomatic missions entrusted to him by the duke required a man of the world. He passed, moreover, for a man of letters, reading classic authors and studying geometry. Did he not, by an innocent whim, disguise in Greek letters his modest device, *Als ik kan* (As I can)?

The intellectual and moral life of the fifteenth century seems to us to be divided into two clearly separated spheres. On the one hand, the civilization of the court, the nobility and the rich middle classes: ambitious, proud and grasping, passionate and luxurious. On the other hand, the tranquil sphere of the "devotio moderna," of the *Imitation of Christ*, of Ruysbroeck and of Saint Colette. One would like to place the peaceful and mystic art of the brothers Van Eyck in the second of these spheres, but it belongs rather to the other. Devout circles were hardly in touch with the great art that flourished at this time. In music they disapproved of counterpoint, and even of organs. The rule of Windesheim forbade the embellishment of the singing by modulations, and Thomas à Kempis said: "If you cannot sing like the nightingale and the lark, then sing like the crows and the frogs, which sing as God meant them to." The music of Dufay, Busnois, Okeghem, developed in the chapels of the courts. As to painting, the writers of the "devotio moderna" do not speak of it; it was outside their range of thought. They wanted their books in a simple form and without illuminations. They would probably have regarded the altar-piece of the Lamb as a mere work of pride, and actually did so regard the tower of Utrecht Cathedral.

The great artists generally worked for other circles than those of the devout townspeople. The art of the brothers Van Eyck and of their followers, though it sprang up in municipal surroundings and was fostered by town circles, cannot be called a bourgeois art. The court and the nobility exercised too powerful an attraction. Only the patronage of princes permitted the art of miniatures to raise itself to the degree of artistic refinement which characterizes the work of the brothers of Limburg and the artists of the Hours of Turin. The employers of the great painters were, besides the princes themselves, the great lords, temporal or spiritual, and the great upstarts with whom the Burgundian epoch abounds, all gravitating towards the court. The ground for the difference between Franco-Flemish and Dutch art in this period lies in the fact that the latter still preserves some traits of simple soberness recalling the little out-of-the-way towns, such as Haarlem, where it was born. And even Dirk Bouts went south and painted at Louvain and Brussels.

Among the patrons of fifteenth-century art may be named Jean Chevrot, bishop of Tournay, whom a scutcheon designates as the donor of that work of touching and fervent piety, now at Antwerp, "The Seven Sacraments." Chevrot is the type of the court prelate; as a trusted counsellor of the duke, he was full of zeal for the affairs of the Golden Fleece and for the crusade. Another type of donor is represented by Pierre Bladelin, whose austere face is seen on the Middelburg altarpiece, now at Berlin. He was the great capitalist of those times; from the post of receiver of Bruges, his native town, he rose to be paymaster-general of the duke. He introduced control and economy into the ducal finances. He was appointed treasurer of the Golden Fleece and knighted. He was sent to England to ransom Charles of Orleans. The duke wished to charge him with the administration of the finances of the expedition against the Turks. He employed his wealth, which was the wonder of his contemporaries, on works of embankment and the founding of a new town in Flanders, to which he gave the name of Middelburg, after the town in Zeeland of that name.

Other notable donors—Judocus Vydt, the canon Van de Paele, the Croys, the Lannoys—belonged to the very rich, noble or burgher, ancient or new, of their time. Most famous of all is Nicolas Rolin, the chancellor, "sprung from little people," jurist, financier, diplomat. The great treaties of the dukes, from 1419 to 1435, are his work. "He used to govern everything quite alone and manage and bear the burden of all business by himself, be it of war, be it of peace, be it of matters of finance." By methods which were not above suspicion he amassed enormous wealth, which he spent on all sorts of pious and charitable foundations. Nevertheless, people spoke with hatred of his avarice and pride, and had no faith in the devotional feelings which inspired his pious works. This man whom we see in the Louvre kneeling so devoutly in the picture painted for him by Jan van Eyck for Autun, his native town, and again in that by Rogier van der Weyden, destined for his hospital of Beaune, passed for a mind only set on earthly things. "He always harvested on earth," says Chastellain, "as though the earth was to be his abode for ever, in which his understanding erred and his prudence abased him, when he would not set bounds to that, of which his great age showed him the near end." This is corroborated by Jacques du Clercq in these terms: "The aforesaid chancellor was reputed one of the wise men of the kingdom, to speak temporally; for as to spiritual matters, I shall be silent."

Are we, then, to look for a hypocritical expression in the face of the donor of La Vierge au Chancelier Rolin? Let us remember, before condemning him, the riddle presented by the religious personality of so many other men of his time, who also combined rigid piety with excesses of pride, of avarice and of lust. The depths of these natures of a past age are not easily sounded.

In the piety interpreted by the art of the fifteenth century, the extremes of mysticism and of gross materialism meet. The faith pictured here is so direct that no earthly figure is too sensual or too heavy to express it. Van Eyck may drape his angels and divine personages with ponderous and stiff brocades, glittering with gold and precious stones; to call up the celestial sphere he has no need of the flowing garments and sprawling limbs of the baroque style.

Yet neither this art nor this faith is primitive. By using the term primitive to designate the masters of the fifteenth century we run the

risk of a misunderstanding. They are primitive in a purely chrono-
logical sense, in so far as, for us, they are the first to come, and no
older painting is known to us. But if to this designation we attach the
meaning of a primitive spirit, we are egregiously mistaken. For the
spirit which this art denotes, is the same which we pointed out in
religious life: a spirit rather decadent than primitive, a spirit involving
the utmost elaboration, and even decomposition, of religious thought
through the imagination.

In very early times the sacred figures had been seen as endlessly
remote: awful and rigid. Then, from the twelfth century downward,
the mysticism of Saint Bernard introduced a pathetic element into
religion, which contained immense possibilities of growth. In the rap-
ture of a new and overflowing piety people tried to share the sufferings
of Christ by the aid of the imagination. They were no longer satisfied
with the stark and motionless figures, infinitely distant, which romanesque art had given to Christ and His Mother. All the forms and
colours which imagination drew from mundane reality were now
lavished by it upon the celestial beings. Once let loose, pious fancy
invaded the whole domain of faith and gave a minutely elaborate shape
to every holy thing.

At first verbal expression had been in advance of pictorial and plastic
art. Sculpture was still adhering to the formal rigidity of preceding
ages, when literature undertook to describe all the details, both physical and mental, of the drama of the cross. A sort of pathetic naturalism
arose, for which the *Meditationes vitae Christi*, early attributed to
Saint Bonaventura, supplied the model. The nativity, the childhood,
the descent from the cross, each received a fixed form, a vivid colouring. How Joseph of Arimathea mounted the ladder, how he had to
press the hand of the Lord in order to draw out the nail, was all
described in minute detail.

In the meantime, towards the end of the fourteenth century, pictorial
technique had made so much progress that it more than overtook literature in the art of rendering these details. The naïve, and at the same
time refined, naturalism of the brothers Van Eyck was a new form of
pictorial expression; but viewed from the standpoint of culture in
general, it was but another manifestation of the crystallizing of thought
which we noticed in all the aspects of the mentality of the declining
Middle Ages. Instead of heralding the advent of the Renaissance, as is
generally assumed, this naturalism is rather one of the ultimate forms
of development of the medieval mind. The craving to turn every sacred

idea into precise images, to give it a distinct and clearly outlined form, such as we observed in Gerson, in the *Roman de la Rose, . . .* controlled art, as it controlled popular beliefs and theology. The art of the brothers Van Eyck closes a period.

*     *     *     *     *

The fifteenth century in France and the Netherlands is still medieval at heart. The diapason of life had not yet changed. Scholastic thought, with symbolism and strong formalism, the thoroughly dualistic conception of life and the world still dominated. The two poles of the mind continued to be chivalry and hierarchy. Profound pessimism spread a general gloom over life. The gothic principle prevailed in art. But all these forms and modes were on the wane. A high and strong culture is declining, but at the same time and in the same sphere new things are being born. The tide is turning, the tone of life is about to change.

## Suggestions for Further Reading

BLOOMFIELD, MORTON, *Piers Plowman as a Fourteenth-Century Apocalypse* New Brunswick, N.J.: Rutgers University Press, 1962.

FERGUSON, W. K., *Europe in Transition, 1300–1520.* Boston: Houghton Mifflin Company, 1962.

FOCILLON, HENRI, *The Art of the West in the Middle Ages.* 2 vols. Greenwich, Conn.: Phaidon Publishers, Inc., 1963.

HAY, DENYS, *Europe in the Fourteenth and Fifteenth Centuries.* New York: Holt, Rinehart, and Winston, Inc., 1967.

OBERMAN, H., *The Harvest of Medieval Theology,* rev. ed. Grand Rapids, Mich.: William B. Eerdmans, 1968.

PANOFSKY, ERWIN, *Gothic Architecture and Scholasticism.* Cleveland: World Publishing Company, 1966.

PERROY, E., *The Hundred Years' War.* Bloomington: Indiana University Press, 1959.

ROBERTSON, D. W., JR., *A Preface to Chaucer.* Princeton, N.J.: Princeton University Press, 1962.

ZIEGLER, PHILIP, *The Black Death.* New York: John Day, 1969.